Organizational Decision Processes

Organizational Decision Processes

Concepts & Analysis

Ronald J. Ebert
&
Terence R. Mitchell

C̦R

Crane, Russak & Company, Inc.
NEW YORK

Organizational Decision Processes
Published in the United States by
Crane, Russak & Company, Inc.
347 Madison Avenue
New York, N.Y. 10017

ISBN 0-8448-0619-6 cloth edition
ISBN 0-8448-0620-x paper edition

LC 74-13324

Printed in the United States of America

Contents

Preface

The past two decades have seen an increasing interest in organizational decision making, particularly in schools of business and administration. The topic has been of concern, directly or indirectly, to scholars and students of various disciplines. Decisions and related processes are frequently treated as ancillary topics in numerous courses throughout university curricula. From such settings we have found two trends which inspired the effort represented in this book. First, a number of students and colleagues have expressed interest in decision making as a focal topic of study. Second, we have witnessed many expressions of concern about how decision-related topics from many disciplines "fit together." It was in consideration of these trends that the foundations of this work were developed.

Initial drafts of our work were used and reviewed in graduate seminars at the University of Washington. Helpful comments were provided by many students and colleagues. We wish to express particular gratitude to Professor Jim Rosenzweig for having laid the groundwork for many of the necessary materials and concepts. Likewise, we appreciate the efforts of Joel Champion, John Dittrich, Gary Green, Newman Peery, Bob Zawacki, and the many others who contributed directly or indirectly with their ideas and criticisms.

We wish to acknowledge the considerable support that was volunteered by our wives, Mary and Sandy. Mary was particularly tolerant during initial drafts of the book, serving both as editor and part-time typist. We are also indebted to our typists, Joanne Beaurain, Marsha Deering, and Sandra Goodman.

It is our fondest hope that this work will foster and facilitate further exploration of the many unanswered issues in organizational decision making.

RJE
TRM

Part One

Chapter 1

Introduction

INTERDISCIPLINARY FOUNDATIONS

In recent history we have witnessed a proliferation of interest in decision making. This topic has been of concern not only to organizational practitioners, but also to many authors and students in diverse disciplinary fields. Today we find a flurry of decision-oriented interest that cuts across such areas as economics, political science, psychology, social psychology, organization theory, management, public administration, mathematics, and applied quantitative methods. As might be expected, authors in these various disciplines differ in the focus of their interests in the general topic. Some have concentrated on the study of one or a few specific aspects of decision processes, while others have been concerned with a broader view of many such dimensions. Differences are found not only in the breadth of interest, but also in the level of abstraction at which the topic has been approached. Some have been involved with constructing theories of decision making; others have been interested in investigating empirical descriptive phenomena in laboratory or field settings; still others have been concerned with the development of technologies to assist or enhance the effectiveness of decision makers.

These differences in disciplinary orientation, breadth of focus, and level of abstraction (see Figure 1-1) present considerable difficulties when one seeks to synthesize the many aspects of decision making into a coherent whole. We believe that attainment of a meaningful synthesis is more likely to result from a prior exposure to, or sampling from, key subcomponents of the phenomena of interest. Consequently, our presentation is an analysis which identifies and examines major subcomponents of decision making.

Our primary focus is on behavioral foundations that underlie decision making in the organizational setting. However, we have found it useful and necessary to also draw upon selected contributions from the many disciplines mentioned above. Each has provided insights that are potentially applicable to decision-making processes in organizations. In addition to the problems of integrating across disciplines, we are faced with the task of integrating the diverse empirical results into theoretical frameworks to provide a logical, meaningful, integrated "whole." We want a picture of organizational decision making that is comprehensive in coverage, helps to develop a unified understanding of what organizational decision making consists of, and illustrates what we know and what we do not yet know about organizational decision making. But what exactly are the major trends from different disciplines that are blended into current ideas about organizational decision making?

Philosophy. One central theme running through much of philosophical thought has been a concern with man as a rational being. In early philosophical studies, rationalism was seen as a dependence upon reason as the route to knowledge, as contrasted with empiricism in which experience was considered necessary for the verification of statements. These ideas recur in discussions of epistomology, theology, and ethics.

Two main ideas generated by philosophical debates have had important implications for today's theories of decision making. First, the idea of rational man implies a dearth of emotional involvement. Our view of a rational person is one who is detached and able to weigh sources of information without undue

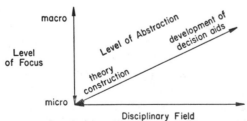

Figure 1-1 Dimensions of Different Orientations in the Study of Decision Making

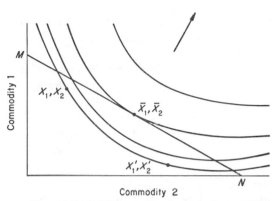

Figure 1-2 Indifference Map for Two Commodities

influence by his emotions. A second equally important idea is that this rational man can make decisions based on some sort of agreed-upon criterion. For some philosophers, such as the British utilitarians, correct decisions were those which resulted in the greatest good for the social aggregate. Other authors believed that the criterion was economic self-interest, and a body of literature developed pursuing this line of inquiry.

Economics. In much of the eighteenth- and nineteenth-century literature on economics, we can see this view of man as a rational being. It is, in fact, this Man in the Market place conceptualization which laid the foundation for many of the current decision models. Adam Smith in the *Wealth of Nations* portrayed man as acting in terms of self-interest with respect to economic affairs. Nineteenth-century summaries of this literature depict economic man as one who bases his decisions on deliberate and reasoned consideration of the possible results of his actions. His final choice was based on his perceptions of what could be expected to produce the maximum economic gain.

More recent research reflects these economic aspects clearly. For example, consider the theory of consumer choice where the individual can exchange a fixed amount of one resource for another resource at a given rate. Indifference curves can be drawn showing the points where the consumer should have no reason to prefer one set of values over the other (see Figure 1-2). In this figure, pairs of quantities on the same curve (e.g., X_1, X_2 or X_1', X_2') are assumed to be of equal value to the individual. If he has M amount of commodity 1 and N of commodity 2 and the rate of exchange is depicted by the hue MN, then it is predicted that he will choose $\bar{X}_1$, $\bar{X}_2$. This prediction is made on the assumption that other things being equal, more of a commodity is preferred to less and the consumer wishes to maximize his payoff. Most current theories of economic decision making, of course, realize that man behaves in a suboptimal way relative to economic criteria. That is, other considerations enter into the picture. These economic foundations, however, still serve as models against which individual decision behavior is contrasted.

Mathematics and Operations Research.   One way in which current decision making has been greatly influenced is through the use of statistics and mathematical procedures. A clear impact has been made in two major areas. First, there are mathematical conceptualizations of how man's mind works. These models appear in various forms, including systems of equations and computer simulation programs. Various assumptions from economic man, psychology, and physiology are built into these models and they have helped to advance the understanding of the decision process. Thus, we have come to know in what ways and by how much actual decision processes differ from the models we generate.

A second and equally important contribution based on mathematical foundations is the attempt to make the decision-making process more objective, measurable, and controllable. Measures of system effectiveness have been developed and studies are underway to determine the character of operating influences from the environment. Models are available that evaluate various alternatives in terms of identifiable decision variables. Other models are used to determine production lot quantities, startup times, as well as to estimate the potential impact of uncontrollable variables. These tools allow the individual decision maker to deal with highly complex information flows in a systematic way.

Psychology.   There are perhaps four major trends in psychology which contribute to the current literature on decision making. The first, and perhaps historically most important contribution, was made by Sigmund Freud. His was an emphasis on man's irrationality. People were seen as being controlled by subconscious thoughts and beliefs; repressed emotions guided much of man's behavior. Sex, aggression, and anxiety were all seen as major determinants of even the most innocuous actions. While current thought in psychology and psychiatry has changed our beliefs about the pervasiveness of these influences, their original statement radically modified the underlying views of man as a rational decision maker.

A second field of research, centered in physiological psychology, has dealt with capacities and functioning of the brain. How information is perceived, recorded, stored, transmitted, and combined are areas of major concern. Thus we have come to realize that the brain is composed of perhaps ten billion neurons which perform man's thinking functions. This research, combined with mathematical and technological sophistication, has produced computerized models of mental functioning which are important in our overall view of the decision process. From these efforts an orientation has emerged toward viewing man as an information system.

Another area of investigation has concentrated on the individual's cognitive processes, such as how do we make judgments, how do we combine bits of information. Much of the early work in learning theory is now used as the foundation for current decision theories.

A final contribution has been made by those psychologists interested in the social nature of decision making. Most organizational decision behavior involves interpersonal interaction. The believability of information is influenced by how much we like someone or how much influence he has over our behavior. Effective decisions are partially based upon efficient implementation, a process which calls for the right type of leadership. Thus, investigators began to see decision making in a broader social context.

Organization Theory.   The beliefs about man's rational and economic nature were the major influences on early theories of organizational functioning. In Europe around 1900, there were great changes in the social, economic, technological, and industrial forces that guided the structure and operation of organizations. There was greater commercialism and urbanization. An urban proletariat increasingly replaced the rural peasant class. Mass markets were created to consume the output of mass production which was pushed along by the ever increasing impact of technology.

Max Weber (1864–1920) in the *Protestant Ethic* and *The Spirit of Capitalism* presented a landmark description of early organization theory. Looking at organizations as large aggregates of semiskilled employees producing relatively simple output, he suggested the principles of bureaucracy as a method of organizational analysis. Central to this analysis were the division of labor, centralization of authority, and a rational program of administration and decision making. Written records, rules, and regulations were highlights of the formal organization. The idea of unemotional, economic, rational decision making was directly incorporated into the most important theory of organizational functioning of its time.

In the United States, under somewhat different economic conditions, the school of scientific management developed. While man was still viewed as basically economically oriented, he was also seen as malleable and changeable. Ideas about the division of labor, coupled with the engineering backgrounds of many of the important proponents of the theory, resulted in the idea that training and indoctrination should become an integral part of organizational planning and design. Decision makers were influenced by the system that surrounded them and they found that they, in turn, could influence it (Gantt, 1910).

Also incorporated in the scientific management doctrine was the perspective of man having specific and limited physical capacities. The knowledge of man's physiological capabilities could be used to build better man-machine systems. Motivation could be manipulated through organizational design.

So organizations were set on establishing functional rational systems based on economic and scientific rationales. But two main trends of thought, one from within organizations and one from outside, developed to change this conceptualization. First, in the process of studying the effects of the physical environment on man's behavior, the impact of social factors was discovered. The now-famous Hawthorne studies indicated the effects of social expectations and pressures. Non-economic factors, considered by some to be non-rational, were seen as important determinants of individual behavior in organizations.

From outside, we had the writings of Freud and other psychologists which uncovered man's irrational behavior. These humanizing forces were first elaborated by F. J. Roethlisberger and W. J. Dickson in their book *Management and the Worker*. Man was viewed as a social being, motivated by many more factors than simple economic concerns. Later philosophies suggested by Maslow, Bennis, Argyris, and others see man's striving for economic gain as a rather minor part of his overall motivation system. Of greater importance are issues of social interaction and more meaningful work. Thus, we can see how the views of numerous disciplines have come to influence, mold, and change our picture of man's place in organizations.

But where does this history place us today in terms of decision making? We will attempt in this book to include those rational, scientific, and social elements which constitute current organizational thought. To some extent, they are still independent areas of research; in many other ways, however, they are highly interrelated. Of greatest importance is the fact that they have blended and co-existed rather than completely replaced one another. Many current decision models attempt to incorporate both the rational and irrational and the individual and social aspects of organizational life. We see our role as one of attempting to integrate and summarize these various trends.

DESIGN OF THE BOOK

Our treatment of decision processes assumes that the reader is familiar with the fundamental concepts and terminology of organizational behavior and organization theory. Only a modest background in mathematics, probability, and statistics is required to grasp the quantitative elements that are presented. The implications of our presentation, however, will be more meaningful to those who can draw upon a richer background in these areas.

Subject Orientation of the Book

The primary focus of our analysis is on the principal actor in the organization, the individual decision maker. Our overriding intent is to develop an integrated conceptual view of his decision processes, the organizational environment in which he operates, and the kinds of decision problems he faces. This integrative foundation relies heavily on concepts from organization theory, psychology, and organizational behavior. It is within this integrated structure that we qualitatively analyze selected major dimensions of the individual and his decision-making behavior. The analysis considers (a) ways in which the individual acquires a system of beliefs and values and the significance of these to decision making; (b) characteristics of the individual's information processing activities; and (c) characteristics of the judgment and inference processes in the individual's decision making. The analysis of each of these dimensions has an empirical orientation drawn from research results in management and the behavioral sciences. Research results, rather than methodology, are emphasized. We attempt to identify the implications of these findings for decision-related behavior in organizations.

In the course of studying decision processes, one is impressed with certain limitations of man's decision-making abilities. This leads to a consideration of various decision-making aids—models—which offer promise for overcoming such limitations. However, problems arise concerning when and how to employ such models. To help overcome these difficulties, we have found it useful to first identify specific sources and types of decision-problem complexities. The problem complexities can then be matched with models which are well-suited for handling these types of complexities. This approach is also useful for pointing to worthwhile directions for future model development.

Although individuals are the central figures of decision making, they do not function in isolation in organizations. Group processes, social influence, attitude change, power, and leadership are interpersonal phenomena that profoundly affect organizational decision processes. A large base of theoretical and empirical information about these phenomena is available for enriching our study of decision behavior.

Chapter Organization

The book contains four major sections. This first chapter introduces the reader to the foundation on which the following material is based. It provides an historical perspective and an overview of the book. The second chapter describes individual decision-making processes as we see them. In general, this description integrates individual and social perspectives of the decision process with an emphasis on the individual's perceptual and cognitive contributions. The third chapter deals with the organizational environment and its impact on decisions.

Part Two elaborates on individual decision-making processes within the frameworks of preceding chapters. Chapter 4 describes beliefs and value systems as the fundamental guiding foundations that permeate all phases of decision making. We discuss their acquisition, their role in the decision process, and the implications of such a role. The fifth chapter elaborates on individual information processes, such as perception, motivation, information acquisition, and information utilization. Chapter 6 focuses in more detail on the judgment aspect of the decision process. Here we describe in some detail the factors that influence one's judgment. Such factors as the amount, type, and simplicity of the information that is gathered are considered. Finally, Chapter 7 concludes this section with a description of how certain decision-making models can be used to overcome some of the problems discussed throughout Part Two.

In Part Three, we review the impact of social processes on organizational decision making. Chapter 8 begins with a discussion of how the individual behaves differently in a social context than he does alone. Also included is a review of the major social or group variables which influence decision making, such as interpersonal attraction and group heterogenity. Chapters 9, 10, and 11 carry this elaboration to greater detail. First, we deal with the processes of social influence and attitude change. Since attitudes are seen as an integral part of beliefs and values, how they are changed becomes a major component of the decision process. This extends to a consideration of power and leadership.

Our treatment concludes with a summary of issues for organizational design and action. These issues are derived from the many unanswered questions that appear throughout the book.

Decision Making: An Individual Analysis

So long as people remain the chief instrument of corporate policy a key feature of management decisions will be the choice processes of individual human beings.

Peer Soelberg

The intent of this chapter is to establish a preliminary understanding of individual decision processes. Several important definitions and ways of representing these processes are presented. Later we will build upon the basic frameworks of this chapter to show how the individual fits into the organizational decision setting. To accomplish this goal we must examine the individual in some detail.

DECISION MAKING DEFINED

A number of definitions of *decision* can be found, and the appropriate one depends upon its intended use. For the psychologist, the statistician, the administrator, and the researcher, variations in the "appropriate" definition can be

11

expected. However, common elements do exist among these definitions and our intent here is to provide a more coherent foundation for relating the many facets of organizational decision making that will be elaborated in subsequent chapters. Perusal of the diverse literature on the topic also reveals close intertwinings and, indeed, frequent interchangeability among terms such as decision making, problem solving, and choice behavior. Problem solving has been defined as follows:

> Problem solving, as we will use the term, is thinking activity directed toward reaching some goal; it generally involves thoughtful effort to get around or overcome an obstacle (Costello and Zalkind, 1963, p. 334).

We contrast this definition with Costello and Zalkind's (1963) definition of *decision making* as the choice process; choosing one from among several possibilities (p. 334). This suggests that problem solving is the more pervasive activity which may involve decision making at its culmination, or at other points in the problem-solving process. Problem solving as defined above emphasizes the thought process that precedes terminal choice.

We are now able to explore both choice behavior and problem-solving behavior along a number of dimensions and to attempt to integrate the many dimensions into a coherent structure. Not all choices should be included as part of our concern, but only those related to the organization. We then would define *organizational* decision making as the *choice processes* that occur in the organizational setting together with *choice-related behaviors* and the processes producing them that are directed towards the resolution of organizational problems to reach organizational goals. It is this shared concern for organizational matters that narrows our definition and helps to accurately describe what we will pursue throughout the book.

In developing our view, we will examine both the process and the structure of decision making in the context of organizational settings. It is useful for these purposes to refer to decision problems,[1] situations that demand elements of both decision-making and problem-solving behavior. Since individuals are important actors in the resolution of organizational decision problems, it will be useful to provide frameworks for understanding their decision-related behavior.

DECISION MAKING VIEWED AS A PROCESS

Choice behavior, when viewed as choosing one from among several alternatives, is a relatively narrow and time-specific phenomenon in the context of the "total" decision problem. Choice may appear as the culmination of the larger problem, or at intermediate phases of the problem-solving process. Observation

---

[1] Similar usage can be found in Cyert and March, 1963 and Soelberg, 1966.

of the choice, in itself, is of restricted value for understanding choice behavior. It may not reveal the underlying rationale of the chooser, nor the factors that entered into the choice, nor the manner in which these factors were integrated in making the choice. The study of terminal choice usually provides information of an associational, as opposed to causational, nature, and is therefore of limited value in understanding and predicting this behavior. Consequently, we will view choice behavior or the process of choosing as the culmination of a broader process. The study of this broader process will enable us to relate the final outcome of the choice process to numerous antecedent variables which may effect that choice, and may help to direct future studies of organizational decision behavior.

A COGNITIVE VIEW
OF INDIVIDUAL DECISION PROCESSES

Much of the history of psychology has been ruled by "behavior theorists" who emphasized a non-cognitive, deterministic view of the relationship between stimuli and response.[2] The individual's behavior is theorized to be completely predictable from the knowledge of past positive and negative reinforcements received as a consequence of performing similar acts in similar situations. This view of decision making (and other behavior) as stimulus-response reflexive activity has been criticized for its inability to account for certain behaviors.[3] Alternative views of behavior, which have received increased emphasis in the recent literature (e.g., Mitchell and Biglan, 1972; Dulany, 1967), have been offered by cognitive theorists. One such theoretical framework for behavior in general has been adopted here to help explain individual decision behavior. This cognitive orientation attempts to identify, explain, and interrelate the deliberative processes of this behavior.

We introduce first March and Simon's (1958) "general model of adaptive motivated behavior." Although their model (Figure 2-1) was presented in the more general context of the motivation to "produce," we apply it here to the narrower context of "decision-making activity."

The underlying idea of the model is that individuals attempt to reach satisfied states. Relatively low levels of satisfaction are accompanied by searching for alternative actions. Through the process of searching the environment and his past experiences, the individual is able to assess what will be the likely outcomes (expected value of reward) of various actions. These outcomes are of course more or less attractive depending on numerous factors, including the individual's values and aspirations. Satisfaction and level of aspiration will

[2]See Watson, 1913.
[3]See Miller, Galanter, and Pribram, 1960.

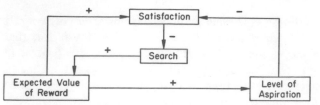

Figure 2-1 General Model of Adaptive Motivated Behavior (*Source:* March and Simon, p. 49.)

increase with increases in the expected value of reward. Through various cognitive processes the individual develops beliefs regarding the behaviors most likely to lead to a desired level of satisfaction, and he behaves accordingly. The model " ... postulates a 'desired' level of satisfaction ... at which search for increased satisfaction would cease" (p. 49). Note that the theory does not argue that the individual will attain ever-increasing levels of satisfaction, but simply that it is his *anticipation* of satisfaction which induces his decision behavior.

In addition to viewing behavior as a process, the model is important in that it introduces an integration of psychological states of the organism (satisfaction, expectations, and level of aspiration) and cognitive and/or overt activity of a specific type (search). Furthermore, it views the individual as adaptive; that is, the interaction of behavior, the situation, and psychological factors provides the means for adaptations to diverse situations.

As pointed out by March and Simon and others, many individual and organizational variables influence the behavioral processes depicted in the general model. Decision-related activities of the organizational actor are initiated in part by his "psychological state" or personality characteristics. But there are also various social and organizational forces that set such activities into motion. To understand this activation process we will first present a broad categorization of individual decision-making activities and identify the various problem stages in which the individual's cognitive processes are applied. We will then elaborate on these cognitive processes.

PHASES OF DECISION PROBLEMS

In Figure 2-2 are shown what Simon (1960) has identified as the *phases* of the decision-making process. These phases identify the various "things" that decision behavior is directed toward, as opposed to identifying the processes involved in behavior. *Intelligence activity* includes scanning the environment and maintaining an awareness of the occasion for decision. Environmental cues from many sources are integrated into an organized whole, serving as the basis for intended search and discovery of the need for goal-directed decisions. Gathering, categorizing, and processing information are the major components of this phase. The phase of *design activity* includes the development and examination of

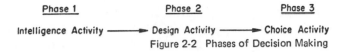

Phase 1   Phase 2   Phase 3

Intelligence Activity ————▶ Design Activity ————▶ Choice Activity

Figure 2-2   Phases of Decision Making

courses of action available to the decision maker. The individual at this point attempts to assess what sorts of consequences are likely to occur as a result of various alternative decisions. He must also attend to the values or attractiveness associated with these consequences. Finally, *choice activity* is the phase of decision making involving the choice itself. Either because of internal or external pressures the choice must be made. The individual will use the information he has gathered to compare the alternatives and choose the one that he believes will best accomplish his goals.

Viewed from the time perspective of the individual these activity phases need not occur in the strict uninterrupted sequence shown in Figure 2-2. He may engage in two phases concurrently or may repeatedly cycle between two phases as he grapples with an ongoing decision problem. Furthermore, since individual decisions influence other elements in the organizational setting, we can expect activity in any of the phases to initiate related sub-activities. Without regard to their order of occurrence, these broad activity categories of intelligence, design, and choice are useful descriptions of different activities to which the individual devotes his intellective processes while he is making decisions.

Cognitive Processes. Laying out the phases of decision making, as in Figure 2-2, begs the question of identifying the individual's cognitive processes that are activated in these phases. We can further refine our "picture" of the individual in the organization by attributing to him certain higher-level intellective capacities: abstraction, assimilation, and projection (foresight). These higher-level processes operate on the "evoked set"[4] (March and Simon, 1958) of the memory and the perceptual experience of the individual. Higher level mental processes result in inferences and judgments which themselves become cues for the individual. The decision maker's cognitive processes are viewed as unfolding in the sequence shown in Figure 2-3.

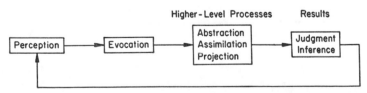

Figure 2-3   Individual Cognitive Processes in Decision

[4]A detailed definition of "evoked set" is presented in the following pages.

Relating this view of the individual to the preceding categorization of phases of decision making (Figure 2-2), we note that the individual's judgments and inferences may pertain to intelligence, design, or choice activity. That is, through the process of perceiving information, processing it, and making judgments or inferences about it, he may be engaging in any of our three phases of decision activity. He may make judgments about the existence of a problem, where to gather information, whether to include various strategies, or the likelihood of certain events occurring. Since we are implying that the same underlying processes are operating in all three phases, we will proceed to define and elaborate upon each of the variables mentioned in Figure 2-3.

COMPONENTS OF THE COGNITIVE MODEL

Perception. All of us are constantly receiving information from our environment. This information reaches us through our senses; somehow we manage to incorporate and interpret these inputs without great confusion. This process is known as perception and can be defined as "the experience people have as the proximate result of the sensory inputs. The process is one of selection and organization of sensations to provide the meaningful entity we experience."[5] The important factor to note is that perception is distinct from what one might call the "real world" or the physical reality of stimulus information. Perception is our interpretation or experience of that objective reality. It includes processes of receiving and filtering inputs from the external world. We will return to this point later in the chapter.

Evocation. Borrowing the notions of March and Simon (1958), one's internal state is a function of his history and experience and is recorded in his memory. This memory includes programs for selectively responding to perceived environmental stimuli. Perceived stimuli trigger or activate only a portion of the information from one's total memory content. These selected portions of one's memory are activated in response to the particular environmental elements that have been perceived by the individual. Changes in the content of the evoked set can occur over short time periods.

> We call the part of memory that is influencing behavior at a particular time the *evoked set,* and any process that causes some memory content to be transferred from the second (unevoked) category to the first a process for *evoking* that content (p. 10).

Higher-Level Processes.[6] Operation of the evoked set of programs for responding to perceived environmental elements is dependent upon several types

[5]Kolasa, 1969, p. 211.

[6]For a more extensive discussion of "higher-level" processes see J. S. Bruner, Goodnow, and Austin, 1956.

of cognitive processes. For instance, perceived environmental stimuli are not internalized as "wholes" but are represented in "summary" form by a small number of distinctive attributes. This process of representation we will denote as the process of "abstraction." It is a simplifying device which enables the individual to record the essence of the stimulus without being encumbered by a large number of its highly detailed attributes, subsequently permitting cognitive organization and categorization.

"Assimilation" is a process by which cognitive organization occurs. Abstracted elements are matched and combined into meaningful representations of the "whole" and are related to previously acquired ideas and concepts. "Projection" is viewed as a process in which previously assimilated inputs are reorganized into varieties of new configurations.

Results. The outputs of higher-level processes we call "judgment" and "inference." These terms refer to the generalizations which are produced through the other processes. These generalizations frequently imply summary statements of how things are, ought to be, or will be. They can further serve as predictions or explanations of one's own actions or of the actions of human and non-human elements in the environment.

Figure 2-3, then, is a representation of individual cognitive processes involved in decision making. During the decision-making phases of searching, defining alternatives, evaluating, choosing, etc., the individual is constantly involved in sifting, categorizing, and processing information from the environment and from his past experiences. We further note the circularity of relationships in this process. More specifically, the resulting judgments and inferences may themselves be regarded as environmental stimuli which can influence the cognitive system from which they were derived.

A DYNAMIC MODEL: THE TOTE UNIT

So far we have identified some of the significant cognitive activity which precedes choice behavior. We have noted that decision making is a process involving cognitive activities in the various phases of decision making. The individual searches, perceives, assimilates, and makes judgments in these various phases. The reason the individual engages in these activities was attributed, in the model represented by Figure 2-1, to his striving to achieve some desired level of satisfaction. But now it would be desirable to explain *how* these cognitive processes work and to show how all of these activities are internally organized in moving the individual to a more satisfying state.

Obviously, our current capabilities for understanding and explaining human behavior, including decision behavior, are limited and inexact. On the one hand, we have unobservable cognitive activities such as perception, evocation, abstraction, etc., that occur in the individual. On the other hand, we have his observable overt behaviors and actions. In order to understand and predict his overt behavior, it would be desirable to show how this overt behavior is related to the unobservable processes that lead to it. Accordingly, we will examine a model which attempts to represent the *structure* of behavior.

The behavior model of Miller, Galanter, and Pribram (1960) is concerned with the " . . . theoretical vacuum between cognition and action" (p. 11), and proposes one rationale for linking this gap. To understand individual behavior they have presented a fundamental unit of behavior called the TOTE (*T*est-*O*perate-*T*est-*E*xit) unit. The TOTE unit is a theoretical attempt to represent the basic structure underlying all individual behavior. It suggests a psychological theory that is an alternative to other theories such as the stimulus-response approaches. We will not become involved in a discussion of this controversy. But because the TOTE concept is a useful way of visualizing the underlying structure of decision-related behavior, we shall discuss it and selected aspects of the psychological theory of which it is a part.

The TOTE Unit. The theory applies to the most simple individual behaviors, including elementary thought processes and simple motor activities such as walking, as well as to the highly complex behaviors involved in decision-making activity. The most simple behavior may be structured as a TOTE unit shown in Figure 2-4.

Two central concepts of TOTE are: (1) phases of behavioral control and (2) the feedback loop.

1. Phases of Behavioral Control Even the most basic behavioral activity, whether mental or physical, involves at least two phases—a "test" phase and an "operate" phase that occur in sequence. Primary control over the individual's behavior resides in one of these phases at any point in time. Upon receipt of input (information) from the environment, control of the individual's behavior resides in a "test" phase in which at least two types of evaluations are performed:

(a) The first part of "test" asks, "Are the stimulus inputs (the perceived state of the relevant world) congruent with the individual's image of what *should*

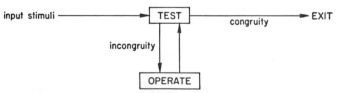

Figure 2-4 The TOTE Unit (*Source:* Miller, Galanter and Pribram, p. 26.)

be?" If such congruence exists, then no further behavior is elicited with respect to the stimulus input.

(b) If an incongruity is perceived between the state of the world and the individual's belief of what the state should be, then we can expect the individual to engage in activities, i.e., to perform certain "operations" that are intended to eliminate the incongruence. But to do this the individual must first "test" to determine that the "operation" that is to follow is indeed an appropriate one for eliminating the incongruence.

> The test phase can be regarded as any process for determining that the operational phase is appropriate. . . . In order to ensure that an operation is relevant, a test must be built into it. Unless the test gives the appropriate outcome, control cannot be transferred to the operational phase (p. 29).

If the operation is relevant and if incongruity exists between stimulus inputs and "test" criteria, primary control of the individual's behavior is then passed to the appropriate "operate" phase.

In "operate," the individual's behavioral activities are directed toward modification of the state of the world. Simple examples might include taking a shower to increase one's alertness, or studying for an extra hour in an attempt to understand a difficult concept. Although the "operate" activity may be either physical or mental, the main point is that the dominant focus of behavior is on "doing something." You have already determined that something should be done and thus, at this stage (operate), the primary focus of behavior is not directed toward answering that question. Rather, having answered that question affirmatively, dominant control of behavior has been passed to the operate phase.

Our discussion thus far has illustrated a central concept in TOTE, the concept that behavior related to particular stimulus inputs resides in distinctive phases, one of which is in dominant control at a point in time. We now turn to a second major concept that is an integral part of the TOTE construct, the feedback loop.

2. The Feedback Loop Continuing with our sequence of activity phases, subsequent to the "operations" performed by the individual, control of behavior is returned to the "test" phase where the evaluative assessments described earlier are repeated. After fifteen minutes you may discontinue the "operation" of studying and ask "Where is this getting me?" or "Have I now developed a sufficient understanding?" These questions indicate that primary behavioral control has been passed from the "operate" (studying) phase back to the "test" phase which now dominates your behavior. An important distinction, however, is that you are no longer "testing" the same stimulus inputs as were "tested" before. You are now "testing" stimulus inputs which have been at least partially affected (revised) by your own "operations." If a state of congruence exists, behaviors related to this set of stimulus inputs are discontinued. Incongruence between desired and actual "states of the world" call for return to the "operate" phase. Thus, control is passed back to "operate" and your dominant behavior focuses again on studying the materials and concepts with which you are concerned.

The important point in this discussion is that the results of "operate" are directly linked to "test." The "test" phase subsequently acts as a comparator to determine whether further "operation" or exit from the TOTE is appropriate.

We thus see at the most fundamental level that " . . . the operations an organism performs are constantly guided by the outcomes of various tests" (p. 29). Behavior is viewed as highly organized activity in which the "test" phase includes some criteria for evaluating input stimuli, the criteria being a reflection of the individual's cognitions about how the "world" is and how it should be.

We must now consider where the "test" criteria that are used by the individual come from, and we will illustrate how the basic TOTE unit can be used to represent the more molar—rather than molecular—behavior that is common to decision-making activity.

The Image. The TOTE concept assumes that the individual is sensitive to the larger environment in which he exists. He acquires an internal representation of his environment through his past experiences and he also has expectations about the future. The kinds of behaviors that can be expected from an individual depend upon his view of the environment: "a human being . . . builds up an internal representation, a model of the universe, a scheme, a simulacrum, a cognitive map, an *Image*" (p. 7). It is this organized experience base (cognitive organization) which guides individual behavior.

Image. The Image is all the accumulated, organized knowledge that the organism has about itself and its world (p. 17).

The Image plays a central role in the TOTE concept. The Image is the source from which the evaluative criteria for the "test" phase of TOTE are derived. Input stimuli are the basis for perceiving the existing state of the environment which is then compared to the criteria, residing in the Image, of what the environmental state should be. The individual also relies upon this accumulated base of knowledge, the Image, for the criteria needed to determine the appropriateness of alternative "operations." Recalling momentarily the previously discussed higher-level processes of abstraction, assimilation, and projection, we can see that their continual operation over time determines the content of the Image. The higher-level processes result in judgments and inferences which reflect the individual's orientation to the future, and this orientation is a significant part of the Image.[7] Your expectations of what lies ahead coupled with your accumulated reservoir of "operations" that have proven appropriate for various stimulus energies result in the formation of more intricate structures for guiding highly complex behavior. Such complex structures have been defined as *Plans* by Miller, *et al.*

Plans. Having developed an understanding of the structure of the basic unit of behavior, the TOTE, it can now be used to build descriptions of more complex mental processes and behaviors such as those related to decision making. The behaviors represented by several TOTEs may be combined to represent larger, more complex behaviors. Such combinations of TOTEs are called Plans.

A Plan is any hierarchical process in the organism that can control the order in which a sequence of operations is to be performed (p. 16).

The individual possesses an accumulation of Plans that have been developed from his experiences and that vary in complexity and frequency of activation. Plans consisting of a single TOTE are the least complex set in the individual's repertoire. Regarding one's orientation toward the future, " ... you have expectations of what lies ahead ... you construct a Plan to meet those expectations ... as time progresses you develop subplans to elaborate on major activities in your overall Plan" (p. 5). Although complex, or molar, behavior has a more complicated structure, this structural complexity is nonetheless patterned. Molar behavior is represented by compounding several TOTE units. Thus the TOTE unit, as the smallest fundamental unit of behavior, is always present. However, the number of such units and the ways in which they are interrelated increase as we attempt to represent the structure of more molar behavior. The resulting Plans enable the individual to cope with his expectations in an organized way:

In all cases, however, the existence of a TOTE should indicate that an organizing, coordinating unit has been established, that a Plan is available (p. 29).

To use the TOTE concept to depict behavior in a hierarchical fashion Miller, *et al.* allows that

... the operational components of TOTE units may themselves be TOTE units. That is to say, the TOTE pattern describes both strategic and tactical

[7]The Image concept has been operationally defined and measured in a study of decision making in a research and development environment. See Cravens, 1970.

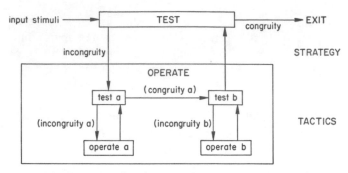

Figure 2-5   Compound Plan (Adapted from Miller, *et al.,* p. 36.)

units of behavior. Thus the operational phase of a higher-order TOTE might itself consist of a string of other TOTE units, and each of these, in turn, may contain still other strings of TOTEs, and so on (p. 32).

Compound Plans are formed by expansions within the "operate" phase of a TOTE unit, as shown in Figure 2-5. The major TOTE hierarchy "tests" and "operates" on other TOTE hierarchies. Within the hierarchy of TOTEs we can distinguish between tactical and strategic units:

The molar units in the organization of behavior will be said to comprise the behavioral strategy, and the molecular units, the tactics (p. 17).

Let us look at a simplified example of one problem confronting a manufacturing supervisor to illustrate the structure shown in Figure 2-5. The supervisor receives news (input stimulus) of a customer complaint about the quality of the product manufactured by the company. This information is adjudged by the supervisor in the "test" phase as being incongruent with the information that he should have received if his manufacturing process was operating correctly. Dominant control of the supervisor's behavior is passed to a compound "operate" phase consisting of two subplans, a and b. In "test" phase "a" he realizes that he should know whether or not his manufacturing process is under control. Without reports to the contrary he has been assuming that it is operating correctly. However, this recently acquired information causes him to question this assumption, resulting in "incongruity a"; he is unsure whether the stimulus was indicative of random or assignable causes. "Incongruity a" results in his sampling of current production output and procedures, "operation a"—which is one kind of action that will allow him to determine whether the stimulus was indicative of random rather than assignable causes. If, from the observation of current output ("operate a") it was concluded that the equipment was being improperly used, then an incongruity exists between actual and desired states of the environment ("test a"). Having arrived at an explanation of the source of the defective unit (represented by "congruity a"), control of his behavior is passed to TOTE unit "b." In "test b" the supervisor knows that proper operation of the production equipment is necessary for maintaining process control. "Operation b," retraining the equipment operator, is undertaken until such time as proper equipment utilization is realized. The achievement of a state of congruity for TOTE "b" results in "exit" from the Plan when the information he receives about his current output is congruent with what should be received under properly controlled conditions.

We note several points regarding our example. First, the search behavior of subplan "a" was a necessary preparatory phase which preceded subplan "b." It is only after the assignable cause is found that the conditions are appropriate for initiating the next, or corrective action, part of the Plan. To be more realistic our search subplan, phase "a," should be further subdivided to represent a larger number of search objects, such as past production records, examination of the defective unit, laboratory analysis of the defective unit, etc. Thus, phase "a" may be refined to include a hierarchical list of related TOTEs for determining the source of the defective product. Regardless of the amount of detail used to represent the search phase, the supervisor's search operations must continue until a reasonable explanation of the defective source has been found, an explanation that is consistent with his Image.

In addition to having Plans operating on subplans in the TOTE hierarchy, we should also note the generality of use of the TOTE phases. "Operate" may, as in our example, include search for information, alternatives, or problem clarification and identification.

> . . . a creature is executing a particular Plan when in fact that Plan is controlling the sequence of operations he is carrying out. When an organism executes a Plan he proceeds through it step by step, completing one part and then moving to the next. The execution of a Plan need not result in overt action—especially in man, it seems to be true that there are Plans for collecting or transforming information, as well as Plans for guiding actions (p. 17).

As stated earlier, the original concern of this cognitive theory was providing a way of relating cognitive and overt behaviors. The Plan, structured as TOTE units, relates the individual's actions (behavior responses) to his Image of "self" and "environment" as summarized below:

a. The Plan is structured as a set of TOTEs,
b. Test is one phase of TOTE,
c. Test is a comparator of "what is" and "what is desired,"
d. "What is" and "what is desired" is part of the individual's Image.

Sub-conclusion: The Image is part of the test phase and includes an evaluative component, and

e. Incongruities arising from c and d result in individual action, either
further cognitive activity or overt behavior.

It now becomes clearer how the TOTE concept relates to our earlier
discussions. We had noted that only selected portions of total memory are
activated—evoked—in response to environmental stimuli. We may now picture
this "evoked set" as consisting of organized, although possibly incomplete,
Plans.

... when we choose a Plan and begin to execute it we may be unaware of
some of the detailed tactics that will be needed to carry it through ... (p. 63).

Furthermore, the individual is motivated to act by a discrepancy between
incoming information and his beliefs of how the world has been in the past and
how it ought to be. The Image thus contains both beliefs and values which direct
behavior toward the reduction of these discrepancies, thereby permitting the
attainment of a more satisfied state. We will find in later chapters that this idea
has provided the theoretical rationale for much of the social psychological
literature on motivation, attitudes, and attitude change. We will also have more
to say about the acquisition and nature of beliefs and values.

BEYOND COGNITION: INPUTS AND OUTPUTS

Having developed a view of the individual's cognitive activities we wish now to
reorient our discussion to consider the "ends" of our conceptualization, i.e., the
"perception" and "results" in Figure 2-3. What are the sources of information
which are perceived and what are the behavioral consequences of all this
cognitive activity? Let us first explore the nature and sources of environmental
stimuli that enter the individual's cognitive processes.

Inputs: Objective and Subjective Reality.   To date our individual has future
expectations, has acquired a knowledge base called an "Image" (and continues
to build upon this base), and continues to develop a repertoire of Plans for
coping with the environment in an organized fashion. But what is this "environment" which is so influential on the individual? We are concerned with a very
special environment, that of the organization into which we will insert the
decision maker. This environment consists of a myriad of human and physical
elements of such great number that complete comprehension by an individual is
prohibitive. Furthermore, the elements vary as to their significance to the
individual's role in the organization. In order to cope with such vastness one
employs a process of cognitive simplification as was discussed in reference to

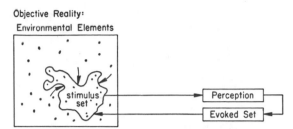

Figure 2-6   Environmental Stimuli at a Point in Time

Figure 2-3. This simplified view of the environment we call "subjective reality." "Objective reality," on the other hand, consists of all environmental elements that actually exist. Viewed at a point in time, some of the environmental elements are influencing one's behavior while others are not. Those elements which are influencing behavior are *stimuli*. As to the question of which of the possible environmental elements will be stimuli at a point in time and which will not, March and Simon comment:

> The stimuli that are present at a given time are major determiners of what set will be evoked or maintained; conversely, the set at any given time will be a major determiner of what parts of the environment will be effective as stimuli. There is no circularity in this relation—just the usual kind of mutual interaction among variables of a dynamic system (p. 10).

These interrelations are portrayed in Figure 2-6. The stimulus set consists of selected elements of the environment at a point in time, a set which includes only part of "objective reality."[8] The individual's perception of this set mediates the evoked set of memory. The evoked set, in turn, influences the composition of the stimulus set. The perception of a scheduled meeting date on one's calendar may result in the evocation of a set of preparatory tasks that were to have been completed prior to the meeting. This evoked set subsequently results in redirection of attention to previously unattended elements of the environment, elements which now become part of the stimulus set. Over time the bounds of the stimulus set expand, contract, and change in shape to encompass various elements of objective reality. The elements of objective reality in the stimulus set may be "filtered" or altered by perceptual processes which will be discussed later in more detail.

We can now link the constructs in Figure 2-6 to the individual's "higher-level processes" and "results." As shown in Figure 2-7, the Image is seen to include a conceptualization of the relevant environment. This conceptualization is "sub-

---

[8]Unanticipated events in the environment can become effective stimuli and can subsequently trigger off a number of other new stimuli. For a vivid example see Cyert, Dill, and March, 1958.

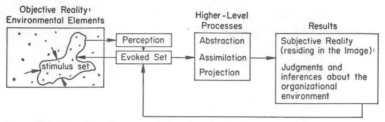

Figure 2-7   Cognitive Processes Related to the *Image*

jective reality" for the organism at an instant in time. We see that the issues and problems to which the individual devotes his energies are mediated by his perceptions. Furthermore, since individuals differ in their higher-level capacities, we can expect them to have different perceptions of the relevance of various environmental elements.

Environmental Forces and Internal States.   We have presented our concepts in a time context; specifically, we have pictured them "at an instant in time." This allows us to better portray the decision maker's adaptive and dynamic features.

> The behavior of an organism through a short interval of time is to be accounted for by (1) its internal state at the beginning of the interval, and (2) its environment at the beginning of the interval. The same two sets of factors, the initial state and the environment, determine not only the behavior but also what the internal state will be at the next moment of time (Miller, *et al.,* p. 9).

As previously stated, the Image is all of one's accumulated organized knowledge about himself and his world. Part of this Image, which resides in memory, is the representation of the "organizational world" in which he participates. The concept of an adaptive organism allows that the Image changes with time. If we stop the "clock," identifiable dimensions of the Image appear to possess "levels" or state-descriptions. At this instant in time, the individual has a fixed set of beliefs and values, expectations of the future, a specific evoked set of memory, and perceptions of relevant elements of the environment. The changes that subsequently occur in these Image dimensions from time to time are functions of their previous levels and various environmental forces that intervene to change these levels. Simon (1957, p. 199) has labeled these latter forces as organizational and social. Organizational forces stem from formal attempts to create a planned environment designed to screen out or minimize random disturbances. Organizational goals, structure, communication and role relationships, etc., are imposed to influence the individuals in the system. However, environmental forces may also arise from unintended "social" sources, as delineated in Figure

2-8. As a consequence of these organizational and social forces, certain behavioral and environmental phenomena arise. Power, leadership, group dynamics, and social influence—the environmental and behavioral phenomena—are derived from, and are attributable to, these social forces. However, the relationship is not one-way. The contents and strengths of the organizational and social forces are influenced, in turn, by the behavioral and environmental phenomena. Note that all the factors found in Figure 2-8 are relevant and meaningful only when there are two or more individuals in the same environment. We have now expanded our conceptualization to include unique phenomena arising from the interactions of numerous people. Interpersonal and group behavior are highly relevant to any discussion of organizational decision processes and we will elaborate on these topics in later chapters.

Returning to the notion of evocation, we can now view the organizational forces as those which are intended to control most of the content of the stimulus set, at least to establish bounds on the content of this set, thereby influencing and modifying the evoked set. The social forces, intended or not, may lead to similar effects on the stimulus and evoked sets.[9] These social forces affect the current status of individual attributes that influence what one does. Characteristics such as attention, creativity, motivation, etc., are jointly determined by past experience and present circumstances. Furthermore, the individual's access to information in the organizational environment is affected by these social forces. So, both the characteristics of the person and his perceptions of the environment are partially determined by social interactions. In summary, these forces, acting overtime, are seen to influence the individual's Image.

Individual Attributes. From the behavioral sciences, we can identify many important dimensions of the individual which may be changed by social forces.

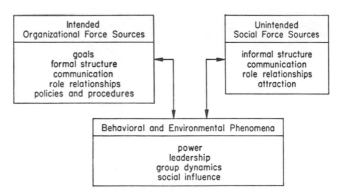

Figure 2-8   Force Sources and Behavioral Phenomena

[9]A study by Pounds (1969) illustrates how various organizational and social forces operate to redirect the attention of the problem solver.

Selected attributes are listed in Table 2-1. At a point in time each attribute may be characterized as consisting of an accumulated level acquired through historical experiences. The current levels of these dimensions determine the individual's predisposition to behave or act in response to current forces in the organizational environment.

Table 2-1   Individual Attributes

Personality Attributes	Motivation	Cognitions
creativity cognitive structure intellectual capacity	adaptation level aspiration	values attitudes expectations

In future chapters we will attempt to identify theoretical and empirical relationships between these and related dimensions where they are believed to exist. We will focus on the significance of these dimensions for decision-making in the organization.

Outputs. We wish to stress that the individual is not a passive instrument within the organizational environment, but rather is directly instrumental and

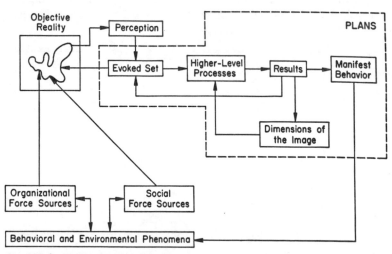

Figure 2-9   The Individual's Decision Processes

predisposed toward influencing its direction. It is suggested that the "behavioral and environmental phenomena" represent one of the media that the decision maker will act upon and through in attempting to influence the organizational and social forces acting upon him. This is depicted in Figure 2-9 as a directed outflow of behavior. Again, this observed behavior may be directed toward the intelligence, design, or choice phases of the decision process. The higher-level processes and the Image dimensions will be related to the intelligence, design, and choice phases of decision making in greater detail in subsequent chapters.

SUMMARY AND PREVIEW

The purpose of this chapter was to provide a framework suitable for a comprehensive understanding of organizational decision processes. We have considered the individual's decision making from both process and structural viewpoints. The orientation is toward a cognitive representation of the decision maker acting on various phases of decision problems in an organized manner. The organizational environment in which he maneuvers has been characterized as having intended and unintended forces which influence, and are influenced by, his decision-related behavior.

Many new terms and concepts were introduced. We will find in subsequent chapters, however, that this framework provides an excellent referent for the work conducted by numerous investigators in different disciplines. This type of integration is one of the major purposes of the book.

The environment of decision will be considered in greater detail in the following chapter. The structure and acquisition of the knowledge base, and the limitations and character of selected dimensions of the individual, will be considered in later chapters. We will also examine ways of assisting a limited-capacity organism in situations which imply the need for Plans of such complexities that they exceed the individual's capacities. For such situations we will endeavor to specify conditions in which such human limitations can be partially overcome by the assistance of various models. Similarly, we will expand upon the nature and roles of the "behavioral and environmental phenomena" in organizational decision-making processes.

The Environment
of Decision

We now undertake the task of describing the "environment" in which the individual operates as a decision-making unit. We are concerned with environment because it is a phenomenon of which the decision maker is a part. As such, it is assumed that decision behavior influences, and is influenced by, the environment.

Although many authors have written about the environment of decisions, it is difficult to find a universally accepted definition. However, we can identify many of the dimensions which should be included in a decision-oriented definition. Wilson and Alexis (1962), for example, use the term environment to encompass the set of contingencies that are not within the decision maker's control, and yet, are partial determinants of the outcome that results from the decision. Dill (1962), in discussing the topic from a somewhat different perspective, suggests that organizations actually have multiple environments, rather than a single environment. This same idea is implied in the following statement by Feldman and Kanter (1965):

Organizational decisions are constrained by the actions of the organization itself, by the physical and mental characteristics and previous experience of its members, and by the social, political, and economic environment of the organization and its members (p. 619).

The diversity of potential sources of influence on decision processes was outlined by Tannenbaum (1950) when he noted that the decision maker's "sphere of discretion" is limited by the structure and authority relationships that are unique to his organization. Such constraints are an important part of the decision environment for each organizational position. External to the organization are groups and institutions which further limit organizational actions. These environmental elements include governmental agencies, parties to contracts, trade associations, and general social customs of the society.

We find from this brief introduction that many elements may comprise the environment of decision. In pursuing these ideas in greater detail, our intent is to discuss how the environment helps to explain differences in decision behavior within organizations.

THE INDIVIDUAL AS AN ENVIRONMENTAL ELEMENT

Internal Environment of the Decision Unit

Recognize first, at the narrowest level, a distinction between the "real" world surrounding the decision unit and the "perceived" world of that unit. As discussed in the previous chapter, a thinking, perceiving, adaptive decision unit engaged in purposeful activity, in whatever setting, is itself a significant environmental subcomponent. The individual's image, his evoked set of memory, and his capacity for higher-level processes may be regarded as the composition of the person's *internal* environment at a moment in time. The composition of this internal environment is changed over time by decision-related behavior. Although many dimensions of this environment may be neither measurable nor directly observable, they nonetheless are postulated to result in different behaviors insofar as they vary with time and across decision makers. Two decision makers may be inserted into a common "larger" environment and yet be said to exist in different environments to the extent that they are internally different. This phenomenon is not a new one, but is a restatement of what is commonly called "individual differences" by psychologists. We wish merely to suggest its relevance to the concept of "decision environment." The psychological make-up of the decision maker, then, is a significant subcomponent of the organizational decision environment. We will later elaborate on various dimensions of the individual's internal environment.

External Environment of the Decision Unit

Still focusing on the individual as a decision unit, we can consider the importance to decision behavior of the stimuli in the world external to the individual. For our purposes, the *relevant external environment* of the individual consists of those external stimuli which effect, or potentially effect, his organization-related behavior. It is apparent from such a definition that the relevant environment is not restricted to elements within the confines of the organization, but includes external elements as well. From the outside world, significant cues impinge upon him through his various roles and social affiliations. Aspects of family, church, school, and other roles in the community may be carried over into one's organizational life (Simon, 1965). Indeed, the culture of which the individual is a part has been cited for its "homogenizing influences," reflected in the beliefs, aspirations, attitudes toward authority, orientations toward time, perceptions, and interpretations of reality among individuals (Thompson, 1967). One's orientation toward his organizational role and how it "fits" with non-organizational roles and affiliations is important in examining organizational behavior. Ultimately, March and Simon have identified these as core considerations in the individual's decision to particpate or to cease participation in the organization (Simon, 1965; March and Simon, 1965).

The roles that are inherited and/or learned in the non-organizational environment are important in forming the personal life-goals that are brought to the organizational setting. To these must be added the cues which emanate from significant organizational elements. These latter cues arise from the formal hierarchy, the task, officially prescribed work rewards, and influences of associates in the organization (March and Simon, 1965). The many sources of cues (intended and unintended) were seen in the previous chapter as forces acting upon the stimulus set of the individual. Hence, they are important effectors of decision behavior.

Having examined the composition of internal and external environmental elements which influence the decision maker, we can now examine specific ways in which his decision-making behavior can be mediated in the organizational setting. A clear picture of how this may be accomplished is the purpose of development of the remainder of this book, and will not be summarized until the final chapter. A necessary antecedent to this end is a consideration of the environment from the organization's, rather than the individual's, perspective.

Multiple Environments of the Organization

The organization is an entity in which decision making is a pervasive ongoing form of behavior. But an understanding of "decisions" and "decision behavior" will remain elusive and weak until we provide a structure—a mechanism—that identifies distinctive characteristic differences among diverse decision situations. We earlier identified a general unit of cognitive behavior for the decision maker, his general phases of decision making, a conceptualization of his Image, and a general identification of variables that influence the "relevant world" in which he performs. But the demands imposed on him change with time, and are dissimilar across various places within the organization. Viewed throughout the organization, decision problems vary in complexity, demanding principal reliance on different sets of skills in varying situations. We can also see differences in the relative importance of the decisions that are made. Similarly, one can readily point to variations in the bounds of decision-making discretion that exist among decision-demanding situations. In consideration of this apparent heterogeneity, a clearer understanding of decision behavior can be obtained by presenting a sufficiently detailed concept of what the organization is. Toward this end, we present a brief model of organizations. Such a model, by definition, identifies the bounds that distinguish the organization from other elements comprising the larger world. It thereby provides one basis for conceptually organizing the sources of intraorganizational heterogeneity.

The Organization as a System

At the core of our picture of the organization are certain concepts from what has been called "general systems theory."[1] The organization is viewed as a configuration of mutually interdependent subunits. The configuration is man-made, as opposed to natural, and its structure is modified by man to accomplish specified purposes. As the entity's purposes may change over time, we witness corresponding structural modifications for maintaining its viability.

Although the day-to-day actions of an organization may be unpredictable, we assume that over longer periods of time they are generally orderly and patterned. Accordingly, we adopt the following characteristic of complex organizations, and will explore its implications for decision making:

> ... we will conceive of complex organizations as open systems, hence indeterminate and faced with uncertainty, but at the same time as subject to criteria of rationality and hence needing determinateness and certainty (Thompson, 1967, p. 10).

Although each of these entities—organizations—has a uniqueness along many dimensions, we wish to focus on some of their general, commonly shared attributes.

---

[1] For an excellent critical survey of general systems theory as related to organization, see the *Academy of Management Journal*, December 1972.

Exchange Relationships. As a subunit of the larger world in which it exists, organizational survival is dependent upon the development and maintenance of exchanges of energy and resources. The organization relies, on the input side, upon the larger environment as the source of human, physical, and other resources needed to accomplish its goals. It likewise depends on the larger environment for consumption of its "products." In a more fundamental sense, the organization depends on the outer environment for its legitimation—the explicit or implied agreement that it can exist. In light of these dependencies, it is understandable that significant organizational action is expended to cultivate, maintain, and modify exchange relationships with the environment.

Three Organizational Decision Environments

Within the organization structure we can abstract three "relevant environments." The distinction arises from Parsons' (1960) identification of *technical, managerial,* and *institutional* levels of organizational activity. Most organizations are structured into specialized subunits, each having primary responsibility at one of these levels. The focus of attention and concern at one level is on different phenomena than at others. Thus, we can expect the nature of decisions to differ across these levels. The primary concerns at the technical level are technology-oriented, with emphasis on attainment of immediate output goals of the organization through the operation of its conversion processes. The institutional level is principally involved with cultivating exchange relationships between the organization and the larger environment, with maintaining legitimation, and with defining the organization's role in the larger environment. The managerial level provides the necessary linkages between the technical level and the exterior environment by procuring input resources and effecting the disposition of organizational outputs.

We see immediately that the decision situations at one level differ from those at another because the "attention-directing" factors and relevant variables are drastically different. This results in three distinctive decision environments. We will explore each of these environments in greater detail.

The Technical Core

Complex organizations are built to operate technologies which are found to be impossible or impractical for individuals to operate. . . . Clearly, technology is an important variable in understanding the actions of complex organizations (Thompson, 1967, p. 15).

The *technical core* is the "layer" of the organization that is concerned with operating its technology to achieve desired outputs in a rational manner. The criteria for technical rationality are: (a) *effectiveness*, the extent to which activities result in desired outcomes; and (b) *economic efficiency*, the avoidance of unnecessary resource expenditures.

To facilitate the attainment of technical rationality the organization seeks closure around its technical core. Complete closure is never possible because core activities are interdependent with the managerial and institutional levels, which are open to environmental impingements. Nevertheless, persistent attempts are made to attain an environment of certainty within the technical core. To the extent that such shielding is attained, the sources of uncertainty are principally confined to the technology itself, and decisions focus upon maintaining and improving the operation of the transformation processes.

Within the technical core, Thompson has identified three types of technologies: (1) long-linked, (2) mediating, and (3) intensive. These different technologies partially determine the extent to which closure of the technical core is possible. The distinguishing feature of *long-linked* technologies is the serial interdependence of subactivities comprising the transformation process. This is exemplified by mass production operations in which standardized precedence relationships exist among sequences of subactivities.

The *mediating* technology is one in which the primary function is to provide linkages between clients who wish to be interlinked. A real estate firm provides such a linkage between buyers and sellers, as does a securities exchange. The operations of the mediating technology must be standardized to facilitate coordination among organizational activities and to facilitate the "matching" of clients. This is particularly crucial since the mediating technology must be operated *extensively*, matching " . . . multiple clients or customers distributed in time and space" (p. 16).

The *intensive* technology consists of a variety of techniques or services which are applied in varying combinations depending upon the state of the client or customer. Whereas one client may need an extensive application of technique A followed by technique B, another client may need numerous combinations of other available techniques. The unique needs of hospital patients illustrate the intensive technology. Whereas one patient may require X-ray followed by surgery, another may require extended laboratory tests and physical therapy.

The long-linked technology is probably susceptible to greater shielding than are the mediating and intensive technologies. In the latter, intrusions of clients present a significant variable over which the organization has relatively little control. For these reasons, diverse degrees and types of uncertainties may exist within technical cores across organizations. The focus and orientation of decision problems in the technical core will depend upon the uncertainties imposed by the type of technology, and upon the success of the organization's shielding efforts to reduce environmental uncertainties.

The Managerial Level. The primary responsibilities at this level are the management of the technical core, determination of the scope of core activities, and servicing the core by mediating the vital exchange relationships between the core and the exterior environment. Considerable effort is expended to assure that core activities are consistent with adaptations made at the institutional level. A dilemma for the managerial level is to provide closure, shielding, and certainty for the core on the one hand, and to modify the core in response to institutional adaptations on the other. Mediating between the technical and institutional levels is a primary focus of managerial-level activity (Thompson, 1967).

To accomplish its objectives the organization must provide the input and output conditions not treated within the technical core. Furthermore, it is concerned with attaining *organizational* rationality, rather than just *technical* rationality. Thus, the managerial level is concerned with providing inputs that are compatible with the core technology and with matching core outputs to environmental consumers. Toward these ends, efforts are made to influence environmental consumption attributes or to adjust core operations to attain appropriate matches. By managing these kinds of transactions, the managerial level "frees up" the technical core, allowing it to act as a relatively closed system. Thompson identifies a number of managerial-level strategies and actions for "closing" the technical core, while at the same time retaining responsiveness to the uncertainties of the outer environment:

(1) buffering the technical core with input and output components;
(2) smoothing input and output transactions;
(3) anticipating and adapting to environmental changes which cannot be buffered or smoothed; and
(4) rationing.

Buffering may involve such managerial activities as stockpiling physical resources, maintaining standby supply sources, cultivating potential sources of employee skills, and pre-training new employees. The establishment and maintenance of programs encompassing such activities provides a buffer between the uncertain environment and the stability of resources required for uninterrupted operation of the core technology. On the output side, disposal facilities, such as warehouses, may be created so that finished output or standardized sub-units may be accumulated until such time as their need is dictated by environmental demand.

Rather than absorb environmental fluctuations, other activities may be used to reduce or smooth fluctuations. Examples are the offering of inducements (such as reduced product price) to customers during slack periods of demand, or the offering of quantity discounts at other times.

If buffering and smoothing are inadequate for stabilizing core operations the organization may resort to activities which will anticipate environmental changes. It may then adapt the core in a planned manner. Under these conditions, the anticipated changes may be used as planning constraints. Accordingly, we see the emergence of forecasting systems and computer programs for adjusting the level of core operations in a systematic manner.

Finally, when environmental impingements are not sufficiently separated from the core by the activities mentioned above, the organization may resort to rationing resources among alternative demands on some priority basis to maintain systematic order in the core.

The Institutional Level. At the institutional level rests the function of establishing the organization's identity in relation to the larger society. Of the three levels, this one is viewed as most open to environmental impingements and thus to uncertainty. In contrast to the technical core, the design and orientation of the institutional level is toward *coping* with environmental uncertainties, rather than being shielded from them. The very right to exist, the organization's ability to procure contributions that are vital for achieving its goals, and its ability to influence "customers" in the disposal of its outputs are sanctioned by diverse extra-organizational elements over which it has little or no legitimate control. The maintenance of satisfactory exchange relationships between the organization and the larger environment suggests the need for flexibility and adaptation to changing legal requirements, codes of proper conduct, and other societal norms. Therefore, the institutional level may set goals reflecting the preferences of dominant organizational members (and perhaps some non-members) for alternative organizational outcomes. The dynamics of goal-setting activities is significant in two respects. First, it reflects the need for flexibility in executing institutional-level activities. At the same time, these goal-setting activities establish the decision premises for lower levels in the hierarchy (Simon, 1965). This is the first step in the sequence of actions which leads to uncertainty reduction for lower levels (March and Simon, 1965). It is here that the interdependence among levels is illustrated. While the institutional level relies upon flexibility for maneuvering in the outer environment, it also makes commitments to, and places demands upon, various intraorganizational elements. It is dependent upon the technical level's capacity to meet commitments to these outside elements. But, at the same time, the technical level's ability to provide depends upon the extent to which it can operate under conditions of relative certainty. The two extremes are mediated and balanced by the managerial level.

Dill (1962) has designated as the "task environment" those elements of the larger world which are "relevant or potentially relevant to goal setting and goal attainment." For decision making at the institutional level, such elements dominate the stimulus set to a greater extent than at other levels. The "relevant decision environment" at the institutional level is distinguished by its focus on those exterior elements related to *goal setting*. While it is true that attention is directed *inwardly* toward organizational factors which may also be of potential relevance to goal setting, there is, simultaneously, a greater emphasis on this unique *outward* focus. As stated by Cyert and March (1963), organizations "learn to attend to some parts of that environment and not to others" (pp. 123–24).

A Summary of the Three Decision Environments. The organization can be viewed as consisting of three basic levels which differ in function, and consequently differ in their interest in, and concern with, numerous variables for the execution of their functions. Variables of concern at one level may be of little or no immediate importance at the others.

The technical core is a relatively closed subsystem which may operate in a world approaching certainty. The reduction of uncertainty is provided by directives from higher organizational levels to promote technical rationality (e.g., the most effective means to obtain one's economic ends). The focus of decision problems is technology-dominated.

The managerial level engages in boundary-spanning activities. It must deal with the extra-organizational environment to acquire inputs for the core, and dispose of core outputs for organizational goal attainment. It is concerned not only with the provision of mechanisms for reducing core uncertainty, but also with attempting to maintain a balance between the conditions for achieving technical rationality on the one hand, and the conditions for adaptability to changes at the institutional level on the other.

Of the three, the institutional level is most open to extraorganizational uncertainties. It is principally concerned with maintaining organizational viability in the larger world. It is acutely "tuned-in" to elements of the larger environment which effect the organization's goals. Thus, it provides the decision premises for the other levels.

Critical Dimensions of Extraorganizational Environment

The *total* extraorganizational environment has now been narrowed to those elements which are of concern to goal-setting and goal-attainment. This relevant subset was called the task environment, and has a diverse composition. Different organizations face different task environments, and a single organization may face a changing task environment. Thompson has identified two task environment characteristics which he suggests are mediators of (a) organizational structure and (b) action strategies of boundary-spanning units. Homogeneity and stability are two such characteristics, each of which is envisioned as a continuum with extremes as shown in Figure 3-1.

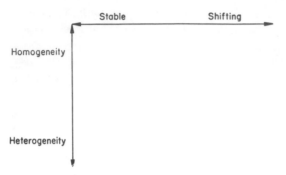

Figure 3-1   Characteristics of Task Environment (*Source:* Thompson, 1967, p. 72.)

First, we can identify differences in homogeneity on the output side. This is where we focus on our reliance upon consumption elements of the task environment. While one organization may have one socioeconomic segment of individuals as primary consumers of its outputs, another may rely upon a number of distinct segments. Whereas the primary customers may be individual members of society in one case, another organization may rely upon individuals or groups, as well as other organizations for output disposal. Organizations may also vary as to the geographic location of customers. While some serve only locally, others are oriented toward market segments scattered throughout a broad geographic region. Multi-national firms face task environments which are culturally heterogeneous, as well as geographically dispersed.

For inputs, the organization may depend on elements of the task environment which are homogeneous/heterogeneous with respect to geographic space, composition of resources available, and resource capacity. This is true not only for suppliers of physical inputs, but also for potential sources of financial support which may have heterogeneous or homogeneous expectations about the manner in which their support will be used. Similarly, some organizations depend upon a single labor union as the principal source of human resources, while others face task environments comprised of diverse unions and professionally affiliated groups of individuals.

The primary sources of community and governmental support may also vary in homogeneity for different organizations. Federal, state, and local regulatory agencies, as well as diverse interest groups may simultaneously impose competing demands on some organizations, while others face relatively homogeneous sets of such demands. Similar differences can be noted in the homogeneity/heterogeneity of competition faced by different organizations. Competitors may vary with respect to size, diversity of product line, methods of distribution, geographic scope of operation, and location, as well as other attributes.

The degree of homogeneity/heterogeneity of the task environment, as discussed above, was viewed at a single point in time. But another important characteristic is its stability, a characteristic that is bound to a time dimension. The degree to which changes occur in the homogeneity/heterogeneity of task-environment elements is an important consideration for organizational decisions. Changes in societal values, the emergence of interest groups at local, national, and international levels, the recognition of threats to limited natural resources, and changes in technology are several of the many factors that can contribute to task-environment dynamics. The homogeneity/heterogeneity of customers, clients, markets, regulatory agencies, competition, and sources of resource inputs can be expected to display various degrees of stability for different organizations.

Implications of Extraorganizational Environment for Decisions

At this point we wish to re-emphasize that the kinds of issues and problems that predominate at one level of organizational action are of a different nature than those at other levels.[2] Furthermore, problems of concern at one level may differ from those at a corresponding level of another organization. Illustrating one difference in orientation, Thompson (1967) states:

> Whereas coordination (of variables under its control) is a central problem for the technical core of the organization, adjustment to constraints and contingencies not controlled by the organization is the crucial problem for boundary-spanning components (p. 81, parenthetical remarks added).

Organizational viability demands an awareness of, and responsiveness to, environmental changes. The degree of adaptiveness required of boundary-spanning units is related to the homogeneity and stability of the task environment.

> The more heterogeneous the task environment, the greater the constraints presented to the organization. The more dynamic the task environment, the greater the contingencies presented to the organization (p. 73).

Attempts must be made, then, to manage the organization's interdependencies with elements of the task environment. In so doing, difficulties arise from a diversity of constraints and contingencies which tend to hinder the attainment of technical and organizational rationality. Such management attempts will take various forms including modifying the organizational structure, undertaking surveillance activities to anticipate environmental fluctuations, establishing power relationships between the organization and environmental elements, shifting the organization's boundaries, and allocating action-discretion among its members. The directions and relative intensities of these actions

---

[2]See Martin (1956) for a documentation of differences in decision situations at different organization levels.

depend upon unique situational circumstances, and are discussed at length by Thompson and by Cyert and March.

The various actions of boundary-spanning units have implications for core activities, due to the interdependencies of these levels. For highly complex task environments, it may be impossible to eliminate significant environmental intrusions. We can expect that the demands placed on core-level decision makers in these organizations will be different than the demands imposed on core decision makers in organizations facing relatively simple task environments.

If, as Thompson contends, "Organizations seek to isolate contingencies for local disposition" (p. 78), then we will find specialized organizational units set up to deal with special contingencies. This in turn calls for special individual skills. Differences in required skills are, in part, likely to be dependent upon task-environment complexity:

> To the extent that the environmental sector is homogeneous and stable, boundary-spanning jobs can be standardized, (and) use common skills. . . .

> To the extent that boundary-spanning jobs occur at points where the task environment is heterogeneous and shifting, however, such jobs require the exercise of judgment to meet contingencies. . . (p. 111).

> To the extent that the organization has handled environmental contingencies through structure, it has removed need for discretion from the boundary-spanning job and thus reduced its dependence on the individual in that job (p. 112).

The above remarks illustrate not only differences in orientation and skills that are partially dictated by the environment, but also show that the task environment is an important determiner of the latitude of action and the extent of the individual's influence in organizational matters.

This differentiation of environments suggests differences in the focus of decision problems at various levels. We would expect corresponding qualitative differences in the sources of decision-problem complexity. Furthermore, referring to our previous chapter, we would expect various features of our general model of individual decision processes to be of differential importance in coping with decision problems in the different environments. Just as the decision-making demands differ, so will the appropriate combinations of skills required for resolving these problems. The behavioral phenomena of greatest relevance in one's role at the institutional level may be of minor significance within the technological and managerial levels.

The existence, then, of various constraints, contingencies, and uncertainties poses the problem of finding appropriate "matchups" of job requirements with individual capabilities. In chapters which follow, we will attempt to delineate significant dimensions of individual capabilities which appear to be closely related to the prominent dimensions that distinguish different decision problems. We will identify different kinds of uncertainty, and specify decision-problem characteristics that signal when various decision-making aids may be of assistance in overcoming human limitations in handling organizational decision problems.

Technology in Task Environment

Our use of Dill's (1962) definition of task environment has been primarily *outer-directed,* referring to extraorganizational elements of (potential) relevance to goal setting and attainment. However, elements *within* the organization may also be relevant. Specifically, the organizational environment houses the core technology which poses contingencies and constraints on organizational action, and impacts goal setting and attainment.

Just as task environment can be usefully examined along dimensions of homogeneity and stability, so can core technology. Whereas some organizations may be principally concerned with one type of technology (long-linked, mediating, intensive), most employ combinations of them. As these combinations increase (heterogeneity), the organization is faced with problems of balancing capacities among them (Thompson, 1967, p. 45). Such problems are of less importance with more homogeneous technologies. Thompson proposes that organizations facing relatively dynamic technologies will experience more frequent changes in organizational goals.

The degree of homogeneity/heterogeneity and stability/instability of the technology would seem to dictate that different skills and orientations are appropriate among decision makers operating within or near the technical core. In the management of heterogeneous technologies, decision makers must consider the problem of balancing capacities to achieve maximum efficiency. This dimension of complexity is less important in managing homogeneous technologies. The individual characteristics required to cope with the shifts in organizational goals that accompany dynamic technologies seem to differ from those necessary for stable technologies.

THE COMPOSITE ENVIRONMENT
OF THE DECISION UNIT

What then is the "environment" of the individual decision-making unit in the organization? For purposes of the development of the remainder of our book, we adopt the following definition:

> The environment of the decision unit is the composite of the interactive factors that determines the source and nature of stimulus cues confronting

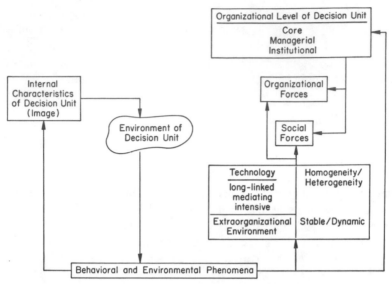

Figure 3-2 Elements of the Composite Environment of Decision

the decision unit, and determines which of those cues will be attended to by the decision unit.

We have depicted this view diagrammatically in Figure 3-2. An important feature of this definition is that it is situation-specific, including not only those elements that the organization intentionally allows by design, but also elements that are unintended, including characteristics brought to the decision setting by the individual decision maker. Although it would be preferable to simplify the definition and delineate its specific content more explicitly, to do so would result in a deceptive oversimplification which would exclude variables that are important for decision behavior.

The organizational and social forces are mediated by the organizational levels, the technology, and the extraorganizational environment, all of which we have previously described. These, coupled with the internal characteristics of the decision unit, result in the content of the unit's decision environment, which includes the set of decision problems confronting the unit. Actions of the decision unit may result in changes in its internal characteristics, the technology, the extraorganizational environment, or its own level in the organization. These changes, operating directly on the environment or indirectly through organizational and/or social forces on various elements, result in modification of the decision-unit environment.

Decision Problems in the Composite Environment

In view of the many concepts in the preceding pages, it is apparent that decision behavior is related to the "environment" in a number of complex ways. To understand and/or predict decision behavior, we must consider more than just the content of the decision problem, per se. Consideration of the organizational context in which the problem arises is also required. This necessitates examining the components of the relevant environments impinging on the individual, including his internal environment, the immediate physical and social environments, the broader environment within the organization (policies, structure, procedures, and so on), and elements of the environment external to the organization. Relevant elements from all of these environments, coupled with the decision problem at hand, comprise what has been called The Total Decision Problem (Ebert, 1972). In this complex context, most decision problems are unique. The decision-related behaviors that will be exhibited are not highly predictable in many instances.

Having recognized all of these complexities, it is helpful, for developments in following chapters, to classify general types of decision problems. We do this by holding constant individual characteristics, while focusing on important distinctions of single decision problems. This is what March and Simon refer to as the "task."

Thompson (1964) argues that decision problems can be classified according to the relative certainty of (a) outcome preferences and (b) cause/effect relationships. As shown in Table 3-1, different decision strategies are appropriate for each of the four types of decision.

Table 3-1 Decision Problems and Strategies

| | | Preferences Regarding Possible Outcomes | |
		certainty	uncertainty
Beliefs About Cause/Effect Relationships	certain	computational strategy	compromise strategy
	uncertain	judgmental strategy	inspirational strategy

Source: Thompson, 1964.

Variations in the degrees of certainty/uncertainty along these two dimensions can be expected at different levels of the organization. As previously discussed, these variations arise from differences in type of technology, in homogeneity and stability of technology and task environment, and in organizational design and structure.

To the above classifications we can relate Simon's (1960) notion of programmed/non-programmed decisions.

> Decisions are programmed to the extent that they are repetitive and routine, to the extent that a definite procedure has been worked out for handling them so that they don't have to be treated *de novo* each time they occur (pp. 5–6).

We can see that recurring decision problems for which there is relative certainty about outcome preferences and cause/effect relationships may be disposed of by standard procedures. This approach is compatible with the "computational strategy" in Table 3-1. In contrast, non-programmed decisions rely upon more general response capacities:

> Decisions are non-programmed to the extent that they are novel, unstructured and consequential. There is no cut-and-dried method for handling the problem because it hasn't arisen before, or because its precise nature and structure are elusive or complex, or because it is so important that it deserves a custom-tailored treatment (p. 6).

Simon's non-programmed category permeates the three remaining categories in Table 3-1 (judgmental, compromise, inspiration). The two dimensions of Thompson's categorization suggest that *sources* of novelty, which render decision problems non-programmable, can be identified. We will expand on this notion in later chapters by identifying further sources of decision-problem complexity, and we will illustrate aids which are available to help cope with various types of complexity. We will also indicate that as our understanding of decision processes increases, technologies will be developed to reduce the impact of certain kinds of problem complexities.

SUMMARY

The preceding chapter provided a basic structure for viewing various aspects of the individual's decision processes. This chapter identified some major parameters of the decision environment in which the individual functions. To portray the significance of the environment for decision behavior we have identified the decision maker as an environmental element. Three levels within the organization were also identified, as were elements exterior to the organization which are relevant to organizational decisions. Some relationships among these parameters have also been presented. Our purpose has been to provide a framework which recognizes "environment" as a significant variable in organizational decision behavior.

Part Two

Chapter 4

Beliefs and Values

We have generally described both the psychological and environmental impacts on decisions. It is time now to examine these areas in more detail. We will deal with the psychological factors first and move to the more global and external influences later in the book.

At the moment there appears to be a fairly common theme running through much of the behavioral sciences. Scheibe (1970) states it as "What a person does (his behavior) depends upon what he wants (his values) and what he considers to be true or likely (his beliefs) about himself and the world (his psychological society)" (p. 1). Using this sort of analysis one would argue for example that the President of General Motors would decide to market a new automobile (behavior) because he wanted to increase sales (value), and he thought that this new car was likely to do that for him (belief).

But to examine all behavior as a function of these psychological processes may be dangerous. It is important that we understand a number of related ideas. First, a given behavior is undoubtedly based upon more than one belief or value. We would like to understand how different beliefs and values combine with one another in order to predict what an individual will actually do.

Second, it is to some extent begging the question to say everything we do is based on beliefs and values. That is, to understand behavior, we must understand how values and beliefs are formed, developed, and changed. For both of these reasons we must learn more about the individual's psychological reality. His beliefs and values are shaped by his past experience and by the way he views his surroundings.

Finally, it is clear that an individual's beliefs and values change from time to time and from place to place. The physical reality of the surrounding environment helps to determine what beliefs and values may be operating at a given time. This orientation results in the familiar sayings in psychology: "behavior is a function of the person and the environment" and "the individual is a product of heredity and the environment."

The foundations, therefore, of almost all voluntary behavior, including decision making, can be defined in terms of beliefs and values. For the rest of the chapter we will discuss these components in more detail, identifying how some decision models directly incorporate beliefs and values and also discussing how these variables are related to other areas of importance in the decision process, such as perception.

HISTORICAL PERSPECTIVE

The components of thought which we have labeled beliefs and values are prevalent in numerous other contexts and have been with us for a long time. One can begin with an analysis of the writings of Plato, who suggested that man's soul was composed of three parts: knowing, wanting, and willing. While the philosophical issues discussed by Plato may not be fully applicable for our purposes, the critical point is that beliefs as knowledge and values as wanting were seen as distinctly separate conceptual units. The question of "What is true?" as opposed to "What is best?" still challenges us today.

If one traces the philosophical development of these ideas we can see that whole schools of thought revolve around these concepts. The field of epistemology is concerned with how man arrives at knowing one thing or another. Ethics, on the other hand, is concerned with questions of value.

In psychology, numerous investigators have wrestled with these issues as well. Early in the twentieth century John B. Watson and the behaviorists who followed him advocated a psychology devoid of all mental concepts. This school of thought, most closely associated today with B. F. Skinner, views the environment as the determinant of behavior. A number of contradictory viewpoints also evolved which dealt with beliefs and values. Kurt Lewin, who came from Germany and was familiar with the Gestalt tradition, shaped much of the work in social psychology. One central tenet of his Field Theory was that only present events influence behavior and that this influence was characterized by valences and subjective probabilities. Valances stood for the attractiveness of various goal states, and the subjective probabilities referred to the possibility of achieving a specific goal. The generalization of these concepts to values and beliefs is obvious.

Other more experimental psychologists, such as Tolman or Brunswik, also postulated cognitive concepts that closely corresponded to beliefs and values. Tolman spoke of the "expectancy" that a particular behavior might lead to particular environmental consequences, and Brunswik discussed "probabilism," a concept that dealt with "What-leads-to-what" in the environment. The groundwork had been laid for a more integrated and perhaps pervasive utilization of these ideas. Before turning to the direct application of these concepts to decision behavior, we will give a more thorough analysis of how beliefs and values are currently conceptualized.

BELIEFS

To understand what we mean by a belief, we must examine its properties more closely. One point that should be made at the outset is that we never see beliefs. That is, we make inferences about a person's beliefs by what he says or does. If a manager consistently decides to employ, praise, and reward white employees, we might infer that he has certain beliefs about minority employees (e.g., they are lazy). Or if we ask the manager about his behavior he might say, "I believe that minorities are lazy." The critical point is that we use either the verbal or behavioral event to infer some cognitive event. Thus the problem of "reality" and the measurement of that reality are important components of the cognitive process which must be confronted. In general, when information inferred from verbal and behavioral events is consistent over time and observers, we feel more confident that an individual does indeed hold a certain belief. Thus, our assessment and knowledge about beliefs are probabilistic, and in that sense, they are beliefs themselves.

Let's take a number of beliefs and analyze their properties more thoroughly:

1. A lawyer in New Orleans states that he believes that President John Kennedy's assassination was planned by a number of different people.

2. A certain environmentalist states that unless we conserve fuel, food, and natural resources we will be facing devastating hardships within two years.

3. The sales manager of an electronic data processing firm believes that his competition will be introducing a new miniaturized computer.

These statements have some things in common and some important differences. First, all of the beliefs reflect an individual's view of the interrelationship of events either past, present, or future. These relationships are shown below:

1. Kennedy's assassination →→→→→→→→→→→→→→→→ number of people
2. Shortages →→→→→→→→→→→→→→→→→→→→→→→→ hardships
3. Competitor →→→→→→→→→→→→→→→→→→→→→→→ miniaturized computer

Thus, there is some object, concept, or thing being related to some other object, concept, or thing. However, the sort of relationship that is being suggested may differ significantly. In some cases we may be imputing causality to events, such as No. 2 above, while in other cases we may be stating what we consider to be a factual statement of interrelationship (No. 3).

Specific distinctions are also made about beliefs concerning future events as opposed to those referring to past events (see Nos. 1 and 2 above). The sub-class of beliefs dealing with future events is usually called "expectancies." In most cases one is predicting what will happen in the future, and therefore these beliefs are frequently subjected to confirmation or disconfirmation. The important role of expectancies in decision making is exemplified by the following excerpt from Scheibe (1970):

> Beliefs about future occurrences are often important determinants of those occurrences, for they influence the choices that are made, the chances that are taken, and the hypotheses that are adopted as working assumptions (p. 26).

There are also differences in the degree to which we feel confident about a proposition. Aristotle, for example, distinguished among certainty, belief, suspicion, and doubt. We may consider beliefs as being probabilistic in their nature. That is, we can assign a probability from zero to one as to the chances of the proposed linkage actually being true. This assessment has an important impact on how we actually behave. Our behavior would differ widely for each of the three beliefs mentioned earlier depending upon this probability estimate.

The components of this probabilistic estimate need clarification. One can, for example, distinguish between the uncertainty that exists due to chance as opposed to the uncertainty attributed to skill. A high jumper on any given day will achieve a certain height because of both factors. A project manager may complete a task by a certain time because of both factors. The problem, however, that confronts many decision makers is an estimate of these chance uncertainties (e.g., how will the market fluctuate, what will my competitors do).

A second major distinction is related to our knowledge about the probabilities of the outcomes of a choice alternative. For example, we may know that the chances are one in ten that a certain play on a roulette wheel will win. On the other hand we often make decisions where the probabilities of various outcomes are unknown. The former decision problems are known as "risky," while the latter can be labeled "decisions under uncertainty." In summary, we have both a subjective probability estimate of the relationship and some feeling of the degree of confidence about the probability.

Finally, we should briefly consider the source of these beliefs. Sarbin, Taft, and Bailey (1960) mention four possibilities:

1. Induction: The development of a belief based on accumulated observations of past experience. For example, over time one might find that Tide produces a whiter wash.

2. Construction: The adoption of a theory about relationships which may or may not be based on factual observations. Sarbin uses the example: "The presence of sunspots may be associated with the potential for homicide" (p. 49).

3. Analogy: Beliefs formed by generalizing from similar objects, situations, or events. A person with a volatile red-haired cousin may believe that all red-haired people are volatile.

4. Authority: Situations in which the information source has enough authority to maintain the belief; i.e., we believe that the earth goes around the sun because we have confidence in the astronomers who tell us so.

Therefore, through our past experience, our imagination, and our absorption of information from others, we come to conclusions about what leads to what. It is just this type of relationship which plays an integral role in the process of decision making. Before turning to this area we must briefly describe our other major component: values.

VALUES

Just believing that certain consequences will follow from various actions or behavior does not tell us all we need to know in order to predict behavior. We must also know how the individual feels about those consequences. The question of "What is good" as opposed to "What is true" becomes important. Thus, beliefs are conceptualized as hypotheses, subjective probabilities, or expectancies, while values are seen as referring to what is preferable, best, or good. The following definitions of values have been cited by Ericson (1969):

Values are normative standards by which human beings are influenced in their choice among the alternative courses of action which they perceive .... values are conceptions of desirable states of affairs that are utilized in selective conduct as criteria for preference or choice or as justifications for proposed or actual behavior (p. 44).

One major difference between beliefs and values is their factual basis. In most cases, beliefs are seen as having factual referents. They may be incorrect, but the individual believes that they are true. Thus a process of disconfirmation is possible. This is not true for values. Personal preference is a matter of individuality and resides in the individual's outlook of what "ought to be." People may disagree with one's value system, and in that sense, the value may be seen as inappropriate, but it is not something which is provable or disprovable.

Our knowledge of an individual's values comes from a variety of sources. People frequently verbalize their long- or short-term desires. One can also observe the choices that an individual makes in different decision settings. These choices or behavioral preferences reflect one's underlying values. Thus, our choice of behavior can be seen as a combination of what we perceive as consequences of our action combined with how much we desire or dislike these consequences.

A couple of limitations to this analysis should be pointed out. When psychologists talk about motivated behavior they usually deal with both the question of what arouses the individual and what path of action he pursues. We are therefore assuming that in the choice situations with which we're concerned there is at least a minimal level of arousal. In terms of our earlier discussion, this arousal often occurs because of a difference between what the individual wants or expects and what he actually gets or perceives. Secondly, we are dealing with situations in which the individual is behaving voluntarily. It is hard to make inferences about beliefs and values of an individual who slips and falls off a bridge. The inferences are somewhat easier for someone who jumps.

In general, most of the research on values attempts to produce a catalog or categorization of values. England and his associates (1971) have suggested two dimensions along which various approaches to the identification of values differ widely. One dimension is the conceptual nature of values:

Preferential Approach (emphasizing likings, needs, desires, and interests)	— — — — — — — — — — —	Normative Approach (focusing on obligatory and/ or moral topics)

The second dimension is the conceptual generality of values:

Very Specific Values	— — — — — — — — — — —	Highly Abstract or General Values

He also says that the conceptual generality of an approach to values will be influenced by where the approach falls on the conceptual nature dimension. For example, his own approach, which will be discussed later, is conceptually a preferential approach and deals with very specific values. Conceivably, another approach might be highly normative, with highly general values.

Early writers often produced lists of basic instincts which were seen as inborn values. Benevolence, ideality, pugnacity, and curiosity are all examples.

The critical problem was that these value lists often become explanations of behavior based on a somewhat circular reasoning. One acted aggressively because of the aggressive instinct, or one twiddled his thumbs because of the thumb twiddling instinct. This type of reasoning did little to further our understanding of behavior. What was needed was a better understanding of where values came from and how they entered into the behavioral choice process.

Today, most social scientists would argue that values develop through our experiences with the world. Things become labeled as good or bad depending upon their reinforcing properties. Thus we come to value objects, concepts, outcomes, or consequences because they are either psychologically or physically rewarding to us. This reward may simply be the putting to rest of curiosity, or it may be the attainment of money. While some things are valued in and of themselves, others are valued because of their instrumentality for achieving other valued outcomes. Consequently, what is "valued" might *change* if it is perceived as being instrumental for achieving other valued things. As we shall see, upon entering the organization certain values may be *assigned* to the individual in his organizational role (profit maximization, loyalty, rationality, etc.). Other values, rather than being assigned to him, are brought *to* the organization by the individual. The critical aspect in any analysis of this type is that from a knowledge of one's beliefs and values we hope to predict behavior, rather than explain it after it has happened. Using this criterion obviously means that the more thoroughly we understand the nature of values and their role in behavior the better our predictions will be. Thus, the question of value assessment becomes of paramount importance. One concept that was developed for doing this was that of utility.

Utility: Individual Choice Criteria

The concept of utility was developed because of the recognition that the subjective value of money often differed from its objective economic value by varying degrees for different people. Like many other psychological scaling problems, the task was to generate a scale which accurately reflects the relationship between the external and psychological dimensions involved. In most cases utility scales are generated either from an ordering of preferences or from an analysis of exchanges (i.e., what will someone trade for another object or commodity). Thus how much someone wants something is couched in terms of how it compares with other things he wants or what he will give up to get it.

In terms of our model of the individual's decision processes (Chapter 2), his value system enters directly or indirectly at several phases. For the moment we will consider the evaluative phase immediately preceding choice. The individual "orders" choice alternatives in accordance with their desirabilities along his internal operational standard of desirability. This internal standard, or "preference function," reflects in some sense the individual's operational value system in this choice role. The importance of individual values in this phase of the decision process is exemplified by the following statement:

> Another way of broadening the closed decision model to reflect a more complete set of elements is through the preference ordering of alternatives by the decision maker. The ordering of alternatives depends on the individual's value system . . . (Alexis and Wilson, 1967, p. 155).

In many decision problems the available choice alternatives have outcome implications along a multitude of value dimensions. In these situations, choices are made which presumably represent the chooser's preference based on the consolidated or aggregate implications of the alternatives. Even though multiple-dimensioned values are considered, it is believed that a common evaluative measure of desirability exists for the individual for each choice situation. As stated by Schiebe (1970), " . . . somehow individuals form a single aggregate preference for an option involving many different kinds of value" (p. 74).

The possible existence of individual preference functions underlies the economists' concept of utility. The extensive attempts to develop theories of utility have derived their impetus from the ultimate possibility of telling us how to choose, and in providing the basis for predicting and explaining choice behavior. This striving for a theory of rational choice has resulted in an impressive array of mathematical developments, but a disappointing record of success in predicting and explaining choice behavior. Only in the simplest of situations[1] have they been shown to be a reasonable representation of choice behavior. As stated by Alexis and Wilson,

> Except where money or some easily measurable commodity can be taken as equivalent to utility or at least related to it in an ascertainable manner, the measurement of utilities, or even the proof of their existence, is a most difficult matter (1967, p. 155).

As is clear from this quotation, existing measurement technology is a major inhibiting factor to the success of utility theory. The problem of measurement as it relates to the multiple dimensions of human value systems results in inadequate representations of the relevant preference function in moderately and highly complex choice situations.

Attempts have been made to formulate "rational decision models" incorporating utility concepts for application in organizational settings.[2] These formulations are typically not comprehensive with respect to the number of values that are included. Those which have attempted a comprehensive inclusion of values

---

[1]See Mosteller and Nogee (1951) for an example.

[2]See Vesper and Sayeki (1973); Matheson and Roths (1967); and Matheson (1969).

have been forced to abandon their efforts due to the great costs and complexity of doing so. The formulations that have been proposed for organizational decision problems are tailored to isolated problems, and are seldom applicable to other decision problems. Furthermore, they are not readily amenable to the dynamics of the decision maker's values. It is understandable that most of these attempts have been made for selected decision problems in relatively stable segments of the organization. The technical core of organizations having stable environments has been the prime proving ground for the application of management science techniques. So long as a conspicuous unidimensional value ("profit") exists, the concepts of utility theory enjoy some operational success. In consideration of the limited success of empirical attempts to develop and use utility theory in choice behavior, Simon's (1959) comment still applies:

> We can interpret these results in either of two ways. We can say that consumers (decison makers) "want" to maximize utility, and that if we present them with clear and simple choices that they understand they will do so. Or we can say that the real world is so complicated that the theory of utility maximization has little relevance to real choices (pp. 258–59).

In presenting our view of the organizational decision maker, we will continue to assume the following:

1. He possesses multiple values that differ in dimensionality.
2. His relevant value set changes with time and circumstance.
3. He is capable, in specific situations, of forming an operational standard of desirability (utility). This evaluative criterion reflects his subjective "balancing" of competing or conflicting relevant values for each situation.
4. He attempts to formulate these evaluative criteria, and apply them in making decisions, so as to maximize his subjective expected well-being over some subjective time horizon.

In our view, then, man is a maximizer in a broad subjective sense. Our inability to predict his behavior and to prescribe normative decision behavior for him is due to current inadequacies in identifying and measuring: (a) his existing value set; (b) the parameters of the process by which this set is acquired and modified; and (c) the parameters of the process by which the values in the set are prioritized. These restrictions preclude the evaluation of the rationality of specific behaviors by anyone other than the individual himself.

ATTITUDES

One major subset of values is that of attitudes. In a 1935 article which reviewed the research on attitudes, Gordon Allport stated that "the concept of attitude is probably the most distinctive and indispensable concept in contemporary American social psychology. In an organizational setting, attitudes are thought to be tied to one's personality and motivation. An employee is said to have a good 'attitude' about his work, or we seek out our supervisor's opinion or attitude about some topic" (Scott and Mitchell, 1972, p. 94). We also have attitudes about the possible consequences of our actions and, in this way, attitudes become an integral part of values and decision making.

Definition

Although Allport uncovered over one hundred different definitions in his review, he also found some consistencies. Social scientists from a variety of fields seemed to agree that attitude could be seen as a *predisposition to respond in a favorable or unfavorable way* to objects, persons, concepts, or whatever. Underlying this dimension are some important assumptions. First, *attitude is related to behavior.* Based upon one's attitude toward something, he is predisposed to behave in a particular way. One could argue that one's attitude about his job is related to his attendance record. Second, *attitude is a unidimensional variable* and that dimension is tied to one's feelings about an object. The particular feeling is one of favorability or affect or attraction—i.e., the degree to which something is liked (a pleasant feeling) or disliked (an unpleasant feeling). Third, *attitude is a hypothetical construct.* It is something which one carries around inside of him. Its consequences may be observed, but the attitude itself cannot.

This definition means that attitude is different from both beliefs and values. Beliefs are typically concerned with the relationships between objects, people, and events. We will find that most attitude techniques use beliefs as a method for inferring attitudes, but they are not the same thing. Values, on the other hand, are ideas about how one should feel about or behave toward something. They have a quality of "oughtness" about them and are usually broader in their conceptualization. A whole set of attitudes can be seen as making up our more general values.

Formation

Discussions of value and attitude development are frequently linked to early childhood behavior. A child has a variety of physiological drives which are satisfied in various ways. The satisfication of these drives becomes linked to the circumstances that surrounded the satisfaction. After a while very complex patterns of behavior may become associated with need satisfaction, and just how specific attitudes are formed will be determined by an individual's personal history.

The central idea running through the process of attitude formation is that these feelings are *learned.* An individual acquires these feelings through his experiences with the world around him. An implication of this idea is that all *objects or concepts acquire an attitude.* One has feelings that may run from positive to negative about everything. Perhaps the most striking support for this idea has been provided by Osgood's research. He and his co-workers were interested in the underlying dimensions of meaning; that is, what dimensions do all people use in their descriptions of things around them. Hundreds of concepts, objects, or people (for example, freedom, house, mother) were rated on hundreds of bipolar adjective scales. An example is presented below:

				Freedom				
Good	___	___	___	___	___	___	___	Bad
	+3	+2	+1	0	−1	−2	−3	
Open	___	___	___	___	___	___	___	Closed
Strong	___	___	___	___	___	___	___	Weak
Pleasant	___	___	___	___	___	___	___	Unpleasant

Using a mathematical process known as factor analysis, Osgood was able to determine what scales seemed to have similar response patterns. These scales seemed to fall into three main groups: one that reflected evaluation (good-bad, pleasant-unpleasant); one that reflected activity (active-passive, fast-slow); and one that reflected potency (strong-weak, heavy-light). Osgood was able to show that this evaluation or attitude factor not only appeared for different stimulus objects but also for different samples of people. Other cultures also use this dimension in their ascription of meaning to objects. Osgood has summarized much of this research by stating, "human beings the world over, no matter what their language or culture, do share a common meaning system, do organize experience along similar symbolic dimensions" (Osgood, 1967, p. 112).

Another important implication is that people ascribe attitudes to things or objects based upon what the things or objects are related to. One's attitudes about an object are formed through the relationship of that object to other things or objects. If those related objects are liked, so is the new object; if they are disliked, the reverse would be true. One's attitude is formed by the degree to which the attitude object is associated with other pleasant or unpleasant objects. We may decide on a given organizational decision, such as developing a training program for minorities, because we think it is the moral or socially responsible thing to do, or because we believe we will avoid litigation and bad publicity. In either case, the evaluations are formed according to the association between the attitude object and other related states, concepts, or objects.

There are two ways that this conceptualization of attitude fits into our larger framework of beliefs and values. First, as we've pointed out, attitudes are formed by their relationship to other objects, concepts, events, etc. Thus, your attitude toward some situation is not independent of other relevant circumstances, people, or events. They are all entwined. Also, to the degree that people strive for consistency in their feelings, these attitudes will be *biased* in a fashion that will maintain consistency. We will return to this point later.

The second issue is how attitudes and values fit together. Since values are broader and more encompassing, they include the concept of attitude. We can conceptualize sets of consistent attitudes as the foundation for values. For example, a manager may believe that everyone ought to put in a good day's work no matter what he or she does. This general value of hard work will have consistent attitudes to bolster it. The individual will probably believe that punctuality is good, that helping the company is good, that keeping busy is good, etc. In this framework, then, we can see a decision as being heavily dependent upon two evaluative processes. First, there are attitudes about specific consequences of the decision; and second, there are broader implications that come under the heading of values. How we change these evaluations is dealt with in a later chapter.

DECISION MODELS USING BELIEFS AND VALUES

The two components we have discussed so far, beliefs and values, have been integrated into a number of theories of decision making. In general, these theories state that an individual's decision may be predicted from the degree to which the different alternatives are seen as (1) leading to various outcomes weighted by (2) the evaluation of the outcomes (expressed as attitudes or values).

The rule which underlies most of these approaches is called the expected value (utility) rule. Stated most simply, the expected value of any action can be found by summing the value of all the possible outcomes, each weighted by the probability of the outcome's occurrence. The probabilities for all the outcomes must equal 1.00. The equation is diagrammed below:

$$ev = \sum_{i=1}^{N} \Psi_i V_i \qquad \sum_{i=1}^{N} \Psi_i = 1$$

where Ψ_i is the probability that outcome i will occur, V_i is the value (utility) of the ith outcome, and N is the number of outcomes for the decision alternative. The overall decision rule is one which suggests that the individual desires to maximize his payoffs and will, therefore, choose the alternative with the highest expected value (utility).

Let's take an example. Suppose you are told by your insurance agent a certain automobile policy is available which will pay you 75 percent of the value of your $4,000 car in case it is stolen. The cost of the insurance is only $25.00 a year. However, you know that the chances are only about one in a hundred that someone will steal your car. Should you buy it? The payoff matrix is presented below:

	Stolen	Not Stolen
Buy	−1,025	−25
Don't Buy	−4,000	0

If the car is stolen and you have the insurance you lose your $4,000 plus your $25.00 premium but you are paid $3,000 by the insurance company. If you buy it and nothing happens you've lost $25.00. If you don't buy the insurance and the car is stolen, you lose $4,000 and, of course, if you don't buy it and nothing happens you neither gain nor lose.

The choice between the two alternatives is obviously dependent upon the chance that the car will be stolen. If it is very likely to be stolen you would, of course, want the insurance. If it is unlikely, you might not. But we already know these probabilities, so let's use them in our equation to determine the proper choice.

$$ev_{buy} = (.01)(-1,025) + (.99)(-25) = -\$35.00$$
$$ev_{don't\ buy} = (.01)(-4,000) + (.99)(0) = -\$40.00$$

In this particular case you should buy the insurance. Your expected loss is less if you purchase then if you do not.

It would be helpful to discuss the properties of the expected value rule in more detail. First, the rule is a normative one; that is, it supposedly tells you how to acquire more or lose less in the long run. It is a rule for how you ought to behave. Thus, over a long period of years (which may be occasioned by the pilfering of your automobile), you would be wise to buy the insurance.

A second aspect of the rule is its simplicity and reasonableness. It may not be a completely accurate representation of your perception of your cognitive processes, but its acceptance should be based on its predictive success. Thus, not only does it reflect what you should do, it also is a fairly good description of how one actually decides to do one thing or another.

But there are some complexities as well. Certain assumptions are built into the rule. Supposedly, if you prefer outcome A to B and B to C you will prefer A to C. This sounds reasonable but whether it is true or not is an empirical question. Several studies have found that this transitivity assumption does not always hold in real choice situations. The rule also assumes that beliefs and values are independent of one another; that is, the likelihood of an outcome does not influence its value. This assumption is even more questionable than the transitivity assumption. Scheibe, for example, argues that the independence of beliefs and values depends upon the level of information available to the individual. For high information levels when the individual is required to express his beliefs, " ... it is unlikely that demands for expression will force a person toward optimistic errors of belief ... " (p. 108). However, when information is lacking or irrelevant, " ... resultant beliefs are likely to be strongly related to values" (p. 108). He also contends that this independence depends upon how correctly the person perceives his degree of control over future events, and whether or not he is given full liberty in expressing his predictions.

Finally, the idea that beliefs and values combine multiplicatively and then are summed to give an overall estimate of expected value depicts a fairly complex cognitive process.

Underlying all of these assumptions is the maximization principle. Other authors have argued that rather than maximize gain some people attempt to minimize the maximum possible loss (von Neumann and Morgenstern, 1947). Others have assumed that the individual will choose the first minimally acceptable choice. In any case, beliefs and values are directly integrated into each approach, and the following steps in the decision process seem appropriate (modified from Schiebe, 1970).

1. Identify the available choice alternatives (only those that are psychologically salient).
2. Identify the possible consequences of each alternative. The number of possible consequences is two only in the simplest cases. A number of evaluatively distinct outcomes in choosing multiple courses of action should be considered as more typical.
3. Determine the expectancy associated with each distinguishable outcome. Represent this as a probability between zero and one. (Of course, the sum of the probabilities for all outcomes associated with a single choice option should equal one.)
4. Determine the psychological value or utility of each conceivable outcome.
5. Determine the expected value for each behavior alternative (after the manner illustrated in the insurance problem).
6. Predict that the person will direct his behavior toward the outcome having the highest expected value.

There are now a number of articles and books which show the breadth of application of the expected value idea for combining beliefs and values (Schiebe,

1970; Mitchell and Biglan, 1971; Lawler, 1971). Lawler (1971) recently reviewed the work of various theorists and their constructs for subjective probabilities. Table 4-1 lists these researchers.

Table 4-1 Labels Used for Theoretical Components

Theorist	Determinants of Impulse to Action
Atkinson	Expectancy X (motive X incentive)
Dulany	Hypothesis of the distribution of the reinforcer X value of the reinforcer
Edwards	Subjective probability X utility
Fishbein	Probability X attitude
Lewin	Potency X valence
Peak	Instrumentality X attitude (affect)
Rosenberg	Instrumentality X importance
Rotter	Expectancy, reinforcement value
Tolman	Expectancy of goal, demand for goal
Vroom	Expectancy X valence; where valence is (instrumentality X valence)

This table is a modification of one presented by Lawler (1971).

In almost every case the subjective probability is combined with an estimate of the value of the outcome and then summed across outcomes. These theories are prevalent in the areas of learning, personality, attitude formation, decision analysis, social power, leadership, and motivation. While the formulations are not exactly the same, one fact is obvious: beliefs and values are an important cornerstone of most areas of psychology.

PRACTICAL ISSUES FOR DECISIONS

How does this emphasis on beliefs and values tie-in with our overall model presented in Chapter 2? First, there is now substantial evidence that what we perceive is influenced by our values and beliefs. In the organizational context, the following comment by Elbing (1970) illustrates one effect of values on the decision-making process:

The decision maker must recognize that situations do not present themselves as prelabeled and predefined problems. A problem is in part defined by the standards (values) each observer applies (p. 240, parenthesis added).

Bruner and Goodman (1947) had earlier noted that *what* is perceived and *how* it is perceived is a function of one's values. England, *et al.* (1971) has called this phenomenon "perceptual screening." Since perception was shown in Chapter 2 to be one component of the individual's decision processes, we begin to see how values can affect decisions. We tend to recognize and select out of our environment those things with which we are familiar and that we like. Second, we note that in the organization the norms and values of one's reference groups are an influence on the individual's view of a decision situation. They will determine what the individual identifies to be relevant alternatives. This is an example of one type of "behavior channeling," a major way in which values can influence behavior (England, *et al.*, 1971). We will review these areas of research more fully in the following chapters.

Clearly, an important area to pursue would be the description and categorization of management values. Two approaches have generally been used. First, we may attempt to describe the values in different professions or at different organizational levels. For example, Porter (1964) found that higher-level managers placed greater emphasis on the values of self-actualization and autonomy than did lower-level managers. There were no differences in the values for security, social, and esteem needs. Guth and Tagiuri (1965) illustrated how personal values influenced organizational decisions. Campbell, *et al.* (1970) also reviewed a number of studies showing that nonmanagement, nonprofessional personnel in the United States tend to value job security, advancement, and interesting work most highly. These different types of values will have a major impact on both the decisions individuals make and their desire to carry them out.

A related area of value assessment looks at cross-cultural differences. Alexander, Barrett, Bass, and Ryterband (1971) surveyed the life goals of managers in a number of different countries. Their data are presented in Table 4-2.

Over the last few years George England has surveyed the values of thousands of managers, students, and labor leaders around the world (England, 1967; England and Lee, 1971; England, 1973). In summarizing his research a number of consistent points were made:

1. There are large individual differences both across and within countries. Individuals differed with respect to the number and kinds of values in their personal value sets. There may be a greater difference between a top executive of a U.S. manufacturing firm and one from an American advertising firm than between the same manufacturing executive and his British counterpart.

2. Personal values tend to be fairly stable and are not conducive to rapid change.

3. Value systems are highly related to behavior on the job. Given various decisions to make, England has shown the direct relationship of choice to values.

4. Values can be used to predict career success within certain organizational settings. They are both measurable and predictive.

5. Personal values of managers are different in different organizational contexts, but the extent to which their value systems are determined by the organization is not known.

Table 4-2 Cross-Cultural Differences in Values

Mean Ranks of Life Goals Assigned to Self

Rank	U.S.		U.K.		Denmark		Norway		Italy		Spain		India	
1	Leadership	4.23	Self-Realization	4.23	Service	4.53	Self-Realization	3.57	Self-Realization	3.75	Self-Realization	2.79	Expertness	4.3
2	Self-Realization	4.27	Security	4.55	Expertness	4.66	Affection	3.80	Inde-pendence	4.19	Service	4.45	Self-Realization	5.0
3	Inde-pendence	5.76	Leadership	4.98	Self-Realization	4.83	Inde-pendence	4.02	Affection	4.60	Leadership	5.04	Service	5.23
4	Security	5.80	Pleasure	5.14	Inde-pendence	4.93	Security	5.11	Leadership	4.82	Affection	5.10	Duty	5.45
5	Expertness	6.02	Inde-pendence	5.20	Security	5.00	Leadership	6.02	Security	5.23	Security	5.74	Leadership	5.59
6	Wealth	6.12	Expertness	5.42	Affection	5.47	Pleasure	6.04	Expertness	6.14	Inde-pendence	5.83	Inde-pendence	5.64
7	Affection	6.14	Affection	5.74	Pleasure	5.61	Duty	6.33	Pleasure	6.75	Expertness	6.03	Affection	5.91
8	Pleasure	6.51	Service	6.30	Leadership	6.00	Service	6.33	Service	7.02	Prestige	6.37	Prestige	6.26
9	Service	6.73	Wealth	7.60	Duty	7.32	Expertness	7.39	Prestige	7.11	Duty	6.88	Security	6.90
10	Prestige	7.10	Prestige	8.16	Wealth	8.80	Wealth	8.52	Duty	7.28	Wealth	8.86	Wealth	7.09
11	Duty	7.44	Duty	8.59	Prestige	8.85	Prestige	8.87	Wealth	9.11	Pleasure	8.90	Pleasure	8.55
N	59		86		59		54		57		78		69	

Source: Alexander, Barrett, Bass, and Ryterband (1971).

6. How personal value systems develop, how they are changed by organizational experiences, and how much disparity among value systems of individuals is best for organizational success are all insufficiently understood at the present time.

There are numerous other studies which substantiate these generalizations. However, the overall message seems clear: Values are an integral part of the decision process. We now turn to a more thorough description of the ways in which decision alternatives are generated and how various beliefs and values are combined into overall judgments.

Chapter 5

Information Processes

Previous chapters have described general dimensions of the individual and environment which are important for decision making. This chapter is devoted to a more detailed examination of some information-related phases of decision processes. In simplest form these phases can be identified as information acquisition, processing, and output, as shown in Table 5-1.

Table 5-1 Information-Related Phases of the Individual's
Decision Processes

I	II	III
Acquisition	Processing	Output
Search behavior	Information utilization	Judgmental inferences

It will become apparent that these artificial phases are, in reality, closely intertwined and largely inseparable. Still, to facilitate the discussion, Stage III, information output, is considered in depth in Chapter 6. Stages I and II, information acquisition and information processing, are the topics of this chapter. They are examined with respect to the following:

(1) individual variations and variables affecting acquisition and processing,
(2) characteristics of human information acquisition and processing, and
(3) the role and scope of acquisition and processing in organizational decision processes.

As a starting point we will discuss the inadequacies, from a descriptive viewpoint, of the "economic man" concept. Thereafter, the principal orientation is descriptive. We attempt to identify common characteristics of, as well as individual differences in, information-related behavior in decision processes.

Although the ultimate interest is on behavior in the *organizational* setting, it is useful and necessary to consider studies of relevant behavior observed in non-organizational environments. Such studies serve to identify potentially significant parameters of decision-making effectiveness in organizations.

THE DESCRIPTIVE ORIENTATION

The study of decision-related information processes has developed along two principal lines in recent years. The first consists of the many *descriptive studies* that examine characteristics of human search and processing activities. This approach emphasizes how people behave when confronted with various decision problems. The second approach is directed toward developing *theories* of search and processing. These two orientations are not unrelated, for in some instances theories have been derived from the findings of descriptive studies.

Our discussion of search behavior begins by briefly considering some of the assumptions of traditional economic man, the "rational" decision maker. Economic man is assumed to be aware of all decision alternatives. He has a preference ordering among the alternatives, and selects the alternative that is, or is likely to be, most desired in relation to his scale of preferences (Edwards, 1954; Simon, 1959). Is such a model an accurate description of human decision behavior? More particularly, is it representative of decision-making processes in organizations? If not, what models are representative? These are central questions of concern.

Barnard (1938) and Simon (1957) were among the early writers to focus on the inadequacy of the traditional model for representing organizational behavior. Observations of real organizations provide ample evidence that the decision maker, in fact, is not aware of all available decision alternatives. Consequently, he searches for various types of information that will subsequently enter into his decision deliberations. Furthermore, information search is not confined to finding decision alternatives. Search is conducted to obtain many other types of information.

One of the first comprehensive studies to question the suitability of the economic model in the organizational setting was reported by Cyert, Dill, and March (1958). Their orientation was toward viewing the *organization* as an adaptive entity, rather than focusing on individuals within the organization. Their interest was on testing three assumptions of rationality in economic models: (a) that the organization scans all alternatives continuously and adjusts to the pattern of available alternatives; (b) that firms have accurate information on costs and returns, and decisions are made on the basis of this information; and (c) that search has a cost and thus can be treated as an investment-decision alternative. In the years preceding their studies, "theories of the firm" were dominated by an economic orientation and, consequently, were of questionable value for explaining business behavior. The underlying issue was that behavioral variables, in addition to just economic variables, have significant impact on organizational actions.

In the first of four extensive case studies, the following observations were found to be in stark contrast to traditional economic theories.

a. The search for alternatives did not take the form of a continuous scanning process, but rather was dormant until a significant environmental change, a crisis, occurred in the organization. This event provided the stimulus for search activity.

b. The proposed solution to the organization's decision problem was not determined by examining all objective solution alternatives on an economic basis. Rather, it was selected because it was a preferred action for many organization members long before the decision problem arose. The decision problem appeared to present an opportune occasion to implement an already preferred course of action.

c. Contrary to the assumptions of the economic theory, initial estimates of costs and returns for the preferred alternative were vague, and were expressed in incomparable terms. It was not until *after* the decision to implement the preferred changes that detailed cost estimates were obtained.

d. Early cost estimates of the preferred alternatives were overly optimistic. With the passage of time the cost implications of the decision were examined more carefully by the organization. Finally, as environmental conditions changed, other decision problems dominated organizational activities, and the implementation program was abandoned.

Their second case study supported some of the findings of the first study, and added some significant further insights into the nature of organizational search activities.

    a. A prior consensus alternative for the decision problem did not exist when the decision problem arose, and the search for decision alternatives was more extensive than in the first case.

    b. Search for decision alternatives was highly restricted; search was far from exhaustive. Simple guidelines were used to narrow the range of alternatives that were considered. No objective evaluation of these guidelines was undertaken.

A third case study seemed to indicate the importance of human perception as an initiator of *search* behavior. The effects of such perceptions are not considered in economic theories of the firm.

The final case study indicated that human perceptions enter into the *evaluation* of decision alternatives. Staff analysts prepared a recommendation for the decision alternative they believed to be preferred by management.

These studies provided the impetus for the development of "A Behavioral Theory of the Firm" by Cyert and March (1963). This theory includes a number of search-related issues in organizational decision making.

1. Search is motivated. Problemistic search is stimulated by a problem, depressed by a problem solution.
2. Search is simple-minded. It proceeds on the basis of a simple model of causality until driven to a more complex one.
3. Search is biased. The way in which the environment is viewed and the communications about the environment that are processed through the organization reflect variations in training, experience, and goals of the participants in the organization (p. 121).

The above elements of the theory include a number of direct, as well as subtle, implications concerning organizational search activities. Let us examine each in turn.

Search is Motivated

Organizational search activities are not accurately characterized as consisting of continual surveillance of all possible alternatives. Search activity is initiated upon recognition of unsatisfactory conditions (problems). Such conditions include failure to achieve one or more goals, the likelihood of such a failure in the future, or dissatisfaction with current decisions. Search, then, is initiated by recognition of problems, and is directed toward resolving those problems. Search activity will persist so long as satisfactory problem solutions are not obtained. It will subside upon resolution of the problem or under conditions of congruence of organizational goals and achievement.

Search Is Simple-Minded

We assume that rules for search are simple-minded in the sense that they reflect simple concepts of causality. . . . search is based initially on two simple rules: (1) search in the neighborhood of the problem symptom and (2) search in the neighborhood of the current alternative (p. 121).

The theory postulates that more complex search behavior will be forthcoming only when simple search fails to uncover a satisfactory alternative. Only then is the organization driven to a more complex search mode.

Alternatives are searched out and evaluated sequentially, not simultaneously. "Only rough expectational data are used to screen alternative actions (initially)" (p. 79). Since search occurs near the problem-symptom, the nature of the problem will effect the order of search and the decisions that will be made. For familiar types of problems, programs for search that have proven successful in the past will be reactivated. Less successful search routines are less likely to be called upon for use in current problems.

Search is Biased

The direction of search is biased by several factors. The desirabilities of alternatives, the interpretation of goals, and hence the search for additional alternatives are mediated by human perceptions. Organizations establish rules which limit the range of decision alternatives that will be considered, and these rules are based on past experience. Furthermore, the rules and the degree of acceptability of alternatives (or the criteria for acceptability) will change with the success and failure experiences of the organization.

The preceding comments, then, indicate the features of a descriptive theory of *organizational* search—search behavior of multiples of people concerned with common organizational problems. Search intensity and direction, in this context, displays certain predominant characteristics which have been summarized. These characteristics are largely non-economic in nature. We will now focus on the information search and utilization processes of the individual decision maker.

Relating the Behavioral Theory to
Previous Concepts of Individual Search

It is well at this point to relate, in a general way, the characteristics of organizational search behavior to the TOTE construct presented in Chapter 2. Considering an individual organization member, an event(s)—stimulus—in the environment is perceived, evoking a TOTE. Incongruity between input stimulus and criteria in the "test" phase (failure to achieve goals, etc.) initiates search through the individual's repertoire of programs for appropriate "operations." This search-initiating incongruity is consistent with the "behavioral theory's" notion that search is *motivated*.

With regard to search being *"simple-minded,"* the "behavioral theory" implies that the Plans (compound TOTEs) for searching will be initially simple in structure. If simple Plans fail to remove the incongruity they will be replaced with more highly complex hierarchical Plans.

Bias in search is a reflection of the Image—the accumulated knowledge—and is an individual parameter for different organizational members. Bias is a reflection of the individual's history of successes and failures, other past experiences, and other individual parameters, which determine his repertoire of plans and programs available for use in the decision problem.

We can thus begin to see parallels between the Dynamic Model (TOTE) of the individual and the primary characteristics of organizational search behavior as specified in the "behavioral theory." Let us pursue these in greater depth.

THE STRUCTURE OF SEARCH

Initiation of Search

Why does search occur? What constitutes the occasion for the initiation of search activity? The answers to these questions center on two general sets of factors: (1) personal characteristics of the individual decision maker, and (2) the environmental and social forces directed toward the individual in the decision setting. Many specific initiators of search can be identified. For example, search may arise due to the curiosity of the decision maker, his "higher order motive" (Feldman and Kanter, 1965). A pervasive stimulus, as previously mentioned, is the recognition of the existence of a decision problem. In general terms, search behavior will arise whenever a discrepancy is believed to exist between the "state of the world" and "what should be." This determination is made in the "test" phase of the individual's cognitions. The source of stimulus input may be the decision maker himself, other organizational members, or extraorganizational individuals who interact with the decision maker.

March and Simon (p. 115) have also identified perceived discrepancies (which they call "conflict") as primary initiators of search behavior in organizations. The intensity and object of the decision maker's search depend on the source of the conflict. These sources are identified as uncertainty, unacceptability, and incomparability of decision alternatives. The individual's perception of conflict generates the motivation to reduce it, and search behavior is a primary vehicle by which this is accomplished.

Costello and Zalkind suggest a different motive, dissonance, for initiating search behavior:

> It has been shown with some attitudes that people who are given information that produces feelings of dissonance will more likely seek additional information on the topic than those who received consonant information. . . . (p. 294).

Thus, curiosity, problem recognition, conflict, and dissonance have all been recognized as initiators of search activity by various authors.

Object of Search

It makes little sense to discuss what initiates search without, at the same time, discussing the object of search; e.g., without considering what is being searched for. Search is an attempt to find "something" that will eliminate incongruity. One object or purpose of search may be to recognize and define decision problems (Soelberg, 1966, p. 5). This may include scanning the environment and maintaining an awareness of the occasion for decision. The following additional objects of search have been suggested by Soelberg (p. 4):

- special purpose decision rules to apply to the choice situation,
- operational decision criteria,
- consequences of alternatives,
- worth of alternatives,
- the nature of an "ideal" solution,
- feedback regarding results of choice implementation, and
- revised problem definition and goals.

In addition to Soelberg, Boulding (1966) has identified the "value function" *or* "value index" to be used in evaluating decision alternatives as one object of search. Zani (1970, p. 95) has identified problem finding, decision alternatives, evaluation criteria, and outcome determination as objects of search, and has identified their relevance to the design of managerial information systems. Many of these same objects of search had been elaborated earlier by March and Simon, including " . . . a search for programs of activity to achieve goals" (p. 179). They also state that one kind of search is to determine who (source) has the necessary information. Similarly, Ference (1970) proposes that when a decision problem arises, part of the organizational decision process will include a search for the appropriate organizational decision-making unit. The direction in which this search proceeds, he suggests, depends upon the type of decision problem that the organization is concerned with. We thus see that search is conducted for a wide diversity of objects.

Medium of Search

Search activity may be physical, perceptual, or cognitive (March and Simon, p. 178). These differ in degree of involvement of higher-level mental processes and in degree of observability of search activity. Whereas physical and perceptual search include involvement between the individual and his exterior environment, cognitive search is restricted to the mind. Cognitive search entails a search of one's memory, a sifting through the individual's repertoire of experiences. This form of search, the subject of much discussion and research in recent years, is of utmost importance to the study and understanding of problem solving. Cognitive search for problem solutions is the key element to problem solving in the many important studies conducted by Simon and Newell and their associates. But is cognitive search for *problem solutions* a search for *information?* It is, since knowledge about the problem is acquired as various alternative solutions are explored. These explorations indicate promising or unpromising directions for further search:

> Subjects faced with problem-solving tasks represent the problem environment in internal memory as a space of possible solutions to be searched in order to find that situation which corresponds to the solution. . . . Each node in the problem space may be thought of as a possible state of knowledge to which the problem solver may attain. The problem solver's search for a solution is an odyssey through problem space, from one knowledge state to another, until his current knowledge state includes the problem solution—that is, until he knows the answer (Simon and Newell, 1971, p. 151).

Inseparability of Search and Evaluation

The preceding remarks serve to illustrate a difficulty arising from our current presentation of the search process. Search is only one sub-component of problem solving (decision making). We have attempted to analyze information processes into subcomponents of acquisition, processing, and output, to facilitate our understanding of each. The difficulties inherent in such an approach have been noted by Cravens:

> A breakdown of an individual's information-processing activities into phases involves the risks inherent in characterizing a dynamic, continuous process as a sequence of discrete phases or steps. Nevertheless, such an approach seems necessary to get at the structure and interrelationships of the total process (p. 657).

Regardless of our analytic approach, we wish to stress that problem solving is an interrelated process featuring interactive search and evaluation. From the previous quote of Simon and Newell, we note that some "evaluation" must precede further search in many decision problems. The individual, they contend, searches locally and serially for promising directions for further search. Upon attainment of a new knowledge state (at some stage of problem solving) the problem solver acquires additional information from his search (*and* evaluation).

The TOTE construct is an asset for portraying the interrelationships among cognitive subcomponents of information processes. It shows logical linkages between these subcomponents. Cognitive search attempts to find appropriate programs (Plans—compound TOTEs) whose "operations" appear to be suitable for removing incongruencies. As the "test" (evaluation) phases indicate that inappropriate programs are being selected, they may be revised, or rejected and replaced by other programs. Throughout the sequence of trying alternative programs, the individual gains insights (knowledge) regarding the extent to which original incongruities are reduced or increased. He thus acquires information regarding the direction in which programs might be revised to reach a solution to the problem.

Two important points, then, are to be concluded. First, search activity need not be confined to physical and perceptual search, but importantly it includes a cognitive mode; i.e., the search of one's memory repertoire for plans and programs for decision-problem resolution. Second, the evaluative phase of problem solving is intimately related to the search phase. It provides the basis for directing future search.

Recognizing the interrelatedness of information acquisition and processing, it is possible to identify some common characteristics among individuals with respect to information-related behavior, and to identify sources of individual differences. Information-related behavior can be better understood by examining (1) some individual variables to which it is related, and (2) environmental characteristics affecting it. Although selected environmental characteristics are considered, a more extensive treatment of these issues is reserved for Chapters 8–11.

INDIVIDUAL VARIATIONS

People differ on numerous dimensions. Not surprisingly, these differences are related to one's beliefs and values and are, of course, reflected in one's decisions. In terms of our model presented in Chapter 2, both perceptual and personality characteristics are important. As Filley and House (1969) state, "the large amount of evidence attesting to the effects on decision making of individual differences—such as in personality characteristics, expectations, risk preferences, need for achievement, motivations, and perception—lends further support to the proposition that decisions are made with respect to the unique frame of reference of the decision maker" (p. 116). These individual differences influence the individual's search for information and the dynamics of interpreting and processing this information.

Perception

Individuals are constantly bombarded by sensory stimulation. There are noises, sights, smells, tastes, and tactile sensations. Yet somehow we manage to process this information without confusion. This process is known as perception. It may be defined as the experience people have as the immediate result of sensory inputs. The process is one of selection and organization of sensations to provide the meaningful entity which we experience.

Factors Influencing Perception

There are two basic components of this definition. First, perception is a system of *selection* or screening. Some information is processed, some is not. This screening helps us avoid processing irrelevant or disruptive information.

The second component is *organization.* The information that is processed must be ordered and categorized in some fashion that allows us to find meaning in the stimulus signals. These categories may be more or less elaborate but their central function is the reduction of complex information into simpler categories. However, to say that perception is a process of selection and categorization begs the question. How exactly does one choose to select and categorize information in his own unique fashion?

There are at least four general factors which are related to what one perceives. The first factor is called response disposition: People tend to perceive familiar stimuli more quickly than unfamiliar ones. Research has shown, for example, that when words are flashed on a screen at high speeds, subjects tend to recognize words that are frequently used more readily than ones that have infrequent usage.

A second factor is one's feelings towards the objects in question. There is considerable evidence that those things for which we hold strong feelings are also recognized more quickly than neutral stimuli. In general, it appears that we perceive things about which we hold positive feelings. In some cases, however, we recognize negative stimuli, especially where recognition leads to the avoidance of a highly negative situation. However, frequency and evaluation are not independent of one another. It appears that the more frequently one is exposed to something, the greater the likelihood that it will be positively evaluated.

Another factor of importance is called response salience. Secord and Backman (1964) define salience as *contemporary* conditions which predispose the organism to make certain responses. Given several possible responses, a particular one may be elicited by experimental instructions, by an immediately preceding sequence of behavior, by the preference of a motivated state, or by some aspect of the immediately present stimulus situation. Frightened people would perceive fearful objects; hungry people would perceive food objects, etc. So, both historical variables such as exposure and evaluation, and contemporary factors such as needs and expectations, influence what one perceives.

A final set of variables are those that represent the physical environment. Research by Segall, Campbell, and Herskovits (1966) has shown that one's surrounding environment is related to his perceptions. They present evidence that people living in situations or cultures called "carpentered" (numerous structures with right angles) tend to have different perceptions of two-dimensional representations of three-dimensional objects than those who live in non-carpentered environments. More specifically, they are able to look at a picture (which is two dimensional) and respond to it as if it were three dimensional. The authors also present data supporting the idea that people who live on plains have different perceptions about the representation of vertical lines than do people living in environments where views of distant territory are absent. In summary, what one perceives is a function of his past experiences. His experiences and environments are determined by his culture.

So, the decision maker is likely to perceive things for which he has an affinity and to perceive those things he has perceived in the past. These perceptions will be modified by current needs and environmental conditions.

Risk Taking

In addition to perception, other dimensions of individual variations can be identified. Certain of the individual's characteristics are associated with persistent and consistent modes of behavior. One such characteristic which is important for decision making is the propensity to take risks.

> ... One can hardly afford to neglect the role that risk and conservatism may play in thinking, however, because of the obvious fact that many of the forms of psychological activity that we customarily call "thinking" eventuate in some kind of decision making. Decision making, in turn, involves the weighing of alternatives in terms of their desirabilities and their likelihoods. Issues concerning the avoidance or acceptance of risks in arriving at decisions hence are likely to be important ingredients in thinking processes (Kogan and Wallach, 1964, p. 1).

Two distinct research emphases have evolved in studying risk taking. The first is concerned with various environmental characteristics associated with risk taking in decision making. The second approach relates riskiness to other personal characteristics such as biographic, intellective, and personality dimensions.

The most frequently investigated environmental variable related to risk has been the amount of information present. When a complex decision must be made, there is usually an opportunity for a trade-off between risk and the attainment of more information. More information is often costly to obtain in terms of time or money, but its acquisition reduces risk. Studies by Irwin and Smith (1957), Pruitt (1961), Lanzetta and Kanareff (1962), and Hoge and Lanzetta (1968) have focused on this problem. A review of these studies by Streufert and Taylor (1971) states that "first, subjects seem to take more risk when information is costly in terms of money or time required to make the decision—secondly, the amount of information available affects the degree of subjective uncertainty and confidence in a decision" (p. 8).

Data on personal characteristics has also produced some generalizations about riskiness. It appears as if people who are rigid and dogmatic tend to be overly confident (Block and Peterson, 1955; Brim and Hoff, 1957). Kogan and Wallach (1964), in a sample of females, found that "associated with risk taking in a strategy context are confidence of judgment, extremity under high confidence, narrow category width, and extremity of self-rating." These data suggest that the overly confident person who also is extreme in terms of a number of different response styles will take greater risks.

Early evidence had suggested that men were less conservative than women (Pettigrew, 1958). A later study by Wallach and Kogan (1959) indicated that women were more conservative than men only when they perceive the situation as ambiguous. Under conditions of certainty, women were less conservative than men. These authors also report that "self sufficiency may be related to conservatism in males, and independence to risk taking in females" (Kogan and Wallach, 1964, p. 186).

Finally, it appears as if age is related to risk taking. Wallach and Kogan (1961) state "one of the important consequences of aging appears to be a greater unwillingness to go out on a limb even though very certain of one's judgment" (p. 29). Their data indicate that older people are more afraid of failure and demand a "surer thing" when dealing with financial risks. A recent study by Vroom and Pehl (1971) with 1,484 male managers employed in over two hundred corporations also supports these findings. They report that "the results show a significant relationship between age and measures of both risk taking and the value placed on risk" (p. 404). Older people were less risky. In summary, both personal characteristics and environmental variables seem to be related to the amount of risk one is willing to take.

Adaptation Level

The idea behind adaptation level (Helson, 1947, 1951) is that the individual, over time, establishes a range of acceptable values for any given stimulus dimension or combination of dimensions. Incoming information is then judged as large or small, heavy or light, important or unimportant. This expected range is the adaptation level. The more a stimulus diverges from this range, in either direction, the more likely it is that some action will be taken to explain or understand the discrepancy. Thus, differences in adaptation levels may result in different search behaviors. Shull, Delbecq, and Cummings (1970) note, however,

> that the adaptation level theory does not adequately incorporate considerations of the need system or affective aspects of human behavior. The emphasis of the adaption level theory is largely on the structural properties of past and present stimulus fields. Moreover, this theory does not adequately account for the selectivity of perception (p. 45).

Achievement Motivation

Atkinson (1957) and McClelland, Atkinson, Clark, and Lowell (1953) have suggested that people and societies differ in their motive to avoid failure. McClelland over the years has provided fairly strong support for the idea that a whole culture's productivity can be partially predicted from the need to achieve, as reflected in the writings of its members. He sees this "need to achieve" as an attempt to "do better than the standard."

The research in the area shows that individuals with a high need for achievement (n Ach) come from families in which they are independent at an early age, are expected to be competent, and are evaluated highly. The predictions and results seem to support the following ideas.

•Individuals with high n Ach prefer situations: (1) of moderate risk; (2) where knowledge of results is provided; and (3) where individual responsibility is encouraged.
•Individuals with high n Ach will be attracted to entrepreneurial roles in which the level of risk, feedback, and responsibility is suitable.

Aspiration Level

Information search behavior is believed to be closely related to the goals for accomplishment that the individual sets for himself. These goals are the individual's level of aspiration.

Katona (1953) has formulated three generalizations about aspiration level which are helpful in understanding its role and function within the individual:

1. Aspirations are not static, they are not established once for all time.
2. Aspirations tend to grow with achievement and decline with failure.
3. Aspirations are influenced by the performance of other members of the group to which one belongs and by that of reference groups (p. 316).

The dynamics of aspiration level are illustrated by considering the individual in a sequential choice situation. The requirements of a satisfactory choice alternative are defined by the initial aspiration level. It may change with the individual's experience as the choice sequence unfolds. If the search process reveals easily discovered solution alternatives, then the individual's level of aspiration, and consequently the standards for a satisfactory solution, will increase. If the discovery of satisfactory alternatives is difficult during search, then the level of aspiration will diminish. If the set of alternatives being considered is unsatisfactory, he can search for other alternatives or he can lower his aspiration level and re-search among the existing alternatives. What he will do depends upon his persistence (Simon, 1955). Lewin (in Costello and Zalkind, p. 71) states that whether aspiration level will rise rapidly or slowly after success varies among individuals. Generally, it is more likely to be raised after success than to be lowered after failure. When man is confronted with a novel situation for which he has no history of success and failure, he usually does not set a definite achievement goal. Hence, strong failure is not experienced.

Level of aspiration helps explain when search will be initiated. It also has been used to explain when search will be terminated. In a problem-solving context the search for solution alternatives is related to the difference between the level of aspiration and achievement. This difference is called the "attainment discrepancy" (Wilson and Alexis, 1962). It is postulated to result in a decrease in the search for solution alternatives when past search has been relatively successful (positive achievement). As stated by Alexis and Wilson (1967), " ... as reasonably satisfactory solutions are reached, search becomes undesirable and unproductive. At some level search activity ceases altogether" (p. 161).

Level of aspiration, then, is a function of the individual's history of success and failure, and his expectations of future success. A subset of these expectations forms the criteria for acceptability of decision alternatives. These criteria reside in his Image.

Conceptual Structure

One of the most significant individual variables related to information search and processing is "conceptual structure." Individuals differ with respect to their capacities for using higher-level processes of abstraction, assimilation, and projection. These differences are due to a combination of life-long learning experiences and biological factors. A decision maker acquires and sifts through bits of information, applying his integrative processes in an attempt to eventually arrive at a choice among alternatives. "Conceptual structure" is a concept that has been used to explain this process.

Schroder, Driver, and Streufert (1967) state that " 'level of conceptual structure' refers to the way an individual receives, stores, processes, and transmits information" (p. 8). In general, there are two main processes going on. First, the individual must distinguish between various parts or underlying dimensions of information inputs. This is called differentiation. Second, the parts must

A. Low Integration Index   B. High Integration Index

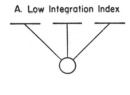 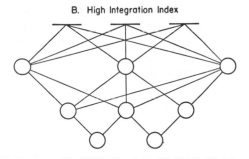

Rules are in a fixed
relationship so that the
whole process can be
reduced to one rule.

Rules are in an interdependent relationship; each
can influence the other singly and in combinations
producing new connections and new rule structures.

Figure 5-1 Variation in Level of Conceptual Structure (*Source:*
Schroder, Driver, and Streufert, 1967.)

be combined through integrating rules. Integration is the label used for this
process. People differ in the ways in which they differentiate and integrate
information from the environment. Figure 5-1 illustrates these differences.

Driver and Streufert (1969) explain that

> . . . information processing systems can be described in terms of (1) the
> number of parts at work in a system (i.e., roles in a group, ideas in a
> personality, etc.), termed *differentiation;* and (2) the amount of interconnec-
> tion between parts, termed *integrative complexity.* The more a system is
> differentiated and integrated, that is, the more system parts are interrelated,
> the more the potential information in the input is utilized in outputs (p. 274).

Various techniques exist to measure an individual's "level of conceptual
structure" (or "cognitive complexity").[1] Many studies have demonstrated that
individuals differ significantly as to level of conceptual structure, ranging from
simple (low) to complex (high).

People with low integrative abilities have the following characteristics:
(1) They tend to be categorical and stereotypic. Cognitive structures that depend
upon simple fixed rules of integration tend to reduce the possibility of thinking
in terms of degrees. (2) Internal conflict appears to be minimized with simple
structures. Since few alternative relationships are generated, closure is quick.
(3) Behavior is apparently anchored in external conditions. There is less personal
contribution in simple structures. (4) Fewer rules cover a wider range of phenomena. There is less distinction between separate situations.

With a moderately high integration structure, we see different modes of

[1]See Vannoy, 1965; and Schroder, Driver, and Streufert, 1967.

cognitive functioning: (1) The cognitive system is less deterministic. Numerous alternative relationships are generated and considered. (2) The environment is tracked in numerous ways. There is less compartmentalization of the environment. (3) The individual utilizes more internal processes. The self as an individual operates on the process.

While these "types" are not pure in any absolute sense, they do reflect different styles of cognitive functioning which are important for decision making.

If we can identify differences in level of integrative complexity (conceptual structure), then we may expect to observe differences in information-search and processing behaviors. Because there are numerous reviews of the research in this area (see Schroder, *et al.*, 1967; Harvey, Hunt, and Schroder, 1961; Bieri, 1955; Vannoy, 1965; Driver and Streufert, 1969), an extensive presentation of empirical findings will not be made here. Instead, we will briefly highlight some characteristics of behavior that have implications for organizational decision processes.

Conceptually simple and conceptually complex persons differ with respect to preferred information-gathering tactics (Streufert, Suedfeld, and Driver, 1965; Suedfeld and Streufert, 1966). One search tactic, relatively simplistic, is to request summary information about various characteristics of a problem situation. An alternative and more complex tactic is to perturbate, or act upon the environment, and to observe the resulting environmental response. On the basis of these observations, conclusions can be drawn about the nature of the environment. Several studies indicate that both search tactics are used by groups composed of conceptually complex or conceptually simple individuals. However, the more complex tactic is preferred by high-conceptual-structure groups, while the simpler tactic is preferred by low-structure groups. It has also been found that individuals low in conceptual structure request information about ongoing events, while high-structure individuals tend to request information about more novel or new situations: " ... simple subjects were more interested in receiving feedback about on-going activities, while complex subjects searched new, hitherto unexplored aspects ... " (Suedfeld and Streufert, 1966, p. 352). Other studies reveal that high-conceptual-structure individuals: (1) spend more time processing information; (2) process and interpret information in more complex ways, resulting in a greater number of interpretations; (3) consider more alternative implications of information; (4) are better able to integrate discrepant information; (5) acquire more information prior to making a decision; and (6) express greater uncertainty about their decisions.

Some important additional differences are revealed by introducing "environmental complexity" into the discussion. Certain general relationships between environmental complexity and the complexity of the individual's decision-related behavior have emerged from various studies. There is a tendency for performance complexity to increase with increasing environmental complexity,

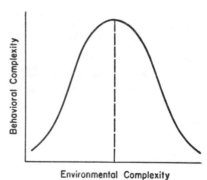

Figure 5-2   Behavioral and Environmental Complexity

up to some optimal level. Beyond that level, further increases in environmental complexity result in decreased performance complexity. The general pattern, resembling an inverted U-curve, is known as the "U Curve Hypothesis" (Schroder, Driver, and Streufert, 1967). It is represented in Figure 5-2.

Several dimensions of behavior have been studied as the ordinate in Figure 5-2, including: (1) complexity of information processing (integration); (2) complexity of perception; (3) amount of information preferred; and (4) quality of decisions. Environmental complexity, the abscissa, usually represents various information loads.

Studies of these phenomena demonstrate that the optimal level of input complexity varies among individuals.

> ... systems have optimal input conditions (neither too complex nor too simple), which maximize their capacity for integrated complexity in output. ... the past experience of an individual or group system determines its unique optimal level ... (Driver and Streufert, 1969, pp. 274–75).

What may be an optimal level of information load (input complexity) for one may be far from optimal for another. Furthermore, extreme deviations from optimal levels may result in negative affect for the individual. This may motivate him to operate on his environment so as to either increase or decrease its complexity toward optimal.

> ... the model suggests that systems differ not only in information-processing capacities, but also in motivation for a particular amount of input complexity (p. 277).

Individuals with a high conceptual structure respond differently to variations in environmental complexity than do low-structure individuals. It appears as if people high in complexity can tolerate and utilize greater information loads. In group task settings, self-initiated search seems to decrease as information load (environmental complexity) increases. However, conceptually simple groups are considerably more sensitive to information load than are the conceptually complex groups (Streufert, Suedfeld, and Driver, 1965). A study by Sieber and Lanzetta (1964) found that complex individuals consistently gathered more information. Furthermore, the complex individual increased the amount of information search as problem uncertainty (environmental complexity) increased, whereas simple individuals did not. In addition, Schroder, Driver, and Streufert (1967) comment,

> The asymptote of searching and processing time occurs at a lower level of uncertainty and external demand [environmental complexity] for concrete [simple conceptual structure] persons. ... Searching and information-processing time of abstract [complex] and concrete [simple] persons are most dissimilar in the middle ranges of uncertainty and external demand (p. 114).

These researches strongly indicate some implications of conceptual structure for the organization. First, we can expect a diversity of "levels of conceptual structure" to exist among individuals in the organization. Second, they suggest the need for mechanisms of organizational design that will provide a suitable match between individual capabilities and task requirements. This "match-up" will be accomplished only when the organization identifies criteria for the kinds of behavior that are best suited to the demands imposed by an organizational role. As stated by Driver and Streufert (1969):

> If the criterion reflects behavior that demands complex search, high levels of perception of input, and complex integrations in decision, then clearly more complex systems are at an advantage. If . . . the criterion is such that simpler search methods and the use of limited information is required for achieving the goal, then there may be no differences or even an advantage for simple systems (p. 280).

Finally, the finding that individuals vary with respect to their optimal level of environmental complexity implies the need for flexibility in the organization's information system. What may be an optimal level of information inputs for one individual may be far from optimal for another. Furthermore, the informational needs of an individual may vary from time to time according to variations in environmental demands placed upon him.

HUMAN BIAS IN SELECTED CONTEXTS

Information-related behavior is a function of the environment, as well as of individual characteristics. We note that certain behavior characteristics have been observed in non-organizational contexts. These observed behaviors have significant implications for organizational informational processes. They indicate additional situations in which specific sources of human bias may be expected. However, many of these characteristics have not been systematically studied to any noticeable extent in organization settings. Available evidence suggests they are worthy of further empirical examination.

Outcome Desirability

In some choice situations, the decision maker has little control over the consequences of outcomes for alternative actions. Here, one of his primary tasks is to assess the chances of occurrence of various outcomes for each alternative. Research studies indicate that decision makers' beliefs and values are not always independently determined in such situations. Morlock (1967) found that individuals' expectations of the occurrence of an event varied positively with the desirability of the event's outcome. Less information was gathered to conclude that a favorable event would occur than to conclude that an unfavorable event would occur. In a similar study it was shown that perceived desirability of outcomes effected predictions (Morlock and Hertz, 1964). The more favorable alternative was predicted more frequently, even though the possible outcomes had identical chances of occurring. This suggests that the "desirability" of environmental outcomes may affect the amount of information search and processing that occurs in choice situations. Extending this to the *organizational* setting, the first case study of Cyert, Dill, and March (cited earlier) also supports the idea that the expectation of an event varies positively with its desirability.

Changing a Decision

If the decision maker receives from the environment some indication that his decision should be reconsidered, we might expect a different intensity of search behavior. Pruitt (1961) found that once a decision had been made and an opportunity existed to change it (or confirm it), decision makers sampled far too much. More information was gathered to change the decision than was needed to decide initially. The existence of this phenomenon, however, is not conclusive. Brody (1965) found that no more information was required to change a decision than to make it initially.

Although the research results are inconclusive, the issue remains relevant: Variations in information search behavior for a decision problem may occur, depending on whether the decision is being made initially or is being reconsidered. Once a commitment to a position is made, the likelihood of modification of that position is diminished. If, as suggested by Soelburg (1966), "remaking" a decision is an affectively difficult phase of the decision process, then we might well expect more information to be required than was needed to make the initial decision.

Unfiltered Information

There is considerable evidence that the relevance of the information acquired from the environment influences decision behavior. Few studies exist on the impact of irrelevant information in organizational settings. Ackoff (1967) states that managers have too much irrelevant information, but explicit studies of its effects are lacking. In a non-organizational setting, Moskowitz (1972) showed that greater amounts of relevant information result in improved decisions. Relevant information is recognized and used in decisions. Extending this, Ebert (1972a) showed that increases in utilization of relevant information are bounded by human capacity limitations. While these and many other studies show that relevant information is used, other studies show tendencies to utilize irrelevant information also. Walker and Bourne (1961) have shown that errors in concept learning increase with the amount of irrelevant information. Ebert (1972b) found that irrelevant information detracted from decision performance, in terms of both level and consistency, when making scheduling decisions. This study showed the improvement in performance that could result from providing a mechanism to ferret out irrelevant information from the environment. Without such a filter we must conjecture that such filtering will occur only as the user (decision maker) learns through experience to distinguish information relevance.

A study by Kleinmuntz (1968) suggests that *experience* at a decision task is crucial for intuitive filtering. In examining information-search behavior, it was found that experienced neurologists had greater diagnostic accuracy and asked fewer questions prior to diagnosis than did inexperienced neurologists. "The neurologist has learned to search his problem environment for those symptoms and signs that yield the greatest amount of information" (p. 181). Their protocols also indicated that they tended to selectively discard data that were irrelevant to the particular diagnosis with which they were dealing. Data were remembered only if they were relevant to the diagnostic decision. These results were more true for the experienced diagnosticians than for the inexperienced. The implications of information relevance to decision making will be considered in greater detail in Chapter 6.

Conservatism

Observations of human information processing reveal, to repeat, a high degree of inter-individual variability. Yet, certain general tendencies have been discovered, one of the most striking being a marked tendency toward conservatism. The meaning of this phenomenon is clarified by referring to a Bayesian model for probability revision, expression [1] below.

$$\frac{P(H_1/D)}{P(H_2/D)} = \frac{P(D/H_1)}{P(D/H_2)} \cdot \frac{P(H_1)}{P(H_2)} \qquad [1]$$

This model, under certain conditions, specifies how one's beliefs should be revised after observing sample information. Consider the simple case in which the decision maker does not know which of two hypotheses (H_1 or H_2) is true, although he knows that one, and only one, can be true. The degree to which he believes each of the alternative hypotheses will be modified as additional sample information is acquired from the environment. Prior to observing sample information, D, the decision maker's opinions (subjective probabilities) regarding the validities of the alternative hypotheses are given by $P(H_1)$ and $P(H_2)$. After observing the sample information, his opinions for the two hypotheses are represented by $P(H_1/D)$ and $P(H_2/D)$, the posterior probabilities. $P(H_1/D)$ represents the probability of H_1 being true, given D. The posterior beliefs, then, represent a combination of prior beliefs and modifications from seeing sample information. The impact of the sample evidence is represented by its probability of occurrence under each of the hypotheses; the conditional probability of observing D if H_1 is true, and if H_2 is true. When the sample information is more likely to occur for one hypothesis than for the other, then the likelihood ratio, $\frac{P(D/H_1)}{P(D/H_2)}$, will depart from 1:1. The extent of this departure is a measure of the *diagnosticity* of the sample datum. Observation of a datum which is much more likely under one hypothesis than under the other is highly diagnostic (informative). At the other extreme is an observation that is equally likely under both hypotheses, and is thus "uninformative." The model, then, explicitly prescribes how sample information is to be combined with prior beliefs in arriving at posterior beliefs. Consequently, the model provides a standard for evaluating human information processing performance.

The behavioral phenomenon referred to as "conservatism" occurs when the individual's prior beliefs are modified to a lesser extent than is warranted by the diagnosticity of the datum. Many studies have revealed the general tendency to revise opinion in the appropriate direction, but by a lesser amount than optimal. Human posterior subjective estimates, following a sequence of data, are revised in the same direction as those of the Bayes model. However, they are less extreme than those of the model. Man behaves as if the data are less informative than they really are. This phenomenon has several implications for information search and processing. With regard to search, it implies that the decision maker will attempt to gather more information than necessary for reaching a criterion level of confidence for certain decisions. As stated by Edwards (1968) "It takes from 2 to 5 observations [of sample information] to do one observation's worth of work in inducing a subject to change his opinions" (p. 18). Secondly, it implies that erroneous assessments of expectation may enter the decision process. These may lead to decisions that are inconsistent with the decision maker's own decision criteria.

Some additional characteristics of conservatism have been reviewed extensively by Slovic and Lichtenstein (1971). Generally, it has been found that as the diagnosticity of the data increases, so does the degree of conservatism. However, at low levels of diagnosticity some studies have found non-conservative information processing. Decision makers also tend to properly use the first datum in a sequence, but then depart toward conservatism after exposure to subsequent data. The foregoing tendencies were supported in a more recent study by Mason and Moskowitz (1972). These researchers went on to question whether or not conservatism could be accounted for by the individual's risk-taking propensity. Their results indicate that no such relationship exists.

The underlying causes of the conservatism phenomenon are not sufficiently understood. Three hypotheses have been advanced to explain its existence (Edwards, 1968; Slovic and Lichtenstein, 1971). The "misperception" hypothesis suggests that conservatism results because humans misperceive the diagnostic impact of each datum. Advocates of the "misaggregation" hypothesis contend that humans have difficulty aggregating sequential data into an accurate summary judgment, although they accurately perceive the diagnostic impact of an individual datum. The third hypothesis contends that conservatism is an artifact that occurs when humans are forced to deal with extreme probabilities. Du-Charme (1970) believes that humans are only conservative when dealing with odds ratios outside the range of 10:1 to 1:10.

Although the reasons for conservatism are unresolved, the well-established fact is that " ... opinion change is very orderly and usually proportional to numbers calculated from Bayes' theorem—but it is insufficient in amount" (Edwards, 1968, p. 18). Attempts to overcome conservatism have been largely unsuccessful. Instructions to information processors reduce conservatism, but the amount of reduction is relatively small (Peterson, DuCharme, and Edwards, 1968).

Some methods have been proposed for improving subjective estimates (Winkler, 1967), but these are relatively cumbersome, time consuming to implement, and have not been extensively tested to date. Failure to eliminate human conservatism has led to the development of methods for minimizing its negative effects. These methods[2] are designed for interaction between man and machine, in which man makes certain estimates of inputs for expression [1]. Thereafter, the machine processes those estimates to arrive at a posterior probability ("belief"). As stated by Slovic and Lichtenstein (1971):

A system where men estimate P(D/H) separately for each datum and the machine combines these into posterior probabilities via Bayes theorem has consistently been found superior to a system where the man, himself, must aggregate the data into a P(H/D) estimate (p. 697).

[2] For an elaboration of these methods see Edwards and Phillips, 1964, and Edwards, Phillips, Hays, and Goodman, 1968.

Capacity Limitations and Simplification

A primary source of human bias arises from man's limited capacities, and the mechanisms he employs for adjusting behavior within these bounds.

> Limits on human intellectual capacities and on available information set definite limits to man's capacity to be comprehensive (Lindblom, 1959, p. 84).

The above statement indicates the need to consider human limitations in the decision process, particularly as they relate to information search and utilization. Man constantly employs devices to simplify environment complexity. He does this at both specific and global levels: (1) in a specific problem context he categorizes objects and events according to their key elements (Bruner, Goodnow, and Austin, 1956); and (2) in broader contexts, he adopts a predominate system of values (his larger behavior premises) from among a large number of possible value systems. Simplification processes at both levels are necessary for instrumental action, and for avoiding overload of human capacities. In the first case, categorizing permits operation of higher-level mental processes and, thus, sets the tone for cognitive search capabilities. In the second case, guidelines are established within the Image to provide the evaluative criteria for the decision process.

The concept of conceptual structure suggests that individuals differ in the level of information load that is optimal. When the amount of information from the environment is at a suboptimal level we can expect information search behavior to ensue. When the incoming level is superoptimal we can expect behavior directed toward simplifying the environment. Miller (1960) has suggested several adjustment mechanisms that may be employed by the individual confronted with an overabundance of information:

> (a) omission—temporary nonprocessing of information; (b) error—processing incorrect information, which may enable the system to return to normal processing afterwards; (c) queuing—delaying the response during a period of high overlap of input information in the expectation that it may be possible to catch up during a lull; (d) filtering—neglecting to process certain categories of information while processing others; (e) cutting categories of discrimination—responding in a general way to the input, but with less precision than would be done at lower rates . . . ; (f) employing multiple channels—processing information through two or more parallel channels at the same time . . . ; and (g) escape from the task (p. 697).

Other writers have noted that organizational man's attempts to simplify are manifest in simplistic modes of search behavior. The greater the cognitive strain imposed by problem complexity, the simpler the search rules become (Alexis and Wilson, 1967, pp. 73–74). In decision problems such as the determination of administrative policy, Lindblom (1959) argues that simplification occurs systematically by reducing the number of alternative policies to be investigated (limiting search to alternatives near the existing policy), and by eliminating the need to investigate some of the consequences of alternative policies. The dilemma for the decision maker is to be sufficiently comprehensive so as to perform well on the one hand, and to employ simplifying strategies to avoid (or reduce) cognitive strain on the other.

For problems involving a large number of possible alternatives, it is difficult to empirically determine the way in which simplifying processes are structured. Simon and Newell (1971) report that search is highly selective. Only a modest number of possible alternatives are evaluated. However, a trial and error search strategy is not used. Instead, search is serial and systematic. Additional information is acquired in successive steps, providing direction and guidance for further search. Furthermore, people tend to pursue an understanding of the implications of a single alternative in some depth (over several stages) before relinquishing that alternative to pursue other alternatives. An alternative strategy would be to examine the next single stage for each of many alternatives. This latter strategy is a difficult one due to limitations of the short-term memory (p. 153).

Kleinmuntz (1968) attempted to uncover the structure of neurologists' search processes as they diagnosed illnesses. This work revealed several characteristics of the diagnostic search strategy:

(a) The neurologist has learned to search his problem environment for those symptoms and signs that yield the greatest amount of information. . . . he radically reduces his problem environment with each question. . . . He cuts his problem environment in half . . . until he reaches a diagnosis (pp. 181–82).

(b) The types of questions he [the neurologist] asked . . . indicate . . . a pattern that moves from general to specific questioning (p. 178).

(c) Kleinmuntz reveals that search efficiency and diagnosis accuracy were found to be related to the amount of hospital-ward experience of the neurologist. Fewer questions (information search) were asked by and fewer diagnostic errors were made by the more experienced physicians. Greater experience led to strategies of selectively discarding data that were irrelevant to the particular diagnosis. Data were remembered only if that piece of data was relevant to the diagnostic decision.

This work clearly illustrates that systematic procedures and strategies evolve for the simplification of the decision maker's environment. It further illustrates that these strategies are refined and modified with experience. We observe, then, that intensity of search and "objectivity" of information processing are functions of individual capacity and situational complexity. It is not surprising, therefore, to observe large differences in behavior among individuals, as well as noticeable variations in an individual's behavior over time. In some situations the individual's decision behavior may appear to be biased and "irrational" from the organization's viewpoint. This same behavior may be quite "rational" when the individual's capacities and the demands of the decision problem are considered. It is true that the individual's environment can be structured to effectively raise his capacities for remembering and for utilizing incoming information to some extent (Yntema, 1963; Yntema and Mueser, 1962). Indeed, organizations attempt to employ information technologies (information systems) to facilitate the simplification process of the decision maker (Burlingame, 1961, p. 124). However, the state of advancement of this technology is inadequate relative to man's requirements. Subsequently, he relies most heavily on his internally derived coping strategies.

INTEGRATION INTO THE ORGANIZATION

The preceding sections have introduced a framework for understanding information processes. Subcomponents have been analyzed in some detail from a behavioral perspective. We cannot hope to concisely integrate each of the many variables into a unified set of causal relationships. We can, however, be aware of their existence and presume that they underlie much of the observed behavior in organizations. With this in mind, it is worthwhile to look momentarily at information processes in organization settings.

Information Sources that Initiate Search

Our review has indicated that individual search is initiated by curiosity, perceived conflict, or by recognition of the existence of a problem. All of these processes are internal to the individual. However, in the organization, problem recognition or identification does not arise solely at his initiative and discretion. Therefore, it is appropriate to consider how the occasion for decision (and search) is signalled.

Motivated problemistic search requires that certain types of information be available to serve as "benchmark" indicators or standards against which a given state of affairs can be assessed. Incongruence between actual and desired status, as indicated by these standards, provides a signal for the occasion for decision. Ference (1970) has postulated four such types (sources) of problem-initiating (recognizing) information: "criterion checks," "repetitive procedures," "policy statements," and "residual sources."

Criterion Checks. The organizational environment typically provides a history of accepted and established "yardsticks." Examples are normal costs of operation, employee turnover rate, accident rates, regulatory constraints, industry standards, etc. Organizational deviations from these performance indicators signal the possible existence of a decision problem. Ference postulates that the ensuing search for problem clarification and solution alternatives is relatively localized. Search occurs in the area where the problem arose, and most consideration is given to solution alternatives that currently exist (p. 89). It is only upon failure of this initial localized search that expanded search occurs.

Repetitive Procedures. Periodically recurring activities throughout the organization are another source of problem recognition. Product quality-appraisal procedures, equipment and personnel evaluation procedures, etc. may signal the existence of a potential problem. The ensuing pattern of search will be similar to that displayed for problems initiated by criterion checks, according to Ference.

Policy Statements. Formal policy statements as sources of problem initiation pose more difficulties than the criterion-check and repetitive-procedures sources. Arising from higher levels of the organization, such statements typically affect several or all areas of the organization. Subsequently, they induce more extended "innovative" search for problem identification and resolution.

Variations with the Environment. The appealing notion that "criterion checks" result in more localized search behavior than do "policy statements" may be an over-simplification. For, as Thompson (1967) proposes, the types of criterion checks employed by organizations vary greatly. The qualitative character of the criteria that are used depends on: (1) characteristics of the organization's task environment; (2) the degree to which the organization's technology is instrumentally perfected; and (3) the means used to control interdependence among organizational subunits. The criteria checks employed under different circumstances range between highly "crystallized" and "ambiguous" (p. 85). These differences may lead to qualitatively different search behaviors, rather than relatively localized search postulated by Ference. This issue remains to be explored.

Pounds (1969) examined the kinds of criteria that are used by organizations to detect the existence of problems. Recent historical performance indicators ("criteria checks" in Ference's terminology) were dominately used in the technically based corporation that he studied. Comparison of the organization's performance with planning models, and with the performance of other organizations, played lesser roles. Undesirable performance departures from the historical criteria commonly resulted in the manager's loss of discretion in defining (searching for) his own problems. Problem definition was imposed on him by his superior in the organization.

Others in the Environment. Of the many recognized problems, the ones to which the individual devotes his energies are significantly determined by others in the organization. The work of Pounds illustrates that managers do not independently search through their "portfolios" of "problems needing attention" and then proceed to embark on programs for resolving one or more of them. Instead, their efforts are predominately directed elsewhere by various environmental and social forces within the organization. Customers, peers, superiors, and subordinates significantly influence the problems attended by the manager.

A problem found by someone in the organization carries with it substantial influence over the problems on which *other* parts of the organization will work (p. 10).

This statement illustrates that the initiation of search does not occur independently among members in the organizational environment. It is not initiated unilaterally by the organizational problem solver on the basis of his problem agenda and interests. The impact of these environmental and social forces will be considered in greater detail in succeeding chapters.

Comprehensiveness of Search

Our preceding review indicates some limitations on the comprehensiveness of search. From the individual's viewpoint, problemistic search is adaptive. The search for alternatives is sequential. Satisficing, rather than optimizing, criteria are used (Cyert, Feigenbaum, and March, 1971). Problem solving involves the use of search strategies (patterns or plans for search) which vary in complexity (Alexis and Wilson, 1967). In the initial phases of problem solving, simplistic search strategies are adopted. The problem solver cognitively scans his repertoire of similar problems from past experience. He considers immediate solution alternatives prior to considering longer-run solution alternatives. The search for alternatives is conducted in the neighborhood of the problem symptom until driven to a more complex (expanded) search strategy (March and Simon, 1965; Cravens, 1970). Further failure to find an acceptable alternative leads to a re-examination of estimated consequences of alternatives already under consideration (search for clarification), and a re-examination of objectives. Subsequent failure leads to a relaxation of criteria of satisfactoriness; i.e., a change in level of aspiration (March and Simon, 1965; Cyert, Feigenbaum, and March, 1971). The speed (motivation) of search will increase with increased time pressure. Legal restrictions, features of the organizational structure, and the locus of search responsibility in the organization impose restrictions on the discretion to act and on the availability of information (Feldman and Kanter, 1965; Wilson and Alexis, 1962; March and Simon, 1965).

In addition to the above characteristics, other provocative issues have been set forth which merit further study.

1. When confronted with a problem, the decision maker engages in two distinct kinds of search. The first is a "sizing-up" of the problem itself—an assessment or appraisal of the problem content (Simon and Barenfeld, 1969). This is followed by a search for alternative solutions. The ensuing search is not exhaustive, but is restricted by constraints imposed by the environment and by human capacity limitations.

2. Many authors have contended that the search for alternatives is sequential and is terminated by the acceptance of the first satisfactory alternative (Simon, 1955; March and Simon, 1965). However, a study by Soelberg (1966) suggests that a revision of the theory of search be considered. The behavior which he observed indicated that search is a "parallel process," rather than occurring in a sequential one-at-a-time manner. More than one satisfactory alternative at a time is held in an "active roster" prior to the time of choice. At the termination of search, the problem solver will have identified a preferred alternative. However, explicit comparisons of alternatives (called the "confirmation process") is deferred until search has ended and choice is imminent.

3. It has been suggested that satisficing occurs because of the contradictory demands placed on the individual by the search and evaluation phases of the decision process (Emory and Niland, 1968). The cycling between alternative-generation and alternative-evaluation phases requires switching between two very different thought processes. The search for alternatives may most appropriately call for an openness of mind, relatively free of restrictive bounds, to permit the discovery of suitable alternatives. On the other hand, " . . . appraisal requires convergent thinking and evaluation, both of which accent rationality, a challenging attitude and the careful weighing of evidence" (p. 73). These contradictory demands have also been noted and discussed in different contexts by Costello and Zalkind (1963, pp. 379–80). This notion that the idea-generating phase (search for alternatives) is inhibited by the evaluation phase has led Maier (1964), as well as Emory and Niland, to suggest that the two phases be separated. By so doing, the quality of generated alternatives may be facilitated. This separation of evaluation and idea-generation phases has been termed "deferred judgment" by Parnes (1964, p. 145). His early research indicated that "initial idea-generation" (the first satisfactory alternative) produces highly useful but non-unique ideas, whereas extended idea-generation produces unique and useful ideas using the deferred judgment concept.

When formal procedures for separating these phases are not provided, man will develop his own simplistic rules to avoid cognitive strain. This strain arises from the demands for systematic comparisons among dimensionally incomparable alternatives. It is identified by Soelberg (1966) as an affectively difficult phase of the overall decision process. The implications of the discomfort from this phase are suggested by the following remarks:

> The existence of the confirmation process also explains the often observed assymetry of administrative decision making: once made, decisions are usually very hard to unmake, or to get remade. A most obvious explanation is that he balks at having to go through all the pain of changing his tailor-made decision rule to fit a new pair of alternatives (pp. 14–15).

Many of the foregoing characteristics of search offer the advantage of providing relatively quick problem resolution, particularly when the individual has a rich background of problem-solving experience. At the same time, however, reliance on his repertoire of potential problem-solving responses may inhibit his propensity to develop new or unusual problem solutions (Costello and Zalkind, 1963, p. 379). The process tends to retard innovation which otherwise may lead to more desirable solutions.

Direction of Search

The search for information leads in a number of directions and to various sources. It has been suggested, for instance, that in searching for programs to achieve organizational goals, attention will first focus on those variables that are within the control of the individual (March and Simon, 1965; Emory and Niland, 1968). Next, attention shifts to variables that are not within the individual's control. A number of more detailed propositions have been set forth, with implications for the direction of search behavior (Ference, 1970). The following characteristics are inferred from those propositions: (a) for ill-defined problems, information will be sought more predominantly through informal than through formal channels; (b) the substantive character of the decision problem, rather than the procedural dictates of the organization, provide primary guidance in selecting information sources; (c) information deemed required by the substance of the problem " ... is more likely to be sought from frequently used sources than from infrequently used sources" (p. 92), and is strongly influenced by the experience of the problem solver. Furthermore, the problem solver is likely to identify frequently used sources (rather than infrequently used sources) as possessing needed information. Ference further proposes that the problem solver prefers, and we therefore infer that he will seek out, information that can be obtained without time lags and without bargaining.

In many instances it is necessary or desirable to obtain relevant information about the organization's environment. Aguilar (1967) conducted an extensive study of the acquisition of such information by top level business managers. The type of environmental scanning that occurred was dependent on the relevance, urgency, and potential consequences of the issue under consideration. Managers were unable to consider all potentially important factors because of the number and complexity of variables involved, and because of the immense number of potential information sources. Some major results of the study are outlined below:

(a) A definite relationship was observed between the subject matter of the manager's search and his functional specialty. Although organizational problems were frequently matters of *shared* concern, search tended toward the manager's area of greatest concern. Technical managers tended to seek out higher proportions of technically oriented information, while marketing managers showed a greater inclination for seeking out marketing information. Similar tendencies have been noted by Ference:

> Persons in the communications network may also be distinguished by their functions; purchasing agents and engineers will perceive and react differently to information received from the same source. . . . Particular interests or concerns will determine if information is to be eliminated, modified, or added to before being transmitted. . . (p. 84).

The observation that the sources of information sought are a function of the individual's functional specialty is not surprising. Such behavior has been noted by others (Dearborn and Simon, 1958). Having perceived a problem in terms of the goals and activities of his area of specialization, the individual sets out to gather relevant information. The same problem, when viewed by other individuals, will have different interpretations. These different orientations will lead to different areas of search.

(b) Personal sources of information were of much greater importance than were impersonal sources. To obtain external information, managers relied upon their personal networks of communication (personal and organizational) to a greater extent than they relied upon formal networks (reports, meetings).

(c) Within the company, subordinates were the greatest single source of information. Superiors were found to be a relatively poor source of external information.

(d) Managers of large companies relied much more heavily on internal information sources than did managers of smaller companies.

Information search in the organization's external environment is a function of its stability. Dynamic environments pose considerable uncertainty. In attempting to reduce this uncertainty, greater search efforts may be expended. It is also expected that more time will be devoted to acquiring information about the relatively controllable segments of the environment than about uncontrollable elements. This latter expectation is derived from the work of Emory and Niland (1968), and that of March and Simon (1958). It was tested in a field study by Kefalas and Schoderbek (1973).

We would expect the characteristics of search to vary among the technical core, managerial, and institutional-level positions. Furthermore, we would expect the stability of the extraorganizational environment to influence the characteristics of search in that environment. Occupants of institutional levels would be expected to put greater emphasis on seeking out more information about the environment than would those in the technical core. Those in the managerial and technical core positions would be expected to seek out information which is oriented toward their functional specialities.

A Concluding Observation

We have seen that the object or focus of search, the sources searched, and the timing of search depend upon characteristics of the individual, upon social and environmental forces, and on the substantive nature of the problem. The organization attempts to find ways of identifying and channelling potentially relevant information to the decision maker. Regarding both external and internal sources of information, the main problem is one of properly locating information-gathering units in the organization structure so as to facilitate decision making (Simon, 1957). The creation of such specialized information (surveillance) units has other organizational implications. The centralization of needed information is a potential source of organizational power (Mechanic, 1964), power which may substantially influence organizational decisions.

Much of the literature on managerial information systems implies an orientation toward standardized reporting procedures on an organization-wide scale. The inertia for such standardization would seem to be abated by the decision maker's needs, as implied by our foregoing developments. We face a significant need for individual tailor-made information to facilitate decisions, information that goes beyond the standardized. This might include information to the individual regarding various characteristics of his decision-related tendencies.

Chapter 6

Judgmental Inferences

We now turn to that stage of our model of individual decision processes called Output or "Results," a stage consisting of "judgment" and "inference." Judgment and inference were identified as "results," but results of what? These "results" were described as emanating from a set of "higher-level processes" in the organism. The processes by which individuals arrive at judgments and inferences have been the subject of considerable research by behavioral scientists since the 1950s. Although much insight has been gained, many questions about this important aspect of decision processes remain unanswered, as indicated in the following pages.

DEFINING JUDGMENT AND INFERENCE

Existence in a world of many complex stimuli can be confusing and distressing without some mechanisms for ordering and relating the diverse events around us. The world is not perceived by the individual as a completely mysterious accumulation of unrelated bits, but rather consists of patterned relationships which are somewhat predictable. *Beliefs* are developed about relationships that exist among the variables around us. Consciously or unconsciously actions and events are observed, interrelated, and integrated to arrive at conclusions or inferences. The following definition of *inference* conveys its intended meaning in the current discussion:

> Let us say that we have a set of statements that we shall denote by A. These statements contain information on the basis of which we can reach another statement, B. Now, when we proceed from A to B, we make an *inference*. An inference, then, is a process by which we reach a conclusion on the basis of certain preceding statements—it is a process of reasoning whereby we start with A and arrive at B. We then have some belief that B is true on the basis of A (McGuigan, 1960, p. 246).

Closely related to inference, and perhaps inseparable from it, is the concept of *judgment*. A satisfactorily precise definition of judgment is elusive, as has been noted by others:

> "Judgment" is an umbrella term, like "perception," "thinking," "learning," and "cognition." ... It is a mistake to believe it can (or should) be a technical term or precisely defined (Newell, in Kleinmuntz, 1968, p. 1).

Rather than attempting a precise definition we will indicate some characteristics of "judgment" to help clarify its meaning for our immediate purposes.[1] First, a judgment is a conclusion, part of the "judgmental *process*" which includes antecedent cognitive activities that lead to the conclusion. Second, our interest is restricted to conclusions and cognitive processes that are based on the individual's experiences and evolve in the absence of explicitly defined normative inference rules. The use of such rules, in fact, constitutes a replacement or substitute for human judgmental processes. Third, "the main inputs to the process, that which is to be judged, are given and available; obtaining, discovering, or formulating them is not part of judgment." This third characteristic distinguishes judgment from problem solving, judgment being a narrower concept. In particular, note that information-search activities are not part of the judgment process. Instead, we are interested in understanding the processes that ensue after information inputs are made available.

The remainder of this chapter examines the role of judgment and inference in organizational decision processes. Attempts are made to summarize what is known about certain aspects of human judgment, focusing on the individual, the "judge," whose judgmental processes are being considered. The information

---

[1] These characteristics of judgment are adapted from Newell (in Kleinmuntz, 1968, pp. 5–6).

inputs to the judgmental processes are called "cues" or "stimuli." Since much of the work in this area has been experimental and conducted in non-organizational contexts, our conclusions are tentative and somewhat speculative regarding their applicability in the organizational setting.

THE LOCUS OF JUDGMENT IN THE DECISION PROCESS

Organizational decisions are typically not made by an individual in isolation, but rather are guided by formal decision premises and are influenced by numerous environmental cues that impinge on the decision unit. The individual, confronted with these various cues, may combine them in a variety of ways in arriving at conclusions as to their implications for his current or future behavior. On the basis of these conclusions the individual decides to act or not to act. It is the formation of these conclusions (judgments, inferences), and not the subsequent related decisions, that concerns us now. The role of judgment in this overall decision process can be put into perspective by distinguishing "first-level" judgments from "higher-level" judgments.

First-Level Judgments

The most readily identifiable linkage between judgmental inference and decision making we call *first-level judgments*. Such judgments are defined as having two distinguishing characteristics: (a) the judgment is directly coupled to the decision; the decision corresponds one-to-one with the judgmental conclusion, and (b) the cues are relatively factual components free of prior judgmental interpretation. As portrayed in Figure 6-1 the judge is confronted with several factual informational cues, $X_1, X_2 \ldots, X_n$ which he assimilates into a judgment (J). This judgment summarizes his beliefs regarding the implications of the information available. For instance, the pathologist's diagnostic decision regarding the malignancy of a growth may be based on the results of a series of laboratory tests. Perhaps ten such test results comprise the sole set of information he uses in making his malignancy versus non-malignancy decision. Another example, somewhat oversimplified, but not too unrealistic, is the personnel officer of an

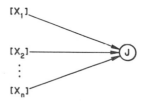

Figure 6-1   First-Level Judgment

organization who must decide which candidate from among several applicants to select for a job position. If his criterion is to select the candidate possessing the greatest likelihood of job success, he may base his judgment on several test indicators and subsequently select the candidate whose "judged likelihood of success" is greatest. In this simplified example, the judgmental result *is* the decision that follows from his assimilating a relatively factual set of cues.

Higher-Level Judgments

It is important to be aware of the pervasiveness of judgmental inferences as they permeate the decision process. They enter into the decision process at various stages and from various sources.

> Judgments may be accepted as direct inputs to the decision process, or they may be regarded as a part of behavior useful in, or essential to, the process of reaching a decision (Shelly and Bryan, 1964, p. 10).

Higher-level judgments are those in which: (a) the judgment is directly coupled to the decision (as with first-level judgments), and (b) at least one of the information cues, called the higher-level *component,* is the result of a prior judgment. Higher-level components are one or more stages removed from the decision and may be thought of as the judgments, previously made, which are cue inputs for future judgments. This is an example of what Newell has called "preparation for judgment" (p. 5). Higher-level components and the manner in which they may enter the decision process are illustrated by expanding our personnel selection example, with particular emphasis on the nature of the information sources (indicators, cues) used by the judge.

In Figure 6-2, the $X_1, X_2 \ldots, X_n$ each represent information items (or cues) that are used by the decision maker in arriving at his judgmental conclusion (HLJ). One such information item might be an applicant's aptitude test score. Others might be personality and psychological test results of various types. In addition to such "factual" first-level components, one or more of the information items may itself be a judgmental conclusion, such as a judgment

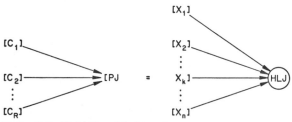

Figure 6-2 Higher-Level Judgments

(rating) of applicant suitability by a person other than the decision maker. In this example, then, one of the information items (X_k) is a conclusion of a previous judgment (PJ), a higher-level information component which was used to make the ultimate judgment (HLJ). This previous judgment was based on several cues ($C_1, C_2 \ldots, C_R$). Note, however, that the result of the previous judgment does not necessarily dictate the ultimate decision since it is only one of several cues, of varying reliability, which will be inferentially combined in the higher-level judgmental process.

The locus of judgments in the decision process can be further illuminated by identifying a class of higher-level components called premise judgments. These prior judgments are characteristically of a broad nature and need not be uniquely associated with a specific immediate judgment. They are developed through the inferential experience of the judge and may be used by him to relatively "weight" other informational items. These "weightings" are based on the judgmental conclusions which have evolved about the relative worth (validity) of various information sources.[2] Premise judgments, then, are the latent evaluative components of the judgmental process. As stated by Rigby (1964),

> ... the process of evaluating the available information may properly involve judgment.... It must be relatively rare for the decision maker to have the opportunity to apply rigorous statistical or other quality tests to his information in a decision situation. If so, the decision maker is commonly reduced to making quality judgments which, although based on good evidence— internal consistency, reputation of source—are still in the judgment category (p. 42).

The manner in which the judge utilizes the immediate cues in a specific situation is presumably a reflection of the premise judgments he has made about those cues, or their sources, on the basis of his prior experiences. This composite repertoire of premise judgments is a significant component of the Image, discussed in Chapter 2. A judgmental problem, as viewed here, can be classified as a first-level judgment problem only in the absence of prior premise judgments, i.e., in the absence of prior experience with the informational items, and/or the type of judgment required. Such occurrences are judgmentally novel and are a principal source of problem complexity best exemplified in organizations by "ill-structured" decision problems. In the following pages, man is initially placed in a judgmentally novel situation and his progress is traced as he gains experience with factual information cues. The analysis indicates how premise judgments are developed and applied to the factual cues in the transformation from first-level to higher-level judgmental processes.

---

[2] For a discussion of the fact that individuals do come to develop beliefs about the "competency-reliability" of various information sources see Cravens, 1970.

CHARACTERIZING JUDGMENTAL LEARNING

In his daily life man continually draws conclusions based on his beliefs about the ways in which certain indicators enable him to predict (are related to) other environmental events. The physician, the stock-market analyst, the economist, and the manager all rely on selected information to make judgments about future events. For certain situations they implicitly believe that various information cues have some relationship to an event that is of interest to them. However, man's beliefs about relationships among variables are not inherent, but are learned through experiences. It is on this learning process that we momentarily wish to focus. Since it is not feasible to observe directly the manner in which he utilizes and combines (assimilates) cue information, man's observable responses must be regarded as the best available reflections of his judgmental conclusions. The approach of most studies in this area is to use a series of the judge's conclusions (responses) to characterize his ability to learn the underlying cue relationships confronting him.

Let us begin by examining relatively basic and fundamental relationships among variables. Imagine an initially inexperienced individual who is given a limited set of informational cues that are, he is told, systematically related to another (distal) variable. He might as a personnel manager, for example, have access to a number of test scores (cues) which are supposed to be indicators of a potential employee's job performance (distal variable). Having seen the initial set of test scores, he is asked to predict the applicant's future job performance. This obviously calls for an inferential judgment by the bewildered judge, a judgment which may initially consist of ill-founded guesswork. After obtaining his initial judgment the judge is told the actual level of job success of the applicant whose test scores he was given. He now has some basis, however scant, for deciphering the "true" relationships between the distal variable and the cues. He may ask, "To what extent are test scores related to job performance?" He may mentally entertain hypotheses about these relationships in an attempt to explain how the performance value could have resulted from the set of test scores. The process is now repeated by providing a second set of test scores for another applicant and obtaining the judge's estimate of the associated performance value, after which he is provided with the "true" performance score. Over repeated trials of this process, through experience, the judge might acquire a "feel" for the relationships that do exist, even though he may not be able to precisely specify the nature of his "believed mental relationship." This basic approach, although perhaps oversimplified here, has been extensively employed by psychologists to study man's ability to learn such fundamental patterned relationships among variables, learning which requires inferential judgments. The sequence of this procedure is shown in Figure 6-3, where at stage 1a, the judge is given numeric values for each of three cues (C_1, C_2, C_3). Following his response he is shown the correct response value (Y, in stage 1b). In stage 2a he is given new cue values, and in stage 2b he is given the correct response associated with them. As the process repeats through numerous stages, will the pattern of responses suggest that the judge is learning the relationships between the distal variable (Y) and each of the cue variables?

By observing the cue values and the corresponding judgments over a series of repeated trials, we can develop descriptions of the way that the judge seems to

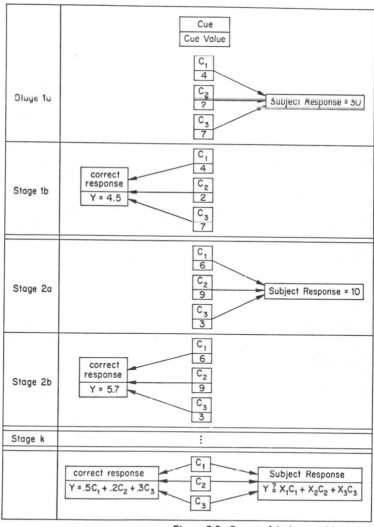

Figure 6-3 Stages of Judgmental Learning

be relating the cue values to the distal-variable values. He may, for example, be relying heavily on one cue (e.g., C_3), while virtually ignoring C_1 and C_2 in making his judgments. In a controlled experimental environment it is possible for the experimenter to design judgment tasks in which he establishes the "true" relationships between the cues and the distal variable. The resulting design specifies the degree of relationship between each cue and the distal variable and may be expressed in the form of a correlation coefficient. A correlation coefficient indicates the amount of linear relationship between two variables and may assume values from −1.00 to +1.00. When the relationship is close to −1.00 it means as one variable increases the other decreases. Supply and demand is a good example. However, in most of the studies with which we will be concerned, these relationships are positive. When the correlation is positive it means as one variable increases the other increases as well. Note, for example, as cue C_1 gets higher (from 4 to 6) that the correct response also increases (4.5 to 5.7). Common-sense notions about height and weight or IQ and school achievement provide other examples. A coefficient of zero between a cue and distal variable indicates that no linear relationship exists between the two variables. A correlation value of plus or minus one indicates a perfect linear relationship between the cue and the distal variable. Furthermore, it is important to note that the relationships may be altered by the experimenter to any numeric value between zero and plus- or minus-one to obtain the desired strength-of-relationship between the two variables. The relationships determined by the experimenter between each cue and the distal variable are called the *cue validities* or "environmental" validities. By appropriate design, one can structure judgmental tasks that are suitable for studying a variety of inferential judgment characteristics. For instance, the relevance of a cue as an information source is frequently varied between the extremes of zero and one to evaluate the influence of relevance on judgments. As we shall see, a number of other task characteristics can be varied.

Now, how does this relate to organizational decisions? The sort of task just described is very common in organizations. The decision maker constantly weighs information from various sources. He may be predicting future sales volume or the performance of a prospective employee. It doesn't matter. What is important is that he must relate information from different sources and he must do it repeatedly; that is, he has many trials, if you like, on a given type of judgment and over time he begins to see that some sources of information are more important than others. It is exactly this process that is being replicated in the experimental settings described below.

Learning Cue Relationships: Human Expertise

Having a measure of the degree of relationship between each cue and the distal variable is significant. It provides a basis for evaluating the way humans interrelate information inputs and may provide a guide for improving individual judgmental processes. Suppose, for instance, that an analyst judges a stock's future rate of return (the distal variable) primarily on the basis of the company's price-to-earnings ratio (cue 1), with only minor emphasis on annual-return-on-assets (cue 2). By analyzing his responses and the associated cue values that were given to him, it would not be surprising to find a high correlation (strong relationship) between cue 1 and his responses and a low correlation (weak relationship) between cue 2 and his responses. These correlations indicate the degree to which each cue is related to his judgments, and by implication they reflect his *beliefs* about the extent of each cue's true relationship to the distal variable. This explicit description of the implied cue-utilization process can then be evaluated by comparison to the true relationships between the cues and the distal variable. Changes in the judge's utilization of the various cues as he gains experience in the judgmental task can also be identified and examined. The variables that we have been discussing and some of the relationships among them are shown in Figure 6-4 for a two-cue judgment task.

C_1 and C_2 represent the two cues that are observed by the judge (J). The left side of the diagram represents the environment that is constructed by the experimenter. He has designed the task so that the environmental outcome (Y) is directly related to the cue values (C_1 and C_2).

Suppose the task has been structured so that the cues are related to the outcome as follows:

$$Y = 1/3\ C_1 + 2/3\ C_2 \qquad\qquad [1]$$

By knowing the values of C_1 and C_2 the experimenter can use expression [1] to determine the associated environmental outcome (Y). On the right side of the diagram the judge does not know how the cue-values are related to the environmental outcome which he is trying to predict. Nonetheless, having seen the two cue-values he estimates the value of (Y) that is associated with them. A series of such judgments permits a computation of the correlation coefficient (r_3) between cue 1 and the judge's responses, and likewise the coefficient (r_4) between cue 2 and the responses. How closely will the judge's use of the cues be to their validities? A number of experimental attempts have been made to determine if

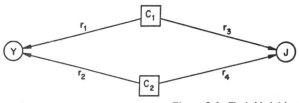

Figure 6-4   Task Variables

people can develop matching strategies; i.e., to determine if the cue weightings implied by the responses match the environmental (experimentally determined) validities of the cues. In Figure 6-4 this would involve a comparison between r_3 and r_1, and a comparison between r_4 and r_2. This is what Summers (1962) has termed "ecological (environmental) vs. functional" validity. Summers' study used cues of different validities to see how dependent on these cues the judgments would be. His purpose was " ... to establish ecological [environmental] validities for originally meaningless cues (to the judge) in a laboratory setting and to observe the responses learned to these cues" (p. 29).

It was predicted that the response weightings would be different and would be ranked in the order of the cue weightings and that the magnitude of the response weightings would approach that of the cue weightings (p. 30).

Summers set up the study with three cues having different environmental validities (high, medium, and low in value). He found that subjects learned to weight the cues in the proper order; that is, the cue weightings implied by subjects' responses were similar in their order of utilization to the order of their environmental validities. Further examination of these experimental data illustrated that the relative weight placed on each cue changed as the learning process occurred (Hursch, Hammond, and Hursch, 1964).[3] Other studies have shown that cues with different environmental validities are responded to differentially, and average subjective weightings of those cues tend to differ accordingly. However, appropriate weightings of stimulus cues are most difficult to learn in situations where the actual cue validities differ only moderately from one another. The judge's utilization of cues more nearly coincides with actual validities in those tasks where the cue-validities are very different (Uhl, 1963). The research also indicates that when irrelevant (zero validity) cues are present, the judge will attempt to utilize them. This observation corresponds to a finding of Hammond (1955), to be considered later, in which experienced clinicians used invalid cues while others neglected valid ones. Certainly, the correlational paradigm provides a valuable tool for assessing characteristics of people in utilizing, or attempting to utilize, irrelevant versus relevant information.

Learning Nonlinear Relationships. The studies cited thus far have involved the learning of linear relationships among cues and the criterion (outcome). What happens when nonlinear relationships are introduced; i.e., a criterion which is related in a nonlinear fashion to one or more of the stimulus cues? It is known, for example, that test anxiety scores are curvilinearly related to performance. People with very high and very low anxiety perform less well than those

---

[3]Hursch, *et al.* also provided a method for assessing the impact of weighting ineffectiveness on the ultimate output of the judgmental process.

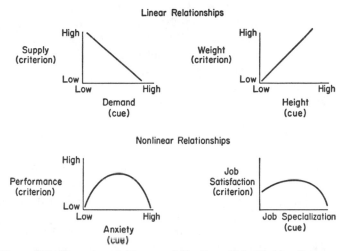

Figure 6-5 Examples of Linear and Nonlinear Relationships Between Cue and Criterion

with a moderate amount of anxiety. Figure 6-5 shows examples of linear and nonlinear relationships.

Hammond and Summers (1965) conducted a study employing two cues, one of which was linearly, the other nonlinearly related to the criterion. The criterion was partly predictable from either cue alone and perfectly predictable from appropriate simultaneous utilization of both the linear and the nonlinear cues. The task was structured such that half of the variation in the criterion was determined by the linear predictor, and the other half by the nonlinear predictor. In the process of learning, both of the cues were under-utilized when compared to the optimal amount of utilization (cue-validity), and "overall, there appears to be a tendency to depend more on the linear cue (than on the nonlinear cue)" (p. 221). Furthermore, dependence on the nonlinear cue increased *only when the judge was told which of the two cues was nonlinear.* The judge tends to increase his dependence on the linear cue but not on the nonlinear cue, even when the nonlinear cue validity is greater than that of the linear cue (Summers and Hammond, 1966). Again, only under conditions where it was known which cue was nonlinear did more appropriate weighting occur. The overall finding of under-utilization of various kinds of cue information in these studies is consistent with the tendency of conservatism that was so commonly observed in the processing of probability information in Chapter 5.

Response Weightings vs. Cue Weightings—Non-deterministic.[4] The cue-

[4]A major framework for understanding probabilistic cue-criterion relationships was presented by Brunswick, 1955.

criterion relationships in expression [1] and Figure 6-3 are deterministic; a specified set of cue values results in a known, invariant, criterion value. That is, the cue values give us all the information needed to perfectly predict the criterion. In contrast, somewhat imperfect relationships are frequently encountered in organizational environments. Some cues are related imperfectly, but somewhat predictably, to certain outcomes, while other cues are more strongly related to the outcomes. In spite of these imperfect relationships, man makes judgments as best he can based on the available information.

Peterson, Hammond, and Summers (1965b) studied the learning of cue relationships in such a non-deterministic judgment task. Three cues were related to the criterion so that the *optimal relative cue weightings* were .50, .33, and .17. By optimal we mean that this relative weighting resulted in the best prediction of the criterion—not perfect, but the best under the circumstances. Analysis of the terminal judgments showed inferred cue weightings (utilization) of .41, .33, and .21, respectively, for these cues. "The response cue weightings quickly separated in the appropriate directions, but the separation was of less than optimal magnitude" (p. 273).

Other studies have revealed additional interesting characteristics of human judgment in non-deterministic tasks. In a simple single-cue environment, judges learned to utilize the cue in accordance with its environmental validity when the cue was *highly valid (relevant) and positively related to the criterion*. However, with lower validity the cue was over-utilized. Again, the judges were relying on comparatively irrelevant information.

Another significant characteristic emerged from this study concerning the direction of the relationship between the cue and the criterion. For negative cue-criterion relationships there was a consistent tendency to under-utilize the cue in comparison to its environmental validity, whether that validity was high or low (Naylor and Clark, 1968). The important factors from this study are twofold. First, it shows a tendency to over-utilize irrelevant information, or to place much more reliance on information than is warranted by its quality. This tendency, if it can be generalized to simple judgmental processes in organizational settings, has implications for the quality of existing inference processes in organizations and identifies elements of the process that might be modified and improved. Secondly, it suggests a hesitancy on the part of human beings to utilize informative negative relationships that exist among cues and criterion in the judgmental process. A negative validity of −.80 is logically just as informative as a positive validity of +.80, and yet the human inference process seems to intuitively treat them as having differential degrees of informativeness.

A more recent study provides additional insights into tendencies to utilize irrelevant information. Humans will frequently make judgments on the basis of non-existent cue-criterion relationships (Castellan, 1973). Judges were given one relevant cue and either zero, one, or two irrelevant cues. In most cases, judgmental performance was lower when more irrelevant cues were present. Furthermore, the tendency to use the irrelevant cues persisted even after prolonged experience. However, when the relevant cue had a high validity judges tended to make less use of the irrelevant cues.

Shifting Cue Weights. What happens if the relationships between the cues and the criterion change rather than remain stable as in the environments we have considered thus far? Relatively few studies of learning have addressed this question. Work reported by Peterson, Hammond, and Summers (1965a) examined such a change by using a two-step procedure. First, judgments were made in a stable environment consisting of three cues of different validities. In this stage of the task, the cues were immediately utilized by the judges in the appropriate order, but the most valid cue was under-utilized and the irrelevant or least valid cue was over-utilized (tendencies that have been found in other studies cited here). In the second stage of the study, the relationships of the cues to the criterion were interchanged. The cue that was previously most valid became irrelevant while the formerly irrelevant cue became most valid. After this shift, the judges eventually utilized the cues in the correct order of their relevance. However, a noticeably greater amount of experience was required to adjust appropriately to the modified relationships than was required to utilize appropriately the original cue relationships. Some individuals were able to make this adjustment more rapidly than others. These findings have potentially important implications for organizational inferences made in dynamic situations where changes in cue-criterion relationships form an extremely complex inferential environment. The quest for organizational decision effectiveness in such an environment indicates the desirability of identifying individuals who are capable of detecting and adapting to relatively unstable environmental relationships.

Summary: Cue-Utilization vs. Cue-Validity in Learning. Studies have been conducted to determine the relative correspondence between the judges' implied cue-utilization and actual environmental cue validities. This "matching" has been observed in both deterministic and non-deterministic task settings. In both settings, individuals learn to correctly discriminate the relative importance of environmental cues. The implied utilization of the cues separates in the appropriate directions, although not to the appropriate degree. Large differences between environmental cue-validities appear to be more easily discriminated than are small differences. Judges also display general tendencies to utilize irrelevant cues, but this proclivity diminishes when at least one of the cues is highly relevant. A tendency exists to under-utilize nonlinear cues, and the extent of this disposition is mediated by the kind of task information given to the judge. Finally, when the cue-criterion relationships are shifting, rather than stationary, a relatively longer period of task exposure is required to relearn and attain "matching" than was originally required. We will now turn to some other dimensions that are important for accurate judgment.

Additional Dimensions of Judgmental Learning: Consistency and Achievement

A number of characteristics of judgmental inference are usefully studied with the help of correlational statistics and regression analysis.[5] In the preceding section we were interested in determining if man, confronted with a set of unspecified patterned relationships, could develop an intuitive "feel" for these relationships. We focused on the relative importance that the judge learned to place on various information sources, compared to the ideal importance (weightings) as specified by the task. His ability to utilize the cues in accordance with their validities was found to be influenced by several task variables. But the implied weights that he places on stimulus variables, and the extent to which they come to approximate the correct weightings, are not the whole story. As the additional insights gained from experience are translated into subsequent judgmental action, we may examine other dimensions of his judgment capabilities. One characteristic that would logically be of interest is the relationship between his judgmental predictions and the environmental outcomes. How closely do the responses correspond to the actual occurrences that the judge is attempting to predict? A measure of this correspondence, called the achievement index (Hursch, Hammond, and Hursch, 1964), is the degree of correlation between the actual environmental outcomes and the judgments. A high correlation indicates a strong relationship between judgments and outcomes. In terms of our previous example (predicting job performance from applicant test scores) the judge's job-performance-predictions can be correlated with actual job performance over a number of cases to obtain a measure of judgmental achievement.

Another interesting characteristic is *consistency*, both for the judge and for the environment (task). Consistency of the judge refers to how well his judgments can be represented by a linear combination of cue values, and is measured by the coefficient of determination R_J. This measure can be interpreted as an indication of how consistently the judge applies his underlying "rule" or system for integrating the cues to reach a judgment. R_J assumes values from .00 to +1.00 with +1.00 indicating that the judge's responses can be perfectly represented by a specific linear combination of the cue values. A similar measure, R_E, can be used to indicate the consistency of the environment, reflecting the degree of determinism in the judgmental task. When the value of R_E is one, it means that the environmental outcome (criterion value) can be completely predicted

---

[5]Hursch, Hammond, and Hursch (1964) present a useful coverage of methodology: Slovic and Lichtenstein (1971) provide an excellent review and analysis of judgmental research.

from a specified set of cue values. Our equation in Figure 6-3 ($Y = .5C_1 + .2C_2 + .3C_3$) is an example. In other cases, when R_E is less than one, it simply means that even when the cues are optimally weighted and combined, the resulting environmental outcome is less than perfectly predictable. By way of summary, Table 6-1 indicates the various components of judgment which have been used up to this point in our discussion.

Table 6-1
Summary of Statistics Used for
Analyzing Judgment

Characteristic	Measure	Interpretation
cue validity	$r_{e,i}$	Simple correlation between the ith cue and the environmental criterion
cue utilization	$r_{j,i}$	Simple correlation between the ith cue and the judgments
achievement index	$r_a = r_{Y_J Y_E}$	Simple correlation between the judgments and the environmental outcomes (criterion)
judgmental consistency	R_J	Coefficient of determination of the judgments and the cues, measures the degree to which the judgments can be represented by a linear combination of cue values
environmental consistency	R_E	Coefficient of determination of the criterion and the cues. Measures the degree to which the criterion value can be represented by a linear combination of cue values

We have introduced, then, measures for two interesting dimensions of judgmental performance: (a) the achievement index indicates how closely the judgments correspond to the environmental outcomes, and (b) R_J indicates how consistently the judge applies some underlying intuitive "rule" for integrating cue values. Both of these characteristics, achievement and consistency, are helpful in understanding how inferential judgment processes are modified with experience, and will be of central concern in exploring how several situational variables influence the judgmental learning process.

Order of Presentation. Preceding sections indicate that when confronted with informational cues of differing degrees of relevance, the judge learns to treat the cues differentially. But what if the cues are presented to him sequentially rather than simultaneously? Consider the most elementary situation in which only one cue is available as the basis for judgment. Later, an additional piece of information is provided so that a revised judgment can be made using both the original cue and the new cue. One study of this situation found that judgmental achievement using both cues was as good as, or better than, judgments that were based on only the original cue, *provided that the original cue was of low relevance* (Dudycha and Naylor, 1966). Furthermore, the increase in judgmental achievement was dependent upon the relevance of the second cue. Achievement was facilitated more as the relevance of the second cue increased. However, when the first cue was highly relevant, the insertion of a second cue frequently resulted in *deterioration* of judgmental achievement, particularly when the second cue was of low relevance. People receiving a relevant cue followed by an irrelevant one appeared to over-utilize this second cue and thus had a lower achievement index. As mentioned previously, man tries to make use of essentially ineffectual information, resulting in lower overall performance effectiveness.

Information about the Judgmental Environment.   Our emphasis has been on situations in which the only information given to the judge, aside from the cues, has been the environmental outcome associated with a set of cue values, and this outcome information is given after he makes his judgment. There are other kinds of information about the judgmental environment that can facilitate his performance. In discussing nonlinear relationships, it was found that if the judge is told which of two cues is nonlinearly related to the outcome, his use of that cue would increase. In more complicated tasks in which the judge was fully aware of several nonlinear relationships, judgmental consistency (R_J) increased substantially as he gained experience (Ebert, 1972a and 1972b). Other research studies indicate various kinds of information that influence judgmental learning.

Recall that judgmental performance was affected when the relationships between the cues and the criterion were changed. The judge detected these changes, his judgment eventually reflecting the modified relationships. However, a relatively large amount of experience was required for adaptation to the new relationships. But a different picture emerges when the judge is forewarned of possible changes in the relevancies of the cues. A study by Summers (1969) shows that the judge, knowing that a change may occur, can readily reorient to such an environmental change, the adaptation being reflected in his achievement index.

Several other facts about the judgmental situation may facilitate learning. In contrast to providing just outcome feedback, in which the actual outcome is revealed to him after his prediction, suppose the judge receives his achievement index, the cue-validity correlations, and his cue-utilization correlations based on past performance (Table 6-1). The effects of these two forms of feedback were studied by Todd and Hammond (1965). They also examined a third kind of feedback consisting of both of the two previous forms. Notice that in two of the information conditions the judge can compare each of his cue-utilization correlations with its corresponding validity correlation. Further, a summary index (r_a) is available to indicate how closely his judgments have corresponded to the environmental outcomes. The study showed that achievement was always greater with the second kind of feedback (r_a, $r_{e,i}$, $r_{j,i}$) than with simple outcome feedback. In addition, this second information condition always resulted in performance that was at least as great as for the third kind of feedback. Thus, although the third condition involved a greater *quantity* of feedback than did the second, nonetheless performance there never exceeded, and was sometimes less than, that under the lesser quantity of feedback. We would conclude, then, that it is not just the quantity of feedback that effects performance but the form of the feedback.

A number of additional studies have attempted to clarify the impact of various types of feedback. Newton (1965) examined such effects on judgmental achievement and on the utilization of the cues. Each judge was given one of the five types of feedback, identified in Table 6-2, after he had acquired judgment experience wihout this feedback.

Table 6-2   Types of Feedback

Type	Content
1	r_a
2	$r_a + r_{j,i}$
3	$r_a + r_{e,i}$
4	$r_a + r_{e,i} + r_{j,i}$
5	$r_a + r_{e,i} + r_{j,i} + $ "rules"

Type 1 feedback consisted of the judge's achievement index, the relationship between his past judgments and actual outcomes. The other types of feedback included either the judge's cue-utilization coefficients, or the cue-validity coefficients, or both. In addition, the judges in condition 5 wrote out an intuitive "set of rules" for predicting the environmental outcome. The effects of all five conditions were evaluated on the basis of the match between cue-validity and cue-utilization correlations before and after feedback. For type 1 feedback, the match was worse after receiving feedback than before the feedback was provided. The after-feedback performance in condition 2 was not significantly different than the before-feedback condition. With types 3, 4, and 5 of informa-

tion feedback, improved matching resulted after feedback. Judgmental achievement was also higher in these cases. In other words, all performances in these
conditions were improved, and it is interesting to note the commonality among
conditions 3, 4, and 5 is that all included the cue-validity correlations which
could then be used as a basis for making future judgments. This result is
supported by a more recent study (Nystedt and Magnusson, 1973) which clearly
showed ". . . that the predictive accuracy of the judges increases substantially
and significantly when they receive information about the validity coefficients
of the cues." Further, the results "do not indicate that information about the
nature of one's own performance provides further improvement" (pp. 107–08).
One final comment is warranted regarding the use of the simplest form of
feedback—outcome feedback—versus alternative types. A study by Hammond,
Summers, and Deane (1973) found that not only was outcome feedback (where
the subject was told the correct response) unnecessary for good performance, it
actually hindered performance. This finding, together with the previous studies,
leads us to re-emphasize the fact that *type* of feedback and not just the *amount*
of feedback in an environmental setting can significantly influence performance.
We further conclude that correlational models can be a very effective device for
communicating information about cue-criterion environmental relationships that
can be meaningfully integrated into the judgmental process.

   Cue Redundancy and Environmental Consistency. Two characteristics that
influence judgmental performance are the redundancy of environmental cues
and the environmental consistency. Redundancy can be considered the degree of
"overlap" of several pieces of data. This overlap is in regard to the informative
content of the cues. When confronted with two cues it is possible that they
provide precisely the same informative content; that is, the environmental
outcome that would result from the value of cue number one would be the same
as the outcome that would occur on the basis of the value of the second cue.
This case, where the cues totally overlap, has a redundancy value of 1.0. At the
other extreme is the possibility of having absolutely no overlap. The value of cue
number one alone implies one environmental outcome, and cue number two
alone implies a different outcome. In other words, the actual outcome is
dependent upon both of the independent cue values. In this case, the redundancy value of the two cues is zero. The degree of overlap or redundancy
between the two cue values in any judgment task can be visualized as lying
between these extremes, zero and 1.0. In the cue-criterion paradigm this redundancy can be measured by the intercorrelation of the two cues. Intercorrelations
near zero mean that the two cues provide non-redundant information. Most of
the previous studies to which we have referred have had a zero value of cue
interrelationships. What is the effect upon the judgmental process when the cues
are more redundant, that is, when their intercorrelations are not zero? The

cue-criterion paradigm has been used to evaluate these effects and to identify, for the judge, the degree of redundancy that exists among the several cues in his environment. One of the important effects is that greater redundancy seems to increase judgmental consistency (R_J) (Dudycha and Naylor, 1966b). Apparently, when confronted with cues having little redundancy the judge must discriminate "clearly and meaningfully" between the cues and he consequently finds the judgmental task relatively difficult since each cue "must be attended to separately" (p. 601). With highly redundant cues the task is somewhat easier since refined discrimination between cues is unnecessary. It has also been shown that in certain environments, to be specified below, average achievement increases greatly as cue redundancy increases (Naylor and Schenck, 1968). In explaining how redundancy facilitates achievement the following reasoning has been suggested:

> . . . the greater the redundancy existing among the cues, the less important it is for the subjects to use all cues in a systematic fashion. Concentrating on the information provided by some cues, they will, by virtue of the existing redundancy, actually be using all of the cues to some degree (Naylor and Schenck, 1968, p. 3).

An earlier comment, that average achievement increases with greater cue redundancy, was qualified—it applied to some, but not all, environments. In particular, the study by Naylor and Schenck found that increased redundancy did not facilitate achievement very much in situations having a low environmental consistency (R_E). In such environments the outcome associated with a set of cue values is difficult to predict, but as environmental predictability (consistency) increases, average achievement and consistency increase noticeably.

Summary of Judgmental Learning: Consistency and Achievement. Cue-criterion learning studies have used measures of judgmental consistency and achievement to evelute the effects of several task variables on learning. The order of presentation of cues affects achievement because judges apparently attempt to utilize low-relevance cues which tend to distort the judgmental process, resulting in lower overall effectiveness. It was also noted that when cue relevance is changed, judges adapt rapidly if they are informed that such a change may occur. Judgmental achievement was found to be facilitated by providing achievement, cue-validity, and cue-utilization correlations rather than revealing only the "correct" outcome following the responses. It appears as if information about cue-validities is a key factor in facilitating achievement. Finally, judgmental response consistency and average achievement were generally greater in environments with larger cue redundancies. Average achievement was also greater for environments of greater certainty (predictability).

We have reviewed this basic research to gain a better understanding of man's abilities and limitations in learning elementary judgmental tasks. This was done in the belief that the processes operating in such tasks are the foundation of the more complex judgmental processes man uses in the organizational environment.

Analyzing the "Expert" Judge: Policy Formation

At least two advantages can be cited for using objectively structured, predetermined (by the experimenter) relationships among the variables in a judgment task: (a) such tasks provide a normative standard against which various performance dimensions can be accurately assessed, and (b) such tasks can be easily altered to study the effects of numerous task variables on judgmental performance. This approach was used extensively in the preceding section. However, our ultimate interest is in judgmental processes that occur in organizational settings, not just in experimental environments. We will, therefore, undertake an examination of studies which, in varying degrees, more nearly approximate the "realism" encountered in organizational life. Our interest will shift in two ways: (a) "experienced" judges will be the focus of attention rather than the judgmental learning of inexperienced individuals, and (b) although the experimental tasks are still somewhat structured by the experimenter, they will correspond more closely to the "natural" judgmental environment of the "expert" judge.

By what processes do experts arrive at their conclusions in complex, uncertain environments? How are the various informational cues combined into the final judgment? The expert frequently has difficulty answering such questions explicitly. But the answers to these and other questions would be valuable for distinguishing between "good" and "bad" judges and for finding ways of improving judgmental processes. As will be seen in the following pages, the correlational techniques that were previously discussed, as well as other related statistical techniques, have proved useful for sheding insights into experienced inferential processes.

Linearity, Disagreement, and Experience

Since the appearance of the work by Meehl (1954), considerable research has been undertaken to study the judgmental processes of clinical psychologists, physicians, businessmen, and others.[6] The significant results of this vast array of work are summarized and evaluated by Slovic and Lichtenstein (1971), and will not be presented here in detail. We do wish to review briefly some highlights and present examples which illustrate some major characteristics of these judgmental processes and the usefulness of the correlational approach.

---

[6] For examples of application to university admissions and court decisions see, Dawes, 1971; and Kort, 1968.

The clinical psychologist is faced with the task of client diagnosis. Such diagnoses may be considered as the culmination of a judgmental inference process based upon certain informational cues designed to reflect the "state" of the client along selected dimensions. The cues may be in the form of client test results on certain psychological instruments such as intelligence tests, Rorschach tests, or personality inventory instruments. In addition to these formal test instruments, certain cues may emanate directly from the client in the form of verbalizations, or other behaviors, in the presence of the clinician. One of the striking results of judgmental research in this environment has been the high degree of diagnostic predictability obtained from simple linear combinations of test cues that are available to the clinician. The judge's implied importance weights and policies for assimilating diagnostic cues frequently account for most of the differences in his judgments from one diagnosis to the next. Another significant finding has been an apparent disagreement among expert judges as to the relative importances of various cues to the final diagnostic judgment. Finally, professional experience has been found to be related to the manner in which informational cues are utilized in the judgment process.

A study by Hammond (1955) illustrates several points of interest and is representative of the approach used in many other studies. Ten experienced clinical psychologists attempted to predict IQ from four Rorschach (ink blot) factor responses by seventy-eight clients. Each client had taken a Rorschach test, and then had taken a subsequent IQ test. Only the Rorschach test results were given to the clinicians as the basis for their judgments of each client's IQ. Several of the important relationships in this task are shown in Figure 6-6.

The cues to the clinician are the four Rorschach factor responses of a client. On the left side of Figure 6-6, representing the true environmental relationships, the experimenter not only knows the Rorschach test results but also the IQ of each of the clients. Therefore, he can determine the correlational relationship ($r_{e,i}$) between client scores, measured on each of the four Rorschach factor responses, and their IQs. Note that these relationships, the cue validities, are empirical manifestations rather than the result of experimenter manipulation. Hammond found that substantial differences existed among the cue validities in his study. He then determined the correlational relationships ($r_{j,i}$) between the four cues and the clinician's estimates of IQ for all clients. A subsequent

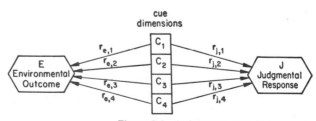

Figure 6-6   Judgmental Task Components

comparison of environmental cue validities ($r_{e,i}$) and judgmental cue utilization ($r_{j,i}$) revealed that "... certain clinicians were found to be using invalid cues, while others were neglecting valid ones" (p. 261). Noticeable variations were found among the ten clinicians with respect to the way they utilized cues that differed in degree of relevance to the environmental outcome. What accounts for such differences among experts? The answer to this question is not fully known but a study by Hammond, Hursch, and Todd (1964) suggests that amount of clinical experience may be part of the answer. Using Grebstein's (1963) data, they found that the "degree of match between ecological validities and utilization coefficients" differed for naive, semi-sophisticated, and sophisticated clinicians who were inferring patient IQs from ten-cue Rorschach test scores. The more experienced clinicians had greater matching scores than did the less experienced clinicians. In addition, it is important to note that judgmental achievement was highly related to the matching scores. Further analysis of the data supported the notion that inferential achievement might be increased by improving the matching process. Thus, experience appears from this study to be an important determinant of matching success and achievement.

Going beyond examination of the judge's cue-utilization, statistical techniques can be used to derive explicit quantitative descriptions of his implied judgmental policy. Reconsider the task represented by Figure 6-6 in which the clinician made judgments of seventy-eight client IQs. His responses can be used to find a regression equation of the form

$$\hat{J} = b_{j,1}\, C_1 + b_{j,2}\, C_2 + b_{j,3}\, C_3 + b_{j,4}\, C_4 + \epsilon \qquad [2]$$

which is one way of describing his judgmental policy. Regression analysis enables us to find values of the $b_{j,i}$ that provide the least-squares fit between his judgments (J) and the regression equation's prediction of his judgment ($\hat{J}$). The resulting $b_{j,i}$s can be interpreted as measures of the importance placed on each cue by the judge. Equation [2] can now be used to predict the clinician's IQ judgments for a set of four Rorschach test scores of any client. If equation [2] is a good representation of the clinician's judgmental strategy, then his judgments would be highly correlated with equation-predictions of his judgments. This correlation, $r_{J\hat{J}}$, when squared, was referred to earlier as judgmental consistency R_J (Table 6-1).

$$R_J = (r_{J\hat{J}})^2 \qquad [3]$$

R_J specifies the extent to which the IQ judgments are predictable from a simple linear combination of the four test scores. The same approach can be used to describe the environmental relationships between client IQ scores and Rorschach test scores:

$$\hat{E} = b_{e,1} C_1 + b_{e,2} C_2 + b_{e,3} C_3 + b_{e,4} C_4 + \epsilon \qquad [4]$$

and

$$R_E = (r_{E\hat{E}})^2. \qquad [5]$$

Environmental consistency, R_E, is an important characteristic of the judgmental environment.[7] It indicates how well environmental outcomes can be predicted by an appropriately weighted linear combination of cue values (as in equation [4]).

From a large number of research studies covering a variety of judgmental situations there has emerged the fascinating fact that simple linear models such as equation [2] account for a very high proportion of judgmental response variation. As noted by Slovic and Lichtenstein (1971), clinicians frequently are not receptive to the conclusion that their judgmental processes are predominantly based on such simple linear combinations of a relatively small number of cues. This, they feel, is an oversimplification of how they assimilate information. The clinician contends that a relatively large number of cues are significantly utilized.

> On the one hand, clinical psychologists behave as if there were virtually no limit to their capacity for inference making. Indeed, the general assumption, only slightly tarnished, is — the more data on which to base the inference, the better the inference is likely to be. (Hammond, Hursch, and Todd, 1964, p. 438).

But the implied judgmental rules of clinicians based upon how they actually behave seem to indicate a relatively heavy reliance upon a small number of cues. Several studies are cited by Gage (1953) which examined the relationships of information quantity to judgments about the interests of others and to predictions of the behaviors of others. The most accurate estimates of performance were based on a relatively small amount of data or information, and not after more detailed information was made available to the judge. Studies were cited in which clinical predictions of behavior were made first on the basis of limited information, and then these judgments were revised upon the receipt of further information; accuracy did not improve in the second case over the first. Nor did it appear that the clinicians had reached the limits of their information integration abilities; that is, the use of just a few cues was not due to information overload. It was found, however, that if all of the data were presented simultaneously, rather than sequentially, better accuracy in judgments resulted. Again, this suggests there is a sequence effect on the utilization of information cues.

[7] Recall that Naylor and Schenck (1968) found that judgmental achievement was positively related to environmental consistency.

Kostlan (1954) experimented with twenty practicing clinical psychologists by giving them the results of three standard psychological tests plus a standard form of patient biographical data for each of a number of patients, in a patient-diagnosis task. The researcher was trying to determine the effects on diagnostic accuracy of the information sources that were made available. In most cases, the results indicated that the biographical data sheet alone gave as good a diagnosis as was obtained by using the three tests in addition to the data sheet. As shall be seen shortly, other studies show that while the expert judge proclaims the need for numerous informational cues, he appears to be using relatively few of them.

A second clinician criticism of the representativeness of the linear model has to do with the model's assumptions of independence and linearity in the use of cues. The issues involved, and their significance, have been investigated in a number of contexts extending beyond the domain of clinical psychology, and are considered below.

Configurality

The linear models have been useful because in many situations they account for a high fraction of the variations in judgment. However, there is evidence suggesting that these models are not necessarily superior to alternative models. In certain judgmental situations it may be inappropriate to conclude that a linear additive model is representative of the way in which cue information is combined, as is heatedly contended by many expert judges. The final judgment may be based on cues which are combined in an interactive fashion. It is also possible that an important cue may be linearly related to the judgment over a certain range of cue values, but beyond that range the cue may be used nonlinearly. In such situations it may be beneficial to uncover the pattern by which cues are assimilated in making the judgment, a pattern referred to as the *configurality*. Consider, for example, a corporate decision maker assessing the attractiveness of further investment in product improvement. Under normal circumstances if his company's brand-share of the market is low, then further product improvement expenditures may be very attractive. If brand-share of the market is very high, then additional product improvement expenditures may be less attractive. In either case, the attractiveness cannot be assessed without concurrently considering the extent to which competition is copying this product. With a high degree of competitive duplication, further expenditures may be relatively unattractive for both high and low brand-share of the market.

In Figure 6-7 we see that having the value of cue 1 alone is insufficient for judging the attractiveness of additional product improvement expenditures. The judgmental implications of the first cue are not clarified without jointly considering the value of the second cue.

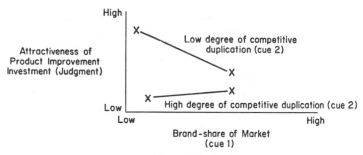

Figure 6-7   Configurality Among Two Cues

Learning.   Although the focus of this section is on "experienced" judges, it is worthwhile to digress momentarily to briefly consider learning behavior in configural tasks. Brehmer (1969) addressed himself specifically to the question, "Can subjects learn configural tasks?" He structured four situations that differed in types and amounts of configurality; they differed in the degree to which outcome variation was attributable to configural versus linear components. At one extreme was a strictly linear additive task with no configurality; at the other extreme was a task having 100 percent configurality. In between was a task having 90 percent linearity and 10 percent configurality, and another with 50 percent linearity and 50 percent configurality. He found that the rate of learning was slower for high degrees of configural relationships. Also, the presence of configural aspects retarded learning of the simpler linear components of the same task; so given a situation that consists of both linear and configural elements, the presence of the configural aspect retards the learning of the linear component of the task. Furthermore, judges learned the configural elements more slowly and less well than they learned the linear aspects. However, there was no evidence that judges' response systems were more linear than the environment; i.e., although the nonlinear aspects were not learned well, we cannot conclude that subjects replaced them with a linear treatment of the cues. Finally, it was observed that judges seemed to inconsistently apply their underlying judgmental rules even though they had learned the linear components of the task almost perfectly. This inconsistency has been demonstrated by Dudycha and Naylor (1966b), by Hammond, Hursch, and Todd (1964), and has been further illustrated in other contexts such as Bowman's (1963) Theory of Management Coefficients, which we will discuss later.

Configurality and Regression.   Several difficulties are encountered when attempting to reveal the configural cue-utilization of experienced judges. Consequently various methods have been espoused for detecting and assessing the significance of configurality in judgmental processes. One approach has been to examine models that incorporate elements of configurality within the framework of regression analysis. Hoffman (1960) sought to discover a configural model to represent the judgmental processes of a clinical psychologist in making judgments based on sets of client predictor variables. First he obtained the clinician's verbalizations of how he used the predictors in his judgmental process. The resulting protocol implied that various cues were used interactively and nonlinearly. Accordingly a hybrid configural model, including interactions and nonlinear components, was developed. Interestingly, this hybrid model was a somewhat poorer predictor of performance than was a linear regression model. This suggests that either the clinician's expression of configural patterns was erroneous, or that an incorrect configural model was used to represent his inferential processes. Either way, it points out the difficulties in trying to derive appropriate configural models to represent judgmental processes when the number of possible configural patterns is extremely large. Another interesting result in Hoffman's study was a discrepancy found between the clinician's subjective (verbalized) cue weightings and his implied nonlinear weightings. The clinician's estimates or beliefs of the extent to which he weighted each of the cues were not accurate reflections of his actual weightings. This raises the question of the value that might be derived from supplying the judge with information illustrating the apparent discrepancy between his subjective and implied cue weightings. Such information may provide insights that would help improve his judgmental processes.

More extensive attempts have been made to accurately represent and describe configural cue utilization. Wiggins and Hoffman (1968) studied the representativeness of three models of clinical judgment for each of twenty-nine clinicians making judgments of "psychotic versus neurotic" on the basis of eleven-cue MMPI profiles.[8] The simplest model was a linear regression in which the eleven cues were the independent variables. A quadratic model included the linear, quadratic, and cross product terms for all eleven variables. A third model was similar to the quadratic except that only systematically selected terms were included. Only the second and third models contained configural relations. The basic research question was, "Does a judge make use of configural or pattern relationships that exist among a set of cues and criterion?" Their definition of configurality included the notion that the weight of a cue in relation to a criterion is not constant but depends on the values of the other cues (non-independence of cues). Thus, they were examining not only nonlinear use of cues, but also non-independence of cue utilization, in an attempt to indicate "the extent to which clinical judgments are configural or non-configural in nature" (p. 71).

Each of the twenty-nine clinicians was classified as linear or configural, in

---

[8]Minnesota Multiphasic Personality Inventory—see Hathaway and McKinley.

terms of cue utilization, according to which of the three models "best fitted" his diagnostic judgments. Sixteen of the judges were best described as configural information processors, and this configural use of information was *not* a function of training and clinical experience. Furthermore, configural use of information was not related to diagnostic accuracy. "Although the differences between linear and configural judges appear to be reliable, their magnitude *is not large. The judgments of even the most seemingly configural clinicians can often be estimated with good precision by a linear model*" (p. 77). Goldberg (1968) concurs with the preceding statement regarding the fact that relatively simple linear, additive models seem to account for the overwhelming proportion of response variance, even in situations in which the clinicians themselves claim to be using configural patterns which should not be well-described by linear models. In re-examining the data for the twenty-nine clinicians in Meehl's study, Goldberg (1965) found that relatively simple linear models were *more* accurate than the *best* diagnosticians. And these simple models were more accurate than were the more complex configural regression models. He also comments:

> Moreover, the fact that staff judges and trainees achieved the same degree of accuracy for this diagnostic task corroborates other studies (e.g., Goldberg, 1959) in indicating that clinical experience is no guarantee of predictive acumen. It seems reasonable to assume that the typical clinical setting does not provide systematic feedback of the predictor-outcome contingencies necessary for optimizing a judge's accuracy" (p. 24).

The above suggestion that "systematic feedback" is necessary for improving judgmental achievement is consistent with our conclusions from the learning studies reported earlier in this chapter. Remember that in the learning studies relatively rapid outcome feedback was provided, usually after each judgmental response. In the "real world" setting such feedback may be delayed for a considerable time before it is available to the judge (if indeed it is ever available).

Configurality and Analysis of Variance. An alternative to the regression methodology for studying cue utilization is the analysis of variance. For judgmental situations involving more than just a few cues, analysis of variance provides a statistically efficient approach to identifying configural cue utilization (Slovic and Lichtenstein, 1971). However, it can also become unwieldly if one is interested in exploring higher-order interactions among cues (see Slovic, 1969). This methodology was employed by Hoffman, Slovic, and Rorer (1968) in a study of nine radiologists' judgments regarding the malignancy of gastric ulcers. The judgments were based upon sets of medical symptoms provided to the radiologists. Analysis of variance was used to discover and describe configural cue utilization, configurality here being interaction in the use of cues. On the basis of expert (radiologist) opinion prior to the experiment, the six symptom-cues were believed to be used configurally in diagnostic judgments. The research results showed that, indeed, diagnoses involved combining symptoms inter-actively (configurally) rather than strictly linearly. Of equal importance, is the fact that diagnosticians differed dramatically in the complexities of the inter-action components that they were, by inference, using. One radiologist appeared to have used a six-way interaction; however, most of the diagnosticians used a relatively small number of the total interactive pattern-combinations that were possible. But again, as in other environments, *the overwhelming variance in the expert judgments was explained by relatively simple linear, additive cue com-binations.*

Extending the concepts of judgmental inference beyond the clinician into the realm of business, Slovic (1969) had two stockbrokers evaluate stock growth potential based on eleven factors taken from Standard and Poor's reports. These eleven factors are commonly used by stock market investors. Slovic suggests that since experts claim to judge on the basis of configurality, our models of inference processes should also do so. If it is possible to uncover and describe the subtle ways in which they process information to reach a judgment, then they, the judges, may learn something about themselves. Further, we may discover how the good judges assimilate information and thus provide a basis for training to improve judgmental performance.

Several interesting results were obtained from this study. First, one broker, before the study, believed that the second broker's approach to selecting stocks was very similar to his own. However, their stock purchase recommendations during the experiment differed markedly. In fact, the correlation between their judgments (recommendations) for 128 stocks was only 0.32. This information alone would be enough to dispel the prior notion of the first broker that his judgmental processes were similar to those of the second judge. Another note-worthy result was that one broker claimed to need a minimum of eleven cues in order to make a recommendation with regard to any stock. Yet the results of the study indicated that his judgments were not influenced significantly by several of these cues. This may also be an enlightening type of information for such a judge. The third major finding was that the two judges had very different information utilization strategies. Both of the judges used mostly linear but also significant configural patterns, and the components in their configural patterns, as well as the relative importances they placed on individual cues, differed noticeably. In the last part of the experiment, the stockbrokers estimated the relative importance they believed they were placing on each of the various cues in arriving at their stock recommendations. One broker accurately estimated the relative weightings he had placed on the cues, while the other made estimates far from the weightings that were implied by his 128 recommendations. This latter result is similar to one that was found by Hoffman (1960) and others, which illustrated that judges' subjective estimates of their weightings may or may not be close to the statistically implied weightings.

Another study of the judgments of stockbrokers was reported by Slovic, Fleissner, and Bauman (1972). Analysis of variance was again adopted to provide a quantitative description of brokers' implied cue-utilization, and to test the role of configurality believed to be imbedded in their inferential processes. Thirteen brokers and five business students, ranging in experience from six months to fifteen years, participated. Common stocks were described by eight ordinarily used factors extracted from Standard and Poor's reports. The brokers, after the experiment, attempted to verbalize the information integration strategies they had used in arriving at their judgments of the appreciation of each stock. These verbal communications were typically vague, at best conveying only hazy insights into their experienced integrative processes. An inexperienced broker would find it most difficult to grasp key components of experienced judgment from these verbalizations. Such difficulties point up the potential value of using quantitative representations of judgmental strategies as communication devices. The researchers illustrated how the methodology could be used to lay bare the vast differences in experienced judgmental processes among experts, identifying the relative influence of each of the cues on the final judgments. The number of cues utilized by two of the experts differed noticeably, as did the number of interactions among the cues; in other words, the amount of configurality differed markedly for these two judges. For all stockbrokers, *the vast proportion of the response variance was accounted for by linear combinations of the cues* used in their judgments. When asked for their subjective beliefs as to how they were weighting each of the cues confronting them, the judges' subjective weightings were far different from the implied weightings of their actual judgments. They apparently were unaware of the manner in which they were weighting these various cues. Furthermore, those judges who had greater experience in the stock market had less valid insights as to the way in which they were weighting the cues.

Cue Consistency: A Source of Configurality.   Slovic (1966) identified inconsistency among cues as a specific source of configurality. In making clinical judgments based on nine cues, when the two most heavily used cues were made inconsistent in terms of their implications for the judgment, one of the cues was discarded and the remaining cue was used more heavily by the judges. Clinicians apparently formed a judgment about the intrinsic validity of a cue. When the two cues were in agreement with one another, that is, were consistent in their implications, both were used. When the two cues were inconsistent with one another, one of the two cues was discarded by the judge in making his judgment.

Even so, "... the linear model predicted the (subjects') judgments quite well within both consistent and inconsistent profile sets. Judgments, however, were slightly more linear for the consistent profiles" (p. 432).

Wyer (1970) similarly studied the manner in which judges discounted the effect of two cues which were inconsistent with one another. If the two cues were inconsistent and one of the cues indicated a median value on some scale while the second cue indicated an extreme value on the scale, then the judge tended to discount the intermediate value and weight the extreme value more heavily. This would lead to more extreme evaluations of the criterion on the part of the judge. However, if the two cues were both extreme and inconsistent with one another, the judge would discount the impact of both cues in arriving at his judgment. Thus, his judgment would end up being less extreme overall than would be the case otherwise.

In general, these studies suggest that the importance-weighting placed on one cue is somewhat dependent upon the values of the other cues. When the cues are consistent in their implications for the judgment, they are "assigned" relatively stable weightings by the judge. If the cue implications are inconsistent, then the cue weightings are modified (Dudycha and Naylor, 1966a). This phenomenon contradicts the linearity principles that underly regression approaches for representing judgmental processes. Hoffman (1968) has noted that the linear models were originally selected to represent judgment because they were simple and readily available for portraying these processes. However, since the linear models assume that responses to cue variability are invariant from a linear pattern regardless of the range of cue values, we must question the validity of using them to represent the true process of weighting, particularly in light of the clear evidence of configural cue utilization in judgmental tasks. Even so, the proportion of response variance attributable to configural patterns is small relative to that accounted for by simple linear combinations of information.

Other Models.   This entire area of judgmental analysis is closely related to the topic of man versus models in decision processes, a topic that will be covered more thoroughly in the following chapter. The striking thing about all of these studies is that man's judgmental processes are well represented by simple linear models. At the same time, the expert judges themselves contend that such simple processes are not the ones that really occur in their diagnostic processes. They contend that one can glean many more cues from the object of the diagnosis than just those from simple test results and standard data, and thus their judgments are not simple linear functions of test scores. In many organizational settings, expert judges may respond in the same way, saying that no simple model could in fact represent their judgmental processes. And yet, the overwhelming evidence in other settings suggests that such simple models will perform as well or better than the judges themselves in many situations.

In discussing this heated topic, Kleinmuntz (1968) states: "My own biases on the matter tend to favor a view which holds that there are certain classes of prediction problems where the clinician's personal touch, no matter how irrational or judicious, adds error variance to the prediction" (p. 151). This view is consistent with much of the research reported earlier and is also in agreement with the notion put forth by Bowman (1963) in his Theory of Management Coefficients. Kleinmuntz reports a study in which the clinician spelled out his "rules-of-thumb," or judgmental heuristics, which were then computerized and made mechanical. One judge was found to be extremely proficient in evaluating the profiles of maladjusted and adjusted college students on the basis of personality test scores.[9] An extensive tape recording of the way in which he made these judgments was obtained by having him verbalize the logic of his thought processes as he made such judgments about a large number of students. From this was derived a set of sequential elementary decision rules representing those used by the expert judge. The composite list of sequential rules was extensive, although not highly complex on an individual basis. Individual rules were extracted from the composite list and structured (combined) to reflect the overall judgmental logic. By use of some additional sorting rules on a computer, it was found that the programmed decision rules were a considerable improvement upon the expert's original judgmental rules and also upon the judgments of the expert himself.

In some subsequent validation studies, Kleinmuntz's work indicated that the computer performed as well as the best of the clinicians and performed consistently better than the average clinician. Performance was measured by the percentage of correct diagnoses from among a large number of diagnoses that were made. The reasons for the superiority of the computer over the individual were twofold: first, the vast number of data processing tasks that had to be performed in interpreting MMPI scores was done much easier by the computer than by a human; secondly, the power of the computer rested in its ability to apply judgmental rules consistently, thus diminishing the error variance inherent in human judgment processes.

The approach described above, involving the derivation of heuristic models, has been extended by Kleinmuntz and is similar to that employed by Clarkson (1962) to simulate decisions of investment trust officers. This work will be discussed further in our coverage of heuristics. Our principal point in this section has been to show that alternative approaches to the study of inference processes are available. We note, however, the rapidity with which their complexities increase, and we are forced to question the relative gains to be realized from the intensified efforts required to develop such alternative models. The argument on the one hand is summarized in the following exerpt from Goldberg (1970):

[9]Minnesota Multiphasic Personality Inventory—MMPI.

... it has been demonstrated that linear regression models of clinical judges can be more accurate diagnostic predictors than are the humans who are modeled. Moreover, even when the model of the judge was constructed on a relatively small subset of cases, and then the clinician and the model competed on the remaining (larger) set of additional cases, this same effect occurred (p. 430).

From a process-*output* point-of-view the rule of parsimony suggests that the development of more complex models is just not worth the effort. However, if our interest is in understanding inferential processes, then the simple rules may not be the answer. Einhorn (1971), considering the notion of cognitive simplification in complex judgmental situations, states:

... a model's mathematical simplicity may have little to do with the cognitive difficulty in using it. . . . It is certainly an intriguing idea that more complex models will have to be developed in order to deal with how cognitive simplification works. In addition, more work will be needed to express complex models mathematically, as well as to deal with the more difficult problem of sequential decision strategies (pp. 24,25).

SUMMARY

It is now necessary to reiterate that judgmental inferences are not always an end in themselves and they may not be conveniently disconnected from other dimensions of the decision process. We must put into perspective, then, the role of judgment in the context of the larger decision processes. At the beginning of this chapter we distinguished between first-level and higher-level judgments, identifying stages at which each enter into the overall judgmental process. We identified a special category called premise judgments. Being broader in nature and acquired through experience these premise judgments reside in the Image, as discussed in Chapter 2.

We have noted that judgmental processes are closely related to the topics of the preceding chapter, information search and utilization. The current treatment of judgmental processes excludes information-search activities and concentrates on the utilization of informational cues of various kinds. In contrast, our coverage of information-utilization in the previous chapter was concerned with the process of probability revision and inferences based on underlying subjective probabilities and utilities.

Practical Implications of Man's Judgmental Processes

We have discussed two major aspects of judgment: (1) methods for representing man's judgmental processes, and (2) man's judgmental capabilities and the influence of the environment on these judgments. In the section below, we summarize some major points and discuss what can be inferred from these findings that will help organizational decision making.

Man's Inefficiency. The previous chapter concluded with a summary of areas related to information search and processing in which man behaved in a less than optimal manner (e.g., satisficing; conservatism, etc.). To this list will be added some major items from the present chapter:

1. Man will use irrelevant information in his judgment. Even after repeated occurrences of a cue being unrelated to some environmental outcome, people will still use this irrelevant cue.
2. Information which is nonlinear tends to be under-utilized. Interactions or curvilinear relationships are not given enough weight even when it is pointed out to the person making the judgment.
3. It also appears that information reflecting a negative relationship between cues and criterion is under-utilized. Logically, this information is just as useful as that which is inherent in a positive relationship.
4. Once a set of weights is learned, it appears to be more difficult to learn changes in these weights than it is to learn the original weights. Once the pattern has been set and been shown to be correct in the past, it is difficult to change.
5. Man is frequently unaware of the way he is using information. Statistical tools can reveal his patterns of information utilization.
6. In many situations a simple linear model explains major proportions of man's judgmental response variation.

Along with these points on human fallibility, we will summarize the effects of task and environmental conditions on judgment.

1. Feedback helps the individual to make more accurate judgments. The type of feedback seems to be more important than the sheer amount of feedback.
2. People tend to give more consistent judgments when there is redundancy in the information; that is, they show less variability in the way they relate the cues.
3. The more configurality in the cues the slower the individual learns the underlying relationships between cues and criterion. Interactions and curvilinear relationships are hard to utilize effectively.
4. Experience by itself does not guarantee accurate judgments. However, with certain types of training, judgmental accuracy can be increased.

Bounded Rationality. It is clear that man does not behave in the manner of a purely "rational" being. He makes errors of judgment, fails to search for all alternatives, misinterprets the information available to him, and estimates incorrectly the likelihood of various events. It was Simon (1957) who perhaps took the initial step in pointing out these problems as they relate to organizational behavior. His principle of bounded rationality states that:

> The capacity of the human mind for formulating and solving complex problems is very small compared with the size of the problems whose solution is required for objectively rational behavior in the real world—or even for a reasonable approximation to such objective rationality (p. 198).

The next question is, of course, how do we deal with this inefficiency and irrationality. One method is through the use of models and it is to this topic that we now turn our attention.

The Role of Models

Preceding chapters identified a number of the decision maker's behavioral characteristics. We now wish to identify how various models can be used to supplement and enhance his decisions by assisting in some of the difficult phases of decision-problem resolution. One approach for doing this would be to comprehensively present numerous models, showing how they are derived and showing the procedures involved in their use. However, the number of existing models is so vast that space limitations alone prohibit such an approach. Instead, we provide a brief sketch of the kinds of assistance various models offer the decision maker.

We have already seen how the demands placed on the decision maker vary across situations, and that his capacities vary along numerous dimensions. To portray the potential usefulness of models we will first identify some characteristic sources of decision-problem complexity. We then attempt to show how selected models may simplify these complexities.

BACKGROUND

At a very general level, models may be defined as abstractions from reality which are used for some purpose. This abstraction, the model, is both a composite of important subcomponents of reality, and a description of how the subcomponents are interrelated.[1] Since the model is developed for a specific purpose, it is understandable that several models of the same object may differ from one another. By recognizing that the content of the model is determined by the modeler's judgment it becomes apparent that modeling is more an art than a science.[2]

Although models can be expressed in many forms, the current discussion focuses on models that are quantitatively oriented. The models that are discussed can be identified as belonging to one of two classes, normative and descriptive. The former subsumes abstractions which are prescriptive; that is, they tell us what is proper, what *should* exist. In contrast, descriptive models are used to portray what *actually* exists. Obviously the two may, but need not, be similar.

The Evolution of Quantitative Decision Models

The era since the 1940s has witnessed a marked emphasis on the desire to use quantitative models to assist in organizational decision making. From these efforts has emerged the professional fields of operations research and management science. Over a period of three decades both the number and variety of quantitative models has accumulated into staggering proportions. The bases of these models are developments in economic theory and the mathematical, statistical, and computer sciences. Scientific developments in these disciplines have paved the way for the development and application of models in organization settings. At the same time, there are limitations to the state of the art in these disciplines which restrict the further development of quantitative models for organizational decision making.

Today, models are capable of fulfilling a variety of roles in decision making. Some provide an "optimum" decision which may be directly implemented in the organization. Others do not directly result in a decision but, rather, provide useful ways of ordering relevant decision information, or provide a means for dealing with selected subcomponents of the decision problem. We can begin to assess the current posture of models from the decision maker's viewpoint by considering the following question: What do existing models do well, and what decision-problem characteristics limit their applicability?

[1] See Bross (1953) for a more complete discussion of models.
[2] See Morris (1967) for a discussion of the art of modeling.

SOME CHARACTERISTICS OF DECISION PROBLEMS

Designated below are several decision-problem characteristics constituting sources of "problem complexity" in organizational decision settings. The list includes only those elements that are of sufficient importance to have been implicitly or explicitly considered in developing the existing "reservoir" of useful decision models.

Content Dimensionality

(a) Number of goals. By goals or objectives we mean the "higher purpose" to which the immediate decision problem relates. Consideration is restricted to organizational goals rather than the personal goals of the decision maker. One difficulty posed by a decision problem is that of identifying the immediate goal(s). Further, major difficulties may be encountered when one is faced with a multiplicity of goals, for here the possibility of goal conflict arises.

(b) Number of criteria. Several difficulties arise in evaluating decision alternatives. The evaluative component of the decision process requires a criterion (i.e., how "good" is an alternative). The criterion and the goal may be one and the same if the goal can be suitably measured. However, in the absence of suitable goal measurement, another variable may be substituted as the yardstick by which alternatives are evaluated. In this context a number of criteria may be appropriately utilized, giving rise to problems of criterial selection and conflict. The vagaries of imperfect criteria will also affect criterial acceptance when the decision impacts multiple organizational subunits.

(c) Number of constraints. Constraints are boundaries circumscribing various aspects of the decision process. March and Simon (1958) have identified organizational goals as one type of decision constraint. Examples of other constraints are time, information, physical and human resources, as well as legal and other environmental restrictions. To the decision maker, constraints may be viewed as both a blessing and a curse, for they serve to decrease decision-problem complexity in some respects, while increasing the complexity in other ways. In searching for suitable decision alternatives, for instance, organizational goals limit the number of feasible alternatives, thus reducing an otherwise vast number of alternatives to more manageable proportions. Similarly, the set of feasible alternatives is reduced under conditions of constrained resources for resource-allocation decisions. But these same constraints may also increase decision complexity. When allocation-decision-alternatives are sets of actions requiring the use of (or competing for) the same set of limited resources, then the decision maker must consider certain *exchange relationships.* Exchange relationships describe the relative rates of usage of limited resources by the decision variables. Such relationships must be understood and utilized by the decision maker in evaluating alternative action sets. As the number of shared resource constraints increases, the number of exchange relationships to be considered increases by an even greater amount, thus increasing one aspect of decision complexity.

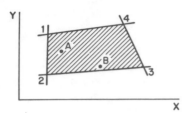

Figure 7-1   Region of Admissable Combinations for Amounts of Two
Decision Variables (X and Y)

(d) Number of alternatives. While organizational constraints eliminate the
need to consider many decision alternatives, the number of remaining alternatives may vary radically in number. Consider the area of feasible alternatives
within the constraints (shaded area) depicted in Figure 7-1. For some problems
this feasible alternative-space may be viewed as being continuous, in which case
an infinite number of unique points (values of X and Y) exist. An example
would be deciding on the average proportion of available productivity time to
allocate to each of two products. In other situations, discrete alternatives—such
as A and B—may be the only feasible alternatives in the solution space due to the
indivisibility of resources. An example might be to decide how many of each of
two types of buildings to construct. Although it may be possible to construct
fractions of buildings, the decision maker may realistically wish to consider only
those alternatives which include whole buildings. Thus, within a given solution
space, variations in the number of feasible alternatives may be a source of
decision-problem complexity. If the individual's decision processes included, for
example, exhaustive search and evaluation of alternatives, the continuous case is
clearly a more complex problem than the discrete.

(e) Number of decision variables. The number of decision variables effects
decision complexity insofar as they are interdependent in effecting the evaluation criterion. Relevant decision variables are identified as those variables under
the decision maker's control which, if modified, result in a change in the value of
the evaluation criterion. Accurate assessment of the desirability of decision
alternatives requires consideration of interdependency relationships among decision variables, as well as understanding the relationships between decision
variables and evaluation criteria. The complexities of these relationships may
increase dramatically with just a modest increase in the number of relevant
decision variables.

Structural Dynamism

Many decision problems consist of an intended (planned) series of sequential
decisions, rather than the single decision required in a static decision problem.[3]
Sequential decisions occur across a succession of stages, where the decision at

[3]See Edwards (1962) for a taxonomy of decision problems.

one stage effects decisions in future stages. The structure of the decision problem is dynamic, thus the term structural dynamism, which is to be distinguished from the dynamics that occur in other aspects of the problem. This is exemplified by the Reader's Control Problem and the production scheduling problem, both of which are presented later in this chapter. The sequential nature of such problems is a special case of interdependence among decision variables, arising from their temporal relationships. Even though the same kind of decision variable may be the object of consideration at each stage, we may differentiate between them since each decision in the sequence is uniquely associated with a single stage. Furthermore, the stage-to-stage interdependencies have implications for the type of solution approach that is "ideal" for the resolution of such decision problems. Whereas the sequential decision problem can be treated as a sequence of single-stage (static) decisions, it is frequently inappropriate to do so. This interstage dependency, then, is an identifiable source of decision-problem complexity.

Uncertainty

The concern with uncertainty in classical decision theory focuses on the decision outcomes (consequences). *Certainty* denotes the case in which the outcome of each decision alternative is known prior to the decision. A condition of *risk* exists when the outcome of each decision is not known, but the probability distributions over the possible outcomes are known for each alternative. That is, we know how likely it is that a given outcome will occur. When the probability distributions of the decision outcomes are unknown, the decision problem is one of *uncertainty*. To further understand how uncertainty effects decision-problem complexity, it is useful to link it to other aspects of decision making, rather than restricting our consideration to decision outcomes.

(a) Anticipation uncertainty (outcomes). It cannot always be presumed that organizational decision problems are approached with complete knowledge of what decision outcomes can occur in a decision problem. Outcome identification is anticipatory, and thus it may be seen as possessing various degrees of uncertainty.

(b) Anticipation uncertainty (variables). Identification of the relevant decision variables is one source of decision uncertainty. Knowledge of the relevance of the many potentially relevant variables may vary from highly certain to uncertain.

(c) Relationship uncertainty. Even with a high degree of confidence regarding the identification of variable relevancy, the decision process requires some understanding (or belief) about the relationships among the relevant variables. The preciseness with which these relationships are known can be viewed along a certainty-uncertainty continuum.

All of these sources of uncertainty have implications for the degree of control that can be exercised by the decision maker. When the relevancy of variables is known with certainty, when the relationships that exist among them are known, and when there is complete knowledge as to which outcomes can occur and which outcomes are associated with each decision alternative, the decision maker is operating under *certainty* which allows the exercise of complete control. Uncertainty with respect to all of these areas represents the extreme condition of *complete uncertainty* and a total lack of control by the decision maker. The significance, then, of uncertainties is the limits they impose on the degree of control that can be exercised by the decision maker. Control may be gained by first identifying the uncertainty in the decision process, and secondly by changing the organization in ways that will reduce uncertainty.

Relationship Patterns

A variety of relationship patterns frequently exists among decision variables, among constraints, and among outcomes, decision variables, and contraints. The forms of these relationships may be highly dissimilar/similar, and may range from relatively simple to highly complex. For example, decision variables may be linearly or nonlinearly related to constraints. Some decision variables may be linearly related to the decision outcome while others are related to outcomes in a variety of nonlinear ways. The number and form of these relationship patterns are a significant source of problem complexity.

Stability

The stability of a decision problem can be considered on several dimensions. We refer to the stability of goals, criteria, constraints, alternatives, variables, uncertainty, and relationship patterns with respect to changes over time. "Highly structured" decisions are those which exhibit stability on many of these dimensions as contrasted to ill-structured and novel decision problems which exhibit substantial instability. The degree of stability effects decision-problem complexity.

Measurement Comparability

We refer here to the *dimensional comparability/incomparability* among existing scales of measurement. Our inability to adequately quantify decision-problem parameters reflects, of course, the current state of development in the science of measurement. The hierarchy of established scales of measurement (nominal, ordinal, interval, ratio) are not equally applicable at all stages of the decision process, or to all aspects of the decision problem. Nonetheless, these phases of the decision process are interrelated, and thus implicitly require some form of integrative scale conversion to provide sufficient structure to cope with decision problems. Scale conversion is needed to precisely relate goals, criteria, constraints, alternatives, and outcomes to one another. Measurement incomparability is a major source of decision-problem complexity.

CHARACTERISTICS OF MODELS

We have just identified several decision-problem characteristics which are sources of "problem complexity." We will now survey some existing quantitative decision aids, identifying the problem characteristics for which the models are well-suited. The alternative to using formal models is, of course, the human intuitive approach. For a few models, human versus model performance has been explicitly evaluated. In most cases, however, such comparisons have not been made, and the relative "usefulness" of the models (vs. human intuition) can only be assumed until a more firm empirical basis is established. The facility with which models handle certain complexities is an intuitively compelling justification for this assumption.

Statistical Models in Decision Making

The potential usefulness of statistical theory, and other quantitative models which incorporate elements of probability and statistics, has been partially demonstrated in our preceding discussions.

In Chapter 6 we discussed the processes by which humans reach conclusions about the implications of proximal events in the environment. These conclusions become man's decision premises. Being based on limited information, they are often inaccurate. Thus, there are risks involved in using them as a basis for making decisions. But how much risk? How much confidence about the "correctness" of the conclusions is warranted by the available information? Statistical models help answer these questions by providing a system for measuring the degree of error in intuitive conclusions (beliefs) drawn from sample evidence. Thus, intuitively formed beliefs about relationships among environmental events and variables can be evaluated against precise descriptions of the strengths of those relationships. From the decision maker's viewpoint, then, statistics may be a powerful tool for sharpening his judgmental processes. In this context, correlation and regression techniques[4] (similar to those used in the judgment models presented earlier) have been found to be helpful for finding and evaluating relationships among variables. In Chapter 6 it was noted that human inferences about relationships among variables closely approximate the statistical relation-

---

[4]Also, related techniques such as factor analysis.

ships in some instances, but the two differ substantially in other cases. To the extent that incorrect human judgments can lead to undesirable decision consequences, we see the potential value of supplementing (or even replacing elements of) human judgment with statistical tools. Statistical methods, then, may be useful for revealing to man certain characteristics of his judgmental processes, and also may help him to arrive at unbiased assessments of the relevance of relationships among environmental variables.[5]

Descriptive statistics, then, may be of assistance in the decision process by coping with the following sources of "problem complexity:"

- helping identify relevant decision variables and potential outcomes;
- detecting relationships, and their strengths, among variables;
- identifying *forms* or *patterns* of relationships among variables; and
- identifying the degree of stability of relationships.

Chapter 5 presented some behaviors used by the decision maker to reduce problem complexity. Of primary importance are his information search and processing activities. Substantial individual differences were observed in the amount of information search and utilization, in time spent processing information, in perceived uncertainty of the implications of the information, and in information-processing capacities. It was further observed that man's conclusions are biased under certain environmental conditions. From these and similar observations arises the question of whether models are available for helping the decision maker select the types and amounts of alternative behaviors in his decision processes. From the field of "decision theory," the response is "yes," with certain qualifications. As stated by Hays (1963):

> The theory of statistics supplies one very important piece of information to the experimenter: the probability of sample results *given* certain conditions. Decision theory supplies another: optimal ways of using this and other information to accomplish certain ends (pp. 11–12).

Many decision-theoretic models incorporate the essentials of the Bayesian model for probability revision illustrated in Chapter 5. It was shown that this model could help reduce unintended bias and conservatism by determining the effect of additional information on a judgment revision. This model is particularly appealing since it allows the decision maker to explicitly incorporate his subjective prior beliefs into the analysis. These beliefs can then be systematically combined with additional information to reach posterior conclusions. If his beliefs and the additional information are expressed in appropriate form,[6] the

---

[5]These basic notions are illustrated by the development of statistical forecasting models See Winters (1960).

[6]See Raiffa and Schlaifer (1961).

model normatively specifies the appropriate conclusions in a consistent and unbiased manner.

Going beyond the revision of beliefs, "decision-theory" models may attempt to specify appropriate courses of action for the decision maker. They provide the means for deciding whether or not to gather additional information, which of several alternative courses of action is most desirable, and they provide specific estimates of the consequences of alternative acts. All of this, however, requires the decision maker to express possible outcomes on a comparable scale of measurement (dollars or utility, etc.). Herein lies a major limitation of the decision-theory models. Outcome-consequences frequently are not conveniently expressed on a common scale of measurement. Nonetheless, these models may facilitate decision processes by:

• combining estimates of outcome uncertainty, expressed as probabilities, with measures of possible outcome consequences to obtain an overall measure of each alternative's desirability in terms of a specific decision criterion;

• providing an explicit basis for guiding information-search activities, particularly in evaluating the desirability of gathering additional information prior to making a decision;[7]

• providing a basis for reducing the number of relevant decision variables. This can be accomplished by performing sensitivity analyses on the models. This procedure reveals parameter-value ranges in which certain variables may be regarded as irrelevant to this decision.

Since some of the elementary statistical models provide unbiased estimates of variables, it is not surprising that these models are used in many ways other than those identified above. They are extensively used as subcomponents of many optimization models, some of which are discussed below.

Other Illustrative Models

In this section the focus shifts to some selected models which are primarily non-statistical. They are presented to illustrate the wide variety of potentially useful properties they offer the decision maker. While some of them are well-known and highly publicized, others have appeared only recently and may be less familiar to the reader. The discussion attempts to match each model with the central "sources of problem complexity" that it assists in surmounting.

Number of Goals: Goal Consistency. Organizational decision makers are frequently faced with a multiplicity of goals, subgoals, a number of alternative actions, and a restricted set of resources for meeting the goals. Surprisingly few

[7]This issue is an example of one type of "structural dynamism;" it involves the question of sequential sampling. See Wald (1947).

models have been developed for assisting in this complex situation. Although the problem of goal-identification, per se, is not directly addressed by existing quantitative models, the *goal-consistency model* can be used indirectly to help reveal goals that should be considered. This model has been developed to permit the decision maker to assess the consistency among his perceptions of goals, policies, and action sets (alternatives) for achieving the goals.

Based on a strategy of problem decomposition, the model provides a set of "rules" for evaluating the relative desirabilities of each set of action alternatives. The decision maker must break down the problem into a set of subproblems with "means-ends" chains, precisely identifying the hierarchical pattern of relationships among actions, goals, policies, and objectives (Vesper and Sayeki, 1973). Let us consider an example consisting of two identifiable objectives for meeting one broader overall organizational goal. The example assumes the existence of three organizational policy areas that can effect the attainment of objectives. The alternative actions that exist within each policy area have also been identified. This example is illustrated in Figure 7-2. Each of the decision alternatives (action sets) consists of one or more actions within the various policy areas. The number of feasible action sets is determined on the basis of resource availability and technological restrictions. The decision problem is to select the action set that will provide the greatest contribution to overall goal accomplishment.

To use the model the decision maker must assign a numeric value, on a prescribed scale, to each action set. These values should reflect his beliefs of the relative value of each action set to each objective. He must also evaluate the relative value to overall goal accomplishment of each action set, expressed in terms of a second numeric scale. Finally, using a third numeric scale, he assesses the contribution that each action element would make to each policy area, and the importances among policy areas, objectives, and the overall goal. Using concepts of utility theory (Sayeki, 1972), the policy utility procedure then permits the computation of desirability ratings derived from the intuitive importance judgments of the decision maker.

The complexities of such a problem arise from the many relationships that may exist among the hierarchy of subcomponents (overall goal, objectives, policy areas, and action elements). The relative desirability of an action set depends on the importance and values of its action elements to each policy area. Similarly, policy areas may be of differential importance to objectives, which, in turn, may differ in importance with respect to overall goal accomplishment. Application of the model provides an explicit identification of the implications of alternative actions throughout the linkages at all levels. The decision maker can use these results to evaluate his appraisal-consistency between adjacent or non-adjacent levels of the problem hierarchy.

Since the model provides a rank ordering of the alternative action sets, it may help the decision maker detect either bias or inconsistency in his evaluation

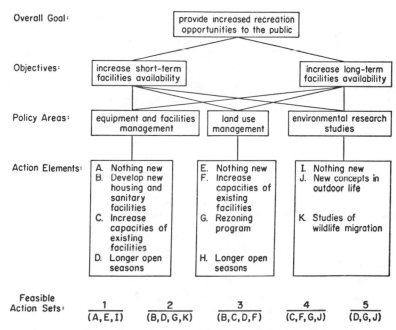

Figure 7-2 A Goal-Consistency Example

processes. It may signal the need for him to re-evaluate his original importance ratings. In evaluating the usefulness of the model, experimental evidence suggests that as the number of levels in the problem hierarchy increases, the value of using the policy-utility procedure also increases:

> The experiment also revealed a possible limitation of human information processing capacity. When subjects were asked to evaluate utilities for a remote goal, their judgments were not consistent with their judgments for immediate goals. Therefore, it may be concluded that when a hierarchial goal structure is given, dependable measures are only the judgments for the adjacent goals between two levels of the goal hierarchy, and if we had to make judgments for some remote goals, it would be best to use some outside aids such as computers. Computers would also be helpful to make the decision maker's evaluations more precise and extensive; a computer may automatically send messages asking to re-analyze subgoals, or to make more careful judgments as soon as the deviation between "calculated" vs. "directly estimated" values exceeds a certain limit. Such consistency checkups would help the decision maker to make more careful judgments, deeper understandings of the implications of each goal, and as a result, to make more "rational" decisions (Vesper and Sayeki, 1973, p. 123).

The potential usefulness of this model arises from its ability to assist in coping with several sources of problem complexity: number of alternatives, number of goals, number of criteria, relationship patterns, and measurement comparability. It also indirectly impacts on the number of alternatives in an important way. The decision maker must identify feasible alternative actions, and relate them to policy areas, objectives, and goals. Iterative use of this approach may result in unsatisfactory ratings (to the user) or inconsistencies, both of which provide impetus for re-evaluating, perhaps adding, additional alternatives. The approach can provide a guide for constraining the number of alternatives to a feasible yet exhaustive set, all stimulated by the motive of greater evaluative consistency.

Although many decision problems require joint consideration of multiple goals, many techniques (decision aids) are operational only for individual alternative-goal-outcome linkages; i.e., an action alternative is considered to have outcome implications for only one goal or objective. The "policy utility" approach will accommodate multiple effects in which actions in a single policy area may have implications for one or *several* objectives, and all objectives may have implications for a single overall goal. Hierarchical goal-subgoal relationships need not be restricted to the case in which one subgoal contributes to only one immediately higher goal (Sayeki and Vesper, 1973). Furthermore, all subgoals, or goals, on a single level need not be considered of equal importance. This type of model helps in determining the implications of these interrelated dimensions.

The model also helps to overcome some complexities of dimensional incomparability, but does so by adopting a linear utility function which may prove unrealistic. But the approach does systematize the otherwise "intuitive mental conversion" that is performed in the judgmental evaluative activity in the decision process. The scaling procedure permits the establishment of intuitive comparisons among economic, material, human, and other alternatives and potential outcomes in terms of their relative importance in the goal-subgoal relationships.

Number of Goals: Goal Programming. Another quantitative model that assists in handling the complexities of multiple goals is *goal programming* (Charnes and Cooper, 1961). It is a specialized version of linear programming. Goal programming provides a set of optimal decision values which satisfies all resource constraints, and simultaneously provides the best feasible solution in terms of meeting the goal priorities of the decision maker. This model has seen increasing application in recent years (Lee, 1971; Lee and Clayton, 1972).

Goal programming is useful for analyzing problems consisting of multiple goals, where alternatives are not readily expressed on a single scale of measurement (such as dollars or cost). As expressed by Lee and Clayton (1972):

> Often, goals set by the decision maker are achievable only at the expense of other goals. Furthermore, these goals are incommensurable. Thus, there is a need to establish a hierarchy of importance among these incompatable goals

so that the low order goals are considered only after the higher order goals are satisfied or have reached the point beyond which no further improvements are desirable. If the decision maker can provide an ordinal ranking of goals in terms of their contributions or importance to the organization, the problem can be solved by GP (goal programming) (p. B-397, italics added).

This mathematical technique assists in coping with the "criterion" problem, as did the goal-consistency model. This is accomplished by using goal-achievement as the criterion for evaluating decision alternatives. These two models, then, are representative of the "state of the art" of quantitative aids for assisting with the "goal problem." Their applicability is admittedly limited when viewed against the breadth and scope of "goal problems" faced by organizational decision makers.

Number of Criteria. Explicit quantitative models for coping with the criterion problem at an operational level are virtually non-existent. This is readily apparent when one recognizes one commonality which exists among virtually all quantitative models: they consist of a single quantified objective (criterion) function. Contrast this condition with the structure of even relatively simple organizational decision problems: (1) a single criterion rarely dominates to the exclusion of others, and (2) due to incomparability of measurement, comparison among multiple and often conflicting criteria are difficult due to inadequate scale conversion capabilities. In short, explicit technology does not exist for precise resolution of multiple criteria and criterial conflict problems.

Number of Constraints. Optimization techniques have been developed to provide decisions for meeting a specified objective when constraints are imposed on the amounts of resources available. Linear programming provides an example of such a technique.[8]

First, we wish to examine some features of linear programming problems and describe some major operations that are used in the technique for arriving at optimal solutions. These components are specific problem dimensions the decision maker must recognize and consider if he is to perform at a level comparable to the model.

The decision maker is faced with:

(1) A well-defined objective function in which the decision variables are linearly related to the decision criterion. This objective function is a mathematical expression of the relationship between the decision criterion and the decision variables. Within an admissable range, the decision maker may assign any value he chooses to each of the decision variables.

(2) The admissable ranges of decision values are specified by a set of linear

[8] For an elaboration of linear programming see Hadley (1962).

constraints. There is one constraint for each scarce (limited) resource. Each decision variable utilizes a known and fixed amount of each resource. The rate of resource usage for each of the possible decision alternatives is prescribed by the constraint equation (relationship) for each limited resource consumed by the decision. The set of all such resource constraints, taken together, identifies the bounds on the decision alternatives that are available.

(3) The decision-making objective is to select values for all decision variables, so long as these values meet the limitations described in (2) above, in such a way as to obtain the highest value of the decision criterion specified in (1) above.

The number of constraints is a source of problem complexity in that all constraints must be simultaneously satisfied in the decision. The solution technique handles this complexity in a simplified routine manner. Beginning with an arbitrary, feasible set of decision alternatives, the technique explores successive solution combinations until no further improvement in the decision criterion can be found. In evaluating a unit change of one decision variable, if the criterion is favorably effected the succeeding improved solution adopts not only the unit change in that variable, but adopts as many units of that variable as are possible within the prescribed limits of available resources. Constraint complexity arises in that the decision variables share (compete for) the available limited resources. By increasing the value of one such decision variable we decrease the amount of resources that may be devoted to the others. As the number of common or shared resources increases so do the complexities of "keeping track" of the exchange relationships that must be considered for all combinations of decision alternatives, if the criterion value is to be optimized. The state of cognitive strain induced by such complexities may trigger a process of cognitive simplification by the decision maker. Simplified heuristics or decision rules, rather than exhaustive search and optimization procedures, could lead to suboptimal decisions. It would seem, then, that a relative advantage exists for models in such complex decision problems. Such a conclusion, although theoretically warranted, is misleading in practice. Assumptions of certainty, criterial clarity, linearity, and goal specificity required of the models are seldom encountered in organizational decision settings. The decision-problem abstraction reflected in the model may or may not be an adequate representation of the total decision problem. Intuitive judgmental decisions may be more nearly optimal than model decisions in the context of the "total decision problem;" inappropriate abstractions will lead to inappropriate conclusions. This does not negate, however, some of the relative advantages of the model. Rather, it points to the need for human judgment to mediate the results of model output in relation to the organizational decision problem. This broader judgmental perspective currently exists in man alone.

Another likely advantage in using optimizing techniques, contrasted to the alternative of using human intuitive approaches, arises from the existence of

Table 7-1 Number of Feasibility Comparisons for Exhaustive Search among
Variables Competing for Shared Resources

Number of Variables	Number of Alternatives per Variable	Number of Feasibility Comparisons per Shared Constraint
1	1	1
	2	2
	3	3
	•	•
	•	•
	•	•
2	1	2
	2	4
	3	9
	•	•
	•	•
	•	•
	10	100
	•	•
	•	•
3	1	3
	2	8
	3	27
	•	•
	•	•
	•	•
	10	1000
	•	•
	•	•
•	•	•
•	•	•
10	1	10
	2	1024
	3	59049
	•	•
	•	•
	•	•
	10	10,000,000,000
	•	•
	•	•

redundancy. If the number of constraints increases problem complexity, and hence effects decision performance, redundant constraints should be omitted from consideration in the problem. In formal optimization techniques such redundancies are treated as irrelevant and no significant problems are posed by their inclusion. In human problem solving, however, such is probably not the case. To the human problem solver, relevancy of constraints is a matter of perception which changes with experience in the decision setting. Perceived constraint relevancy, even though incorrect, may be expected to impede human decision performance in contrast to model performance. Human efforts devoted to consideration of irrelevant task dimensions may detract from relevant dimensions of task performance.

Other programming techniques for optimization are also available. Nonlinear programming, for instance, allows for the relaxation of the linearity assumption of linear programming.[9] Goal programming has already been discussed. Shortly, we will consider dynamic programming.

Number of Alternatives: Linear Programming. Optimizing decisions imply exhaustive search and, for continuous decision variables, exhaustive search and evaluation of alternatives is infinite. If search has a cost, and it usually does, then limited rather than exhaustive search is optimal. Consider the following objects of search that are relevant in many decision problems:

(a)   determination of feasibility of alternatives with regard to explicit and implicit constraints of the decision problem;
(b)   determination of the decision outcomes implied by the decision alternatives; and
(c)   relative comparison of alternative outcomes.

With regard to (a), the complexity is largely a combinatorial problem, illustrated in Table 7-1. Even for problems with relatively small numbers of variables, alternatives, and constraints, the number of feasibility comparisons is significant. This is further complicated by those alternatives that share common restricted resources, as previously described.

These combinatorial complexities identify one role of linear programming as a decision aid. The shaded area in Figure 7-1 is a typical way of representing the set of admissable decision alternatives. For only two or three decision variables, all combinations of alternatives can be readily checked for feasibility. Beyond the three-variable case, however, graphical aids are of limited value. An alternative approach is to use algebraic expressions of the constraints to determine the feasibility of decision alternatives. Linear programming models adopt this ap-

---

[9] For an elaboration of nonlinear programming see Hadley (1964).

proach. Furthermore, they consider only the feasible alternative solutions. In contrast, man in highly complex decision problems must test the feasibility of a myriad of plausible alternatives—some of which may ultimately prove infeasible. One advantage, then, of linear programming and other optimization techniques is a "built-in" capability of restricting search to "feasible" alternatives.

The *number* of relative comparisons required among alternative outcomes was identified in (c) above as one source of evaluative complexity. Consider, again, the number of feasible decision alternatives in the shaded area of Figure 7-1. Theoretically an infinite number of such comparisons are required for an optimal decision. However, it can be logically and mathematically demonstrated that an optimal solution exists at one of four points in the feasible decision space. This and similarly powerful concepts are imbedded in optimization techniques and touch upon the heart of their potential value in the decision process. It is for these reasons that seemingly inappropriate quantitative conceptualizations of decision problems may still prove helpful. In this example, linear programming may rapidly identify a superior decision alternative otherwise not even within the realm of consideration in the face of an endless number of intuitive alternatives. A similar notion underlies the application of classical optimization in the derivation of economic-order-quantity (EOQ) rules for inventory decisions. If the decision criterion can be expressed as a mathematical function of the relevant decision variables, then classical optimization techniques can quickly identify a range of decision alternatives that is highly desirable. This approach removes the necessity of more extensive search and comparison among decision alternatives.

Content Dimensionality: Linear Assignments.   The primary source of complexity for many decision problems is the large number of alternatives, constraints, and decision variables. The many possible combinations of these factors can grow quite rapidly. For other decision problems, these combinatorial difficulties are significant subcomponents.

Several evaluation strategies may be used for solving combinatorial problems. Complete enumeration, for example, involves finding and evaluating every possible combination-set, thus assuring an optimal solution. For small problems this strategy is practical. For slightly larger problems it is still feasible, especially if computing machinery is available. But consider the problems of assigning any of ten resources to each of ten alternative uses in which every use must be assigned one and only one resource. More than three and one-half million (10!) assignment combinations are feasible. A strategy of complete enumeration for moderate and large-scale problems is prohibitive. Complete intuitive evaluation of such problems is beyond man's mental capacities. It is in this context that quantitative approaches can facilitate human decision making, by offering alternative strategies for coping with these combinatorial aspects. Consider an example in

Table 7-2 Cost Matrix for Six Resources and Six Uses

		Uses					
		1	2	3	4	5	6
Resources	A	2	6	3	5	10	12
	B	7	15	2	1	16	14
	C	1	18	12	10	12	2
	D	4	9	10	6	12	4
	E	10	2	8	4	4	7
	F	3	1	6	10	8	10

which each of six resources must be assigned to one of six alternative uses so as to minimize the total assignment cost. The cost for assigning each resource to each use is shown in Table 7-2. There are 6! or 720 possible sets of assignments. Rather than completely enumerating all sets and comparing their cost implications, one may adopt a trial and error procedure. Some obviously bad assignment sets will appear, and these may be immediately discarded from further consideration. By iteratively cycling through the alternatives, the number of alternatives will continue to be reduced until a satisfactory solution is obtained. Humans can and do adopt simple guides (heuristics) to handle such problems. However, such a process does not assure attainment of an optimal set of assignments. Since the optimal solution is unknown to the decision maker, his only clue for evaluating a current solution is the change in cost from previously evaluated alternatives. Instead of intuition, a branch and bound algorithm may be used to resolve such a combinatorial problem. The algorithm consists of a set of simple rules which, if appropriately followed, results in an optimal solution. Although the mechanics of the method are not presented here, the results of its application illustrate how a problem is reduced to successively smaller size. Beginning with the full set of 6! solution alternatives, a simple partitioning rule identifies the lowest possible cost (lower limit or bound) that can feasibly be attained (without yet specifying the assignment set that will attain it).[10] The structure of the problem may ultimately prohibit attainment of this *lower bound* of costs, but at least the decision maker knows that his solution cost cannot be reduced beyond this amount, a powerful piece of information! This phase of the algorithm is portrayed as the top node in Figure 7-3. The next step in the algorithm partitions the full set of feasible solution alternatives into two subsets, or *branches,* one of which contains all solution alternatives in which resource E is assigned to use 5, the other branch containing all other solution

[10]See Gavett (1968) for an elaboration of the partitioning rule and other aspects of the branch and bound technique.

alternatives. The lower bound of cost for all solutions for which E is not assigned to 5 is five units of cost greater than the previous lower bound (14) for all possible solutions. In this example, the lower bound on all solutions containing E5 remains the same as the previous lower bound. Succeeding search focuses on the more desirable of the two branches, E5, since it offers the greatest potential for attaining lowest cost. The procedure is reiterated to identify the next cell assignment that provides the greatest cost-avoidance, followed by further partitioning into those alternatives including F2 and those excluding F2. At this stage we have identified the most promising subset of alternatives as those which assign E to 5 and F to 2. Furthermore, we know the lower bound on the cost of all such alternatives. The process continues until all resources have been assigned

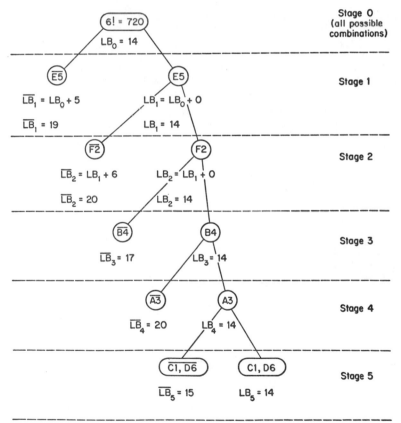

Figure 7-3 Partitioning Characteristic of Branch and Bound Showing Subsets of Assignments (circles) and the Lower Bound (LB_i) of Costs for Each Subset

to the uses. At this point an optimal solution is identified (E5, F2, B4, A3, C1, D6; COST = 14).

We can see, then, that this type of algorithm provides valuable assistance to the decision maker by reducing the complexities of simultaneously considering many decision variables, alternatives, constraints, and evaluations of feasible alternatives. One reason for elaborating on branch and bound is to illustrate the partitioning characteristic employed in the algorithm. The strategy of successively partitioning a large initial set of alternatives into successively smaller subsets results in systematic simplification of search. It is for this reason that this strategy is often employed in heuristic problem-solving models.

Structural Dynamism: Dynamic Programming. Consider the dynamic decision problem whose solution is represented in Figure 7-4. In this figure we see the "state (status) of a system" and a sequence of decisions depicted on a time scale. The system is being described numerically. In some cases this number might represent inventory levels or productivity capacity. The decisions are also expressed numerically and have cost implications since they may be expensive in terms of resources used. Finally, the status can be controlled through our decisions, each of which are made at discrete time intervals 1 through 8. The decision goal is to minimize the total cost of the eight decisions by manipulating the status of the system. The following expression defines how each decision influences the status of the system:

$$X_{K+1} = 1.4\, X_K + 0.1\, Y_K \cdot \qquad\qquad [1]$$

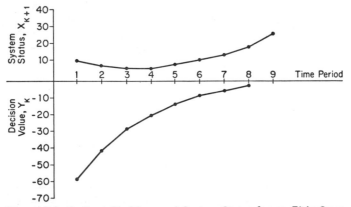

Figure 7-4 Optimal Decisions and System Status for an Eight-Stage Decision Problem

Table 7-3 Optimal Decisions, System Status, and Total Cost for an Eight-Stage Decision Problem

Period	System Status*	Optimal Decision	Total Cost
1	10.0	−58.1	$8,141
2	8.2	−40.9	
3	7.4	−28.7	
4	7.4	−20.0	
5	8.4	−13.7	
6	10.4	−9.0	
7	13.7	−5.5	
8	18.6	−2.6	
9	25.8		

*status at the beginning of each time period.

Relationship [1] shows that the status of the system (X_{K+1}) in the time period subsequent to a decision is determined by two factors: (a) the status (X_K) that existed just before the decision, and (b) the decision (Y_K) itself. This "transformation function" illustrates the role that each decision plays in changing the system over several time periods. Since our decision objective is to minimize the total cost consequences of eight sequential decisions, we are interested in knowing the cost function for the problem.

$$C_K = Y_K^2 + X_{K+1}^2 \qquad [2]$$

Expression [2] specifies the cost resulting from the decision made in time period K. This single-period decision cost is a function of the decision Y_K, and the system status, X_{K+1}, resulting from that decision. In this example the decision cost is determined by summing the square of the numeric decision and the square of the resulting system-status. We should note two characteristics of this cost relationship: (a) before the second cost component in expression [2] can be calculated we must use relationship [1] to determine the system status resulting from the current decision; and (b) even if the decision value for Y_K is zero, decision costs are incurred if the status of the system is non-zero following the decision. Furthermore, although the decisions are to be expressed numerically, they need not be positive; negative decisions are admissable. The optimal decision set is shown in Table 7-3, along with the resulting system status and total decision cost.

The problem specifications are admittedly simple-minded and yet the problem illustrates several important sources of decision-problem complexity. First, note the sequential interdependencies from period to period. The costs attributed to the current period's decision in [2] arise not only from the current decision, but also from subsequent implications of that decision as it modifies the status of the system. At the same time, the modified system status is partially determined by the previous system status. It becomes clear, then, that costs incurred for a *current* period are directly related to the *previous* period's status, which in turn is related to *all prior* decisions and system states. From the reverse viewpoint, the current decision clearly has cost implications for *all* future decisions, since it will effect the system state confronting the decision maker in subsequent decision periods. The implication of all of this is that the decision maker, to perform "optimally," must "look ahead" when making a decision. He must consider the consequences of the current decision for *all future time periods.* Our example would initially require an eight-period time horizon (for optimal performance) at stage one, a seven-period horizon at stage two, etc.—steadily diminishing to a one-period horizon at stage eight. This is particularly important since there exists fairly convincing evidence that the human decision maker intuitively incorporates much shorter time horizons than "optimal" (Rapoport, 1966; Ebert, 1972a, 1972b). Time horizon is a specific dimension in which "cognitive simplification" occurs. In decision problems similar to our example, human time horizons seem to be effectively limited to about four future decision periods, with even fewer being the norm.

This example provides an explicit illustration of the much-discussed notion of sub-optimal decision making. This can occur if one adopts a strategy of decomposing the problem into a series of independent one-stage decisions, attempting to minimize cost for each decision period. Decisions which minimize cost for each period are larger, in total, than the overall cost for optimal decisions. Cost minimization for each period is equivalent to employing a one-stage decision horizon. The resulting decisions, system states, and costs differ dramatically from optimal. An optimal decision strategy, as shown in Figure 7-4, entails making decisions of relatively large magnitudes initially. These large decision values result in high costs during initial periods, followed by smaller decisions and costs in later stages of the problem. It is necessary to sacrifice costs in the early stages to avoid even greater costs in later stages. A study by Ray (1963) illustrates that this "sacrificing" strategy is not immediately obvious to initially naive decision makers in coping with such a problem. After performing several iterations of the problem, the "intuitive" decision maker tends to make decisions of approximately the same relative magnitudes across all decision stages. Succeeding iterations reveal trial strategies that eventually evolve into "sacrificing" decision patterns.

Our example decision problem, known as the Reader's Control Problem (Thomas, 1962), is one which can be solved by "dynamic programming."[11] This

---

[11]See Bellman (1957).

mathematical optimization technique was used to find the optimal decisions and costs in our illustration. The technique derives its usefulness in the decision setting by overcoming the complexities of structural dynamism with greater facility than human problem solvers under the conditions described above. It is able to simultaneously account for interdependencies among: (a) multistage decisions and system states; and (b) decision variables, status variables, and costs in the criterion function.

Confounding of Structural Dynamism with Other Sources of Complexity

It is well to re-state that most decision problems consist of combinations of multiple sub-problems. Consider, for example, the complexities arising from the introduction of outcome uncertainty into the preceding example. Expression [3], the transformation function, includes a stochastic term, ϵ, to reflect an element of uncertainty in the problem.

$$X_{K+1} = 1.4X_K + 0.1Y_K + \epsilon \qquad [3]$$

Expression [3] indicates that the status of the system *next* period is a function of *this* period's decision and status, as well as a probabilistic element whose precise value is unknown to the decision maker at the time his decision is made. This element represents uncontrollable influences of the environment on the decision outcome. The decision maker is now faced with the task of "accounting for" the effects of this new problem dimension, in addition to handling the complexities encountered in the deterministic problem. Furthermore, the stochastic case can be subdivided into at least two categories depending upon the decision maker's information about characteristics of the stochastic element. The case for which the parameters of the probability distribution of the stochastic element are known can be distinguished from the case in which these parameters are unknown. In the latter, the parameters must be learned as the decision process unfolds (and thus additional stochastic information becomes available). These distinctions are summarized in Table 7-4.

Dynamic programming models have been formulated to provide normative solutions for the classes of multistage problems shown in Table 7-4. What are the relative advantages that such models offer the decision maker? This question has been the basis for several experimental studies of sequential decision making. Results reveal interesting intuitive decision-making characteristics relative to the optimal decision behavior prescribed by appropriate dynamic programming models.

For the *stochastic* case the dynamic programming model closely approximates the median of group decisions. Furthermore, this approximation between optimal and actual median decisions increases with decision-making experience

Table 7-4 Classes of Reader's Control Problem, Reflecting Degrees of Uncertainty

Problem-Class	Degree of Uncertainty
Deterministic	Subjective Certainty (no stochastic elements in the problem)
Stochastic	Subjective Risk (parameters of the distribution of the stochastic element are assumed to be known by the decision maker)
Adaptive	Subjective Uncertainty (parameters of the distribution of the stochastic element are assumed to be unknown by the decision maker. It is assumed that the parameters are determined as the process unfolds.)

(Rapoport, 1966). However, there are large variations in performance levels among individuals. Most individuals tend to undercontrol[12] the system with their initial decisions. This behavior is attributable to the use of a relatively short planning horizon.

Comparing performance under stochastic conditions to the results under deterministic conditions, Rapoport (1966) concluded that decision effectiveness is reduced by about half. This reduction of effectiveness indicates that the introduction of a random variable into an intuitive decision system can be costly relative to the alternative of implementing an appropriate model. Intuitive decisions under adaptive conditions seem to reflect a tendency toward "conservatism" by many decision makers. The extent of their revision of subjective probability distributions was less than the amount prescribed by the Bayesian portion of the adaptive model (Rapoport, 1967).

The complexities of the Reader's Control Problem can be summarized by specifying its primary elements. Optimal *adaptive* behavior in the Reader's Control Problem would require that the decision maker learn:

   a.   the meaning and implications of the quadratic cost function [2],
   b.   the meaning and implications of the linear transformation function [3],
   c.   the meaning of statistical independence between successive random variables,
   d.   the effect of (c) on (a) and (b),
   e.   the interrelationships of the current decision to (a) and (b),
   f.   to revise the parameters of his subjective probability distribution over the random generating process in an optimal manner, and

[12]The magnitude of the decision is less than optimal.

g. to meaningfully integrate (a) through (f) at each stage of the process by considering their implications for all periods into the future.

The previous experimental results indicate that some of these conditions are not met in making intuitive decisions.

Another source of complexity which is often found in dynamic decision problems is the number of decision variables. Our previous examples included only one decision variable. Dynamic programming formulations for problems involving multiple decision variables are extremely complex to develop. Extension of the one-variable cases to two-variable formulations presents great difficulties in developing general quantitative expressions for optimal decisions and cost. These difficulties are immensely increased for problems beyond the two-variable case. Thus, decision makers can expect little assistance from dynamic programming for these decision problems. Such decisions must be handled by judgmental experience with, perhaps, the assistance of selected methods for simplifying various subcomponents of the problem.

Structural Dynamism: Two Variables. One well-known organizational problem involving multiple decision variables is production scheduling. As formulated by Holt, et al. (1960), the scheduling decision variables are: (a) the number of workers to employ during the next time period (month), designated as W_t; and (b) the number of units, P_t, to be produced by the work force during the next time period. The decision maker must select values for each of these variables at each decision stage (i.e., month) in the problem. These decisions partially determine the costs that are incurred each month. The problem is composed of many of the basic elements in the Reader's Control Problem: a series of multistage decisions to be made; a cost function (criterion) to be minimized; and a transformation function providing interstage dependencies. It differs from the Reader's Control Problem in that two decisions (decision variables) must be made at each stage, rather than one. The deterministic formulation of the problem may be used for planning purposes, while a stochastic formulation is applicable to short-run scheduling of organizational manpower and output.

The cost function for the model is optimized by applying the decision rules shown below.[13] These decision rules are presented here in detail because they illustrate how models handle problem complexities.

Expressions [4] and [5] specify the mathematical relationships comprising optimal production and work-force decisions for the next decision period. Of special interest is the number of "cues" or variables that enter into optimal decision determination. Inventory level (I_{t-1}), work-force level (W_{t-1}), and expected demand (S_t, S_{t+1}, ...) are the relevant variables to consider when

[13] For the derivation of these rules see Holt, et al. (1960).

$$P_t = \begin{bmatrix} +0.458\ S_t \\ +0.233\ S_{t+1} \\ \cdot \\ \cdot \\ \cdot \\ -0.005\ S_{t+10} \\ -0.004\ S_{t+11} \end{bmatrix} + 1.005\ W_{t-1} + 153.0 - 0.464\ I_{t-1} \qquad [4]$$

$$W_t = \begin{bmatrix} +0.0101\ S_t \\ +0.0088\ S_{t+1} \\ \cdot \\ \cdot \\ \cdot \\ +0.0005\ S_{t+10} \\ +0.0004\ S_{t+11} \end{bmatrix} + 0.742\ W_{t-1} + 2.00 - 0.010\ I_{t-1} \qquad [5]$$

making scheduling decisions. In particular, the bracketed expressions on the right side of [4] and [5] specify the optimal time horizon; i.e., the number of *future* periods of expected demand that must be considered in making *current* optimal decisions. It should be noted that the relative "weightings" of the various "cues" in the decision rules are a function of the organization's cost structure. Hence, the rules that are appropriate for one organizational environment will have different weightings than the rules for another cost structure. Finally, it is important to note the relative "constancy" of the problem and the solution structure. The same set of cues must be consistently interrelated in a fixed manner, from period to period, for optimal decisions. This structure exemplifies a "programmed decision," to which we have previously referred.

The effectiveness of this model, relative to judgmental decision making, has been demonstrated in both organizational and laboratory environments.[14]

Data Organizing Aids. Uncertainties associated with decision outcomes were previously identified as sources of problem complexity. One's ability to anticipate outcomes and their chances of occurrence are an important part of the decision process. Normative models for resolving these difficulties do not exist. However, some models provide guidelines for organizing available data prior to making a decision. By using these models the decision maker is forced into explicit consideration of potential outcomes and their implications. Thus, by carefully organizing relevant data, previously unconsidered factors may emerge.

[14]For applications in organizations see Holt, *et al.* (1960) and Bowman (1963). For laboratory applications see Ebert (1972b) and Moskowitz (1972).

Decision trees are an example of such models. They graphically portray complex decision problems. As seen in Figure 7-5, the tree structure provides an organized view of principal decision elements, and some of their interrelationships, that otherwise might be mentally prohibitive. Circles denote decision points. Emanating from the circles are branches representing the alternatives. Following each decision are events (squares) which partially determine the possible outcomes for each decision alternative.

Use of the tree diagram is intended to induce the decision maker to: (1) identify decision alternatives and uncontrollable events, (2) assess the completeness of his identification of these elements, (3) identify the *sequence* in which decisions and events are expected to occur, and (4) evaluate eventual outcomes. The decision tree approach requires concise consideration of the implications of current decision stages and events for subsequent decision stages. To some extent, then, this approach also provides some assistance in coping with complexities of structural dynamism.

Project-scheduling techniques such as PERT (Program Evaluation and Review Technique) provide another example of data-organizing techniques. The overall task of planning and scheduling a large project may be envisioned as a set of interrelated sub-decisions. Problem complexity may be reduced and clarified by identifying the major sub-activities, and their sequential relationships, which are required to accomplish the overall project. A simple project network is shown in Figure 7-6.

The nodes at the extremes of each arrow depict the beginning and ending points of an activity. Activities flowing from a node cannot be undertaken until the activities represented by preceding arrows have been completed. For instance, activity 12 cannot be initiated until activities 10 and 11 have been completed. The process of deriving the diagram is perhaps more beneficial and informative to the decision maker than any other aspect of the technique. It requires exhaustive consideration of the activities that must occur and the

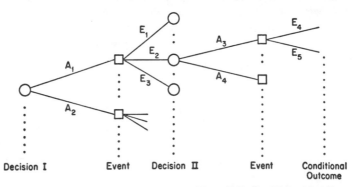

Figure 7-5   Partial Decision Tree

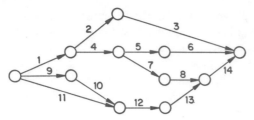

Figure 7-6   PERT Network for a Project Consisting of 14 Activities

precedence relationships that exist among them. It frequently evolves into an iterative process. Inadequacies in initial iterations reveal logical modifications leading to a more accurate representation of the system of activities.

Heuristics. The complexities of many decision problems prohibit their resolution by existing optimization techniques. However, non-optimizing models can be developed to assist. Heuristics is one such class of models. Michael (1972) provides the following definitions:

> Heuristic: As an adjective, heuristic means serving to discover. As a noun, heuristic is an aid to discovery. A heuristic contributes to reduction of search in a problem solving activity. An example of a heuristic is a rule of thumb which aids discovery of a solution.

> Heuristic problem solving: Heuristic problem solving is the taking of a heuristic approach, by using heuristics, in a problem-solving or decision-making situation (p. 75).

Heuristic models can be derived from a careful study of the decision maker's mental processes as he copes with a decision problem. By observation, the modeler extracts key problem elements that are considered by the decision maker and infers key relationships among problem variables. These are then systematically sequenced and interrelated to synthetically replicate the decision maker's thought processes. This approach has been successful in a number of decision contexts.[15] However, a disadvantage of heuristics is the large expenditure of modeling effort required in their development. This is evidenced by the work of Clarkson (1962) and that reported by Kleinmuntz (1968). Nonetheless, these descriptive models often provide the decision maker with valuable information about his own decision processes, as was discussed in Chapter 6.

Although a heuristic model may fail to identify a mathematically optimal solution, it may find a *satisfactory* solution with much less computational effort than is required for optimizing techniques. As stated by Johnson, Newell, and

[15]For a review of applications of heuristic models see Michael (1972).

Vergin (1972), "Heuristic approaches recognize the trade-off between optimal solutions and the cost of problem solving" (p. 149).

Computer Simulation. Computer simulation provides one means for exploring the behavior of various systems. Digital simulation requires the use of logical and mathematical relationships among system subcomponents to represent the system under study. The use of such models has been highly varied and extensive in recent years.[16] Although the output of simulation-modeling efforts has been encouraging, it has been suggested that the very processes of developing such models are equally beneficial (Forrester, 1961). Development of a decision-oriented simulation model requires explicit consideration of all of the sources of problem complexity presented earlier. It further requires an explicit representation of what the decision maker regards as the most important elements (parameters) of the system being studied, as well as the relationships among them. When a model of these initial conceptualizations is constructed and run, the results typically reveal logical misconceptions and omissions. The process of continuously refining the model to obtain representative system performance can sharpen the modeler's beliefs about relevant variables and relationships which should be considered in his decision setting. Simulation affords great flexibility in the use of a variety of complex relationship patterns that is not possible in optimization models. It also permits examination of the effects of "instability" of many parameters on decision outcomes.

SUMMARY

Chapters 5 and 6 identified specific limitations of human information processing and judgmental inference processes. This chapter identified decision-problem characteristics that constitute sources of complexity due to man's limited capacities. Then, we presented a sampling of quantitative techniques, showing how they can supplement specific human limitations. This review has revealed not only man's limitations, but also those of our quantitative technology.

[16]See Naylor, et al. (1966) for a discussion of simulation techniques.

Part Three

Chapter 8

Group Processes

The first part of the book described individual cognitive processes which appear to be most relevant for decision making. However, decisions are only infrequently made in a social vacuum.

> Like the internal elements of the decision itself, the psychological consequences of environmental influences are aspects of the decision process that require study. The environment for a management decision includes the organization structure, the amount and reliability of information that can be communicated by the organization, and the external psychological constraints imposed by traditions, culture and social mores (Fisk, 1967, p. 9)

More specifically, how does the presence of others influence one's decisions? In Table 8-1 we present a variety of possible degrees of influence. On one end of the continuum are situations in which the individual's actions are unobserved and uninfluenced by others. At the other end are situations in which interdependence and coordination are necessary. It is clear that in these latter settings decisions will be partially determined by group contributions.

Table 8-1   Degree of Social Influence on Decisions

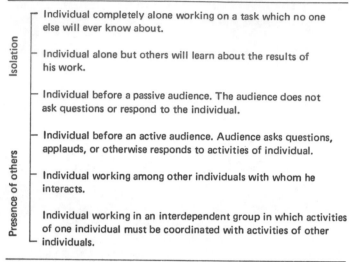

Source: Collins and Guetzkow, 1964.

In terms of the factors that contribute to decisions, we can see how this influence may take place. Recognizing and identifying the occasion for decision may be a result of interpersonal interaction. The search for alternative actions for a decision may involve different people tracing down, evaluating, and reporting suspected consequences. The values attached to any given consequence will be influenced by group contributions. How we feel about these people, the similarity of their goals, and the existing communication patterns will also be important. This chapter is devoted to a discussion of these topics and others, which demonstrate how the individual's decision processes may be modified in a group setting.

GROUPS VS. INDIVIDUALS

The first question is: How do individuals differ in their behavior when they are in a group context, as compared to their behavior alone? To answer this general question we will identify a number of phenomena which have been shown to exist in the group setting, as well as some group variables which potentially effect decision processes. These will be considered under four major topics: social facilitation, group size, brainstorming, and the risky shift.

Social Facilitation

The study of social facilitation concerns the effects of the mere presence of others on individual behavior. The earliest work on this topic was conducted by

Triplett (1897) in his investigation of competitive bicycle racing. He found that competitive races produced better times than paced situations in which the racer had a multicycle in front to set the pace. The times for these paced races were in turn better than those produced by the racer alone. While the "competitive" situation clearly involved more than just the "mere presence" of others, it was the paced vs. non-paced comparison which prompted interest in the area.

Perception and Judgment. The individual's perception and judgment seem to be affected by the presence of other people. Early investigations by Allport (1924) and Farnsworth and Behner (1931) suggest that an individual in the presence of an audience tends to produce more moderate judgments (of weights and odors). Allport suggested that perhaps the individual behaves as if he were reacting *to* the other individuals rather than in their presence. Kelley and Thibaut (1969) suggest that this reaction is an attempt to avoid appearing extreme.

There is also evidence suggesting that the presence of others impacts on attention. An investigation by Begum and Lehr (1963) found that subjects paid greater attention to relevant cues in a monitoring task when they believed they were being observed. The detection rate was 79 percent for the observed individuals as compared to 45 percent for those working alone. Travis (1925) found that eye-hand coordination was better when an audience was present. On the other hand, it is possible that having others around who are either doing the same task, or just observing, may be distracting. Some studies have reported that individuals take longer to respond correctly when they are observed than when they are unobserved (Wapner and Alper, 1952).

Motivation and Response. One way that the presence of others affects behavior is by increasing the individual's level of motivation (Zajonc, 1965). With this increase may come increased activity and a tendency to produce responses which are dominant for that setting. In some cases the dominant responses result in increased performance, while in other cases the responses may inhibit functional effectiveness. Additional research by Zajonc and Sales (1966) supports the idea that our most dominant responses are utilized under increased motivational conditions. Kelley and Thibaut (1969, p. 4) have summarized a variety of findings which relate individual performance to the presence of others:

1. Subjects report that an urge toward greater speed is produced by the activity of others, and they report greater emotional excitement (and distraction) than when alone.
2. Subjects are aroused to activity even after having (in social isolation) reached a point of satiation with it (see Burton, 1941, on children's play activity, and studies on animal eating behavior summarized by Zajonc, 1965).

3. The largest performance gains occur for individuals who give evidence of having least interest in the task itself (those with the lowest solo performance on tasks where performance seems to be a function primarily of how hard the person tries).

4. Intraindividual (time-to-time) variability is higher under social conditions (Allee and Masure, 1936; Allport, 1924; Mukerji, 1940). This would be expected if it is assumed that the heightened motivation carries the person to a performance level where the counterforces (from fatigue, skill limitations, efforts, etc.) are very high. The high level of tension resulting from the conflict between the two sets of pressures would create high susceptibility to severe, though momentary, disruptions and would be manifested in large variations in performance.

In summary, the individual working in the physical proximity of others is influenced by their presence. His motivation appears higher and more dominant responses may be expected to appear. The appropriateness of these responses is dependent on both his past experience and present situational demands. His attention may be heightened, but so may the tendency for distraction. Activity is increased, but its effect is moderated by some other issues that will be discussed later.

Group Size

Two major issues revolve around the research on group size. One concern is whether groups behave differently than individuals, and more specifically, whether they perform better than individuals. The second issue is the degree of change associated with different group sizes. We will review the research in both areas with an emphasis on their relevance to decision-related activities, such as judgment and communication.

One vs. Many. We can compare groups to individuals in terms of judgment, problem-solving performance, and learning—all of which have direct relevance for decision making. Two different techniques have been used to compare the judgments of groups and individuals. First, one can simply average the estimates made by a number of people working independently and compare the average to individual judgments (Lorge, Fox, Davitz, and Brenner, 1958). Studies of this type have investigated judgments of temperature (Knight, 1921) and weights (Gordon, 1924). Note, however, that these results are statistical rather than social-psychological. The increased accuracy is a function of a greater number of observations and the skewness of the distribution of individual responses, not of the group process itself. Other findings show, on the other hand, that group judgments are better than the average individual judgment (Gurnee, 1937). A summary of this research by Shaw (1971) states:

In general, it appears that group judgments are seldom less accurate than the average individual judgment and are often superior. This can be accounted for by the number of judgments contributing to the estimate (Stroop, 1932), by the range of knowledge represented by the individual group members (Jenness, 1932), and by the effects of others on the less confident group members (Gurnee, 1937). It is also apparent that the kind of task may determine whether group judgment will be superior to individual judgments (p. 62).

We will return to the effect of the task in the following section on different group sizes.

The research on problem solving produces somewhat similar findings. Most studies compare the performances of individuals working alone (averaged) with the performance of the same people working together in a group, or with a group of different people of the same size. Performance measures include time to complete the task, the amount produced, or the quality of the solution. The tasks have included investigations on word construction (Watson, 1928), puzzles (Shaw, 1932), code deciphering (Husband, 1940), complex intellectual problems (Barnlund, 1959), and "twenty question" type parlor games (Taylor and Faust, 1952). Again, the overall evidence seems to support the contention that groups do somewhat better than individuals. Certain qualifications, however, should be discussed. First, in many cases groups were slower in their solution times. Since both problem-oriented and social-oriented behaviors occur in the group setting, it is understandable that the solution would take longer to reach. Similarly, more man hours are invested by groups. Also, on some tasks, groups were found to perform less well than the *most competent* individual performing by himself.

Finally, the studies on group versus individual *learning* present comparable findings. Studies of the learning of nonsense syllables (Perlmutter and de Montmollin, 1952), matching behavior (Beaty and Shaw, 1965), and prose (Yuker, 1955) again show that groups learn faster than individuals, both in natural and laboratory situations.

How can we explain these findings? A number of suggestions have been made and empirical support seems to exist for most of them. First, it appears as if groups can reject or correct individual contributions that are wrong. Second, there is a greater amount of total information available to the group. Third, the presence of others arouses motivation to do well; and fourth, the ablest group member frequently has high influence. The degree to which these factors contribute to effective judgment, communication, and decisions partially depends upon the specific size of the group, as well as the task it is trying to solve.

Different Group Sizes. When we move from the individual working alone to groups of different sizes, numerous variables begin to change. One can see, for example, that as size increases so does the number of possible relationships that

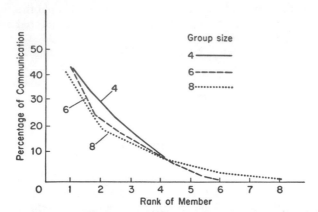

Figure 8-1 The amount of communication by members of a group follows a logarithmic or exponential curve. Regardless of the size of the group, the most talkative member does about forty percent of the communicating and the amount of the other members' communication drops off sharply. The difference between the amount of communication of the first and second most talkative people increases as the size of the group increases. (*Source:* Freedman, Carlsmith, and Sears, 1969.)

may exist among group members. The increased number of relationships bears directly on their content and quality. For example, one variable related to group size is talking time. As the number of members increases, the average time that each member can talk decreases. One has less time to say what is on his mind.

Secondly, the cohesiveness of the group begins to diminish past a certain size. Hare (1962) found, for example, that subgroups begin to form when group size increases past five or six members. It is just too difficult for one to maintain close interaction with all the participants. The tendency becomes one of categorizing people and then attending to their "spokesman" or "representative."

Since the number of potential relationships becomes more complex in larger groups, there is an increased reliance upon a leader (Hemphill, 1950). Studies by Bales and Borgatta (1955) and Carter (1951) show that more forceful and influential members increase their activity in larger groups. Most studies of group behavior show that one member usually speaks around 30 to 40 percent of the time, with the rest of the time distributed among other members. Figure 8-1 shows the results of research by Stephan and Mishler (1952).

Another important phenomenon is that the content of the communication changes with different size groups. It appears as if the intimacy and warmth of interpersonal communication decreases with size (Coyle, 1930; Kinney, 1953). Apparently, as people feel less able to contribute, they also become more impersonal. This may be due, in part, to greater competition for talking time and a greater number of potential criticisms.

These size changes result in changes in the type of communication. Research shows that people appear to be more direct and give more information with increases in group size from two up to seven. There is less showing of agreement and less asking for opinion. In general, a more impersonal, task-oriented process seems to emerge (Bales and Borgatta, 1955) in the larger groups.

Specific Size Characteristics.   Three variables greatly influence the climate in groups of varying size: emotional or psychological comfort; physical freedom; and the requirements of a group decision. As one would expect, in groups with an even number of members (two, four, six, etc.), it becomes more difficult to reach a majority consensus. Empirical studies show there are higher rates of disagreement and antagonism in these groups, as compared to groups with an odd number of members. These effects are less pronounced as the group size increases.

In the dyad we not only need 100 percent agreement to reach a decision, but there are also pressures to please the other person so that the group does not disband. Psychological comfort is at a low point and is indicated by relatively high rates of tension and anxiety.

On the other hand, groups of seven or larger, while psychologically liberating, are physically restrictive for reasons mentioned earlier (talking time, number of relationships). Several studies have now shown that groups of five may produce the greatest satisfaction and performance on various discussion-type tasks (Slater, 1959). Apparently, people feel both psychologically and physically comfortable in a group of five for the types of tasks that were studied.

Task Type and Group Size.   We indicated earlier that the kinds of behavior expected in groups depend on the task. Fortunately, some work has been done to clarify relationships between task type, group size, and productivity. An excellent paper by Steiner and Rajaratnam (1961) describes four types of tasks and suggests the following equation:

Actual Productivity = Potential Productivity − (Coordination and Motivation Decrements)

Potential productivity represents some measure of the aggregate of skills available in the group while coordination and motivation decrements indicate problems that increase with group size. On tasks in which each new member can produce the same additional amount as other members (certain piece-rate systems might be appropriate), we find that performance increases with additional personnel up to the point at which motivation and communication problems begin to offset the additional gain. Graphically, we would expect a relationship of the form shown in Figure 8-2(a). In situations in which the "best member" could solve the problem, we find a somewhat different relationship. Here, increases in size increase the probability of obtaining a highly competent member who can solve the problem. However, after a certain point, increases in group size become less important simply because there is already someone who can do the job adequately. Thus, potential productivity of the group levels off, as shown in Figure 8-2(b).

On some tasks we find that the group's performance is only as good as the "weakest link." Clearly, by adding more people we are decreasing the chances for good performance. Finally, certain tasks require complimentary contributions of members for successful completion. These tasks are similar to the discussion-type tasks described earlier. Because of the psychological and physical forces at work, we would expect a curvilinear relationship between size and actual productivity.

A study by Frank and Anderson (1971) tested the predictions of the best member and worst-member tasks on 288 subjects in groups of two, three, five, and eight. They used both production- and discussion-type tasks and the results support the prediction for both satisfaction and performance.

Shull, Delbecq, and Cummings (1970, p. 148) summarize the benefits and drawbacks of increases in group size:

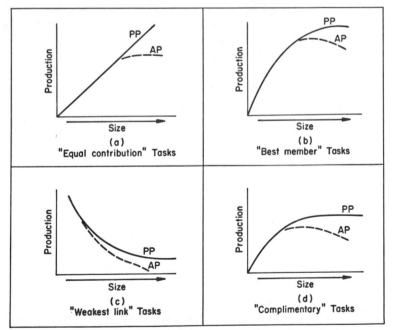

Figure 8-2 Relationships of Task Type, Group Size, and Productivity. Adapted from Steiner and Rajaratnam, 1961.

1. Benefits resulting from summated resources:
   a. An increase in technical skills,
   b. An increase in energy.
2. Benefits derived from increased cognitive resources for problem solving:
   a. An increase in the number of items of information that can be absorbed and recalled,
   b. An increase in the number of critical judgments available to correct errors in inference and analysis,
   c. An increase in the number of suggested solution strategies,
   d. An increase in the range of values brought to bear on the problem, and
   e. An increase in psychological attention due to social facilitation.
3. Benefits resulting from organizational surplus:
   a. An increase in group size may allow for division of labor and specialization.

However, these potential benefits may be mitigated by diminishing returns due to:

1. Increased problems of coordination;
2. Increased feelings of threat, or inhibition of impulses to participate, due to the larger size group and the increased complexity of relationships;
3. Distraction from attention to problem solving, due to attention toward social-emotional relationships; and
4. Increased problems in reaching consensus.

In addition to the effects of group size, we have thus far seen that being in a group influences motivation, the type and amount of information that is generated, the way it is learned and processed, and the value placed on that information. We would expect, in terms of our earlier analysis, that routine decisions made at low levels of the organization will be influenced less by group activity than decisions that are more complex and require interpersonal interaction.

Brainstorming

Another issue with direct and practical relevance for decision makers is the concept of brainstorming. The decision-making process includes phases of problem identification, generation of decision alternatives, and generation of alternative ways to implement decisions. Clearly, the quality of decisions is directly related to the usefulness and ingenuity of ideas that evolve in these phases of the decision process. We have mentioned that group conditions offer the potential for generating more ideas than the individual alone can generate. Clearly, there are greater resources in the group. But a somewhat different question is whether a group can generate more and better ideas than can the same number of individuals acting alone. We have already mentioned that not everyone in the group is heard and that certain people often dominate the discussion. Also, Hoffman and Maier (1964) have found a tendency for group members to evaluate suggestions as they appear, and this process may inhibit a free flow of suggestions. Groups may settle for a solution too early in the life of the problem-solving process. It was Osborn (1953) who first suggested some techniques for facilitating the generation of ideas in a group. The general procedure for a brainstorming group is to consider some problems, such as a brand name for a new product, under the following conditions: (1) ideas are generated without reference to quality, (2) evaluation of ideas takes place only after all the ideas have been produced, and (3) people are encouraged to elaborate on the ideas of others. Under these conditions, it was hoped that more new and creative ideas could be elicited. Not only would the group have access to all the individual ideas that might be thought of alone, but they would also have ideas that were triggered off by other group members, ideas that an individual might not have thought of alone.

Research on this issue at first seemed supportive. Meadow, Parnes, and Reese (1959) found that a greater number of ideas (e.g., uses for a broom) were produced by individuals working under brainstorming instructions than under nonbrainstorming instructions. Cohen, Whitmyre, and Funk (1960) found that pairs of individuals who had undergone training in creative thinking and cohesive pairs who had chosen to work with one another were more effective under brainstorming conditions than two individuals working alone. However, studies of which groups and individuals working alone under brainstorming instructions found little difference between the different conditions. A study by Taylor, Berry, and Block (1958) compared twelve four-person brainstorming groups with twelve four-person nominal groups (sum of individual responses with overlap omitted) on three separate tasks. The nominal groups produced more solutions on all three tasks. An investigation by Dunnette, Campbell, and Jaasted (1963) produced similar findings. Using the same design as Taylor *et al.* (1958), they again found that nominal groups produced more. Group interaction seemed to have an inhibiting influence on idea generation. Further, it was found that group interaction preceding individual brainstorming resulted in greater individual performance.

Finally, a recent study (Bouchard and Hare, 1970) casts further doubt on the hypothesis that group brainstorming is better than *individual brainstorming.* They suggested that larger groups (all the previous experiments used groups of four) might be more apt to show that group brainstorming was most effective. Both nominal and real groups of one, four, five, seven, and nine were tested and both the individuals and groups were given brainstorming instructions. The results of this study are shown in Figure 8-3. It is clear from these results that

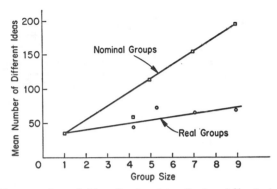

Figure 8-3 Mean number of Ideas Produced by Real and Nominal Groups for Groups of One, Four, Five, Seven, and Nine. (*Source:* Bouchard and Hare, 1970.)

brainstorming was not effective in these situations. However, two qualifications are necessary. First, all groups worked the same amount of time. We have mentioned the fact that groups take a somewhat longer time to solve their problems than do individuals. It is possible that brainstorming also necessitates a longer period to obtain its maximum effectiveness. Bouchard and Hare argue that while this is possible, they feel it is an unlikely explanation of their results. They suggest that certain members tended to monopolize the group process and, consequently, limited idea generation. We earlier pointed out this characteristic of the group process. Perhaps a modification of the brainstorming procedure to correct for this problem might produce better results.

In summary, it appears that brainstorming instructions increase the output of both groups and individuals working alone. It does not appear, however, that brainstorming increases the group output over and above what individuals could generate alone, working under similar conditions.

Risky Shift

One facet of choice behavior that is affected by the group setting is the individual's propensity for risk. A large volume of research has resulted in a "risky shift" hypothesis which suggests that an individual, confronted with a specific problem, will make a more risky decision after participating in a group discussion than he will make alone. If true, this phenomenon would have a significant impact on organizational decision-making behavior.

The research by Kogan and Wallach (1964), discussed earlier, suggests that certain individuals tend to be riskier than others. A student of Wallach's pushed the research even further by suggesting that participation in a group discussion resulted in riskier individual choices (Stoner, 1961). He asked a number of

Table 8-2 Sample Item from Risky Shift Questionnaire

1. Mr. A, an electrical engineer, who is married and has one child
    has been working for a large electronics corporation since grad-
    uating from college 5 years ago. He is assured of a life-time
    job with a modest, though adequate, salary, and liberal pension
    benefits upon retirement. On the other hand, it is very unlikely
    that his salary will increase much before he retires. While
    attending a convention, Mr. A is offered a job with a small,
    newly founded company which has a highly uncertain future. The
    new job would pay more to start and would offer the possibility
    of a share in the ownership if the company survived the compe-
    tition of the larger firms.

    Imagine that you are advising Mr. A. Listed below are several
    probabilities or odds of the new company's proving financially
    sound.

    PLEASE CHECK THE LOWEST PROBABILITY THAT YOU WOULD
    CONSIDER ACCEPTABLE TO MAKE IT WORTHWHILE FOR MR. A
    TO TAKE THE NEW JOB.

    The chances are 1 in 10 that the company will prove
    ___ financially sound.

    The chances are 3 in 10 that the company will prove
    ___ financially sound.

    The chances are 5 in 10 that the company will prove
    ___ financially sound.

    The chances are 7 in 10 that the company will prove
    ___ financially sound.

    The chances are 9 in 10 that the company will prove
    ___ financially sound.

    Place a check here if you think Mr. A should *not* take
    ___ the new job no matter what the probabilities.

Source: Mandler, Mussen, Kogan, and Wallach, 1964.

students in industrial management assembled in small groups to make private
decisions about each of a set of twelve "life dilemma" problems (items). An
example of the first item is shown in Table 8-2. After expressing their initial
judgments, the subjects were grouped together to discuss the problem. When the
group activity was completed, it was found that the group had agreed on choices
having a level of risk substantially greater than the average level of individual
pre-discussion judgments.

At first, it was thought the results could be attributed to some particular characteristics of the subjects or of the setting. But replications by Wallach, Kogan, and Bem (1962) and by others have successfully reproduced the phenomena. Different types of tasks and different subjects have reproduced the results many times, and in some cases it was possible to produce cautious shifts. Lab and field studies also show support (Siegel and Zajonc, 1969) for the idea that group interaction produces shifts in judgments.

Recently, there have been several major reviews of theories purporting to explain group shifts (Dion, Baron, and Miller, 1970; MacKenzie, 1971; Clark, 1971; Vinokur, 1971; Pruitt, 1971). While it is impossible to cover all of the findings here, we will discuss the major approaches and their general empirical support.

First, it is important to list the findings.

1. Groups and individuals make riskier choices after they have participated in a group discussion and reached consensus.
    a. Groups are riskier, even when the group does not reach consensus.
    b. People make riskier judgments after observing a group discussion on the issue.
    c. These findings cannot be attributed simply to "familiarization" with the materials.
    d. The findings cannot be attributed to past discussions of just any topic. When irrelevant topics are used, no shift occurs.
2. Different items (in the Kogan and Wallach problem set) produce different types of shifts. In some cases choice dilemmas produce cautious shifts (Stoner, 1968).
    a. Those items with risky initial averages tend to produce risky shifts, while those with initial cautious averages produce cautious shifts.
    b. Participants tend to favorably evaluate people who take greater risks on the risky items.

Over the last ten years numerous explanations have been suggested for the group shifts. In recent reviews, many of these theories have been partially or completely rejected (Pruitt, 1971) because of a lack of empirical validation. Those theories which seem most prevalent are listed below.

1. *Leadership theory.* This theory suggests that the more confident members assume a leadership role within the group. Their confidence and assertiveness are assumed to cause the shifts, whether risky or cautious. This would mean, of course, that confidence was related to extreme judgments (either risky or cautious). There is some evidence for this approach (Burnstein, 1969; Castore, Peterson, and Goodrich, 1971), but also some problems. One study found that the shifts occur even when group members cannot observe one another (Teger and Pruitt, 1967). So, while leadership may be a partial cause, it is probably not the complete explanation.

2. *Relevant Arguments Theory.* There is considerable evidence that on risky items there are more relevant arguments brought out by the group in favor of risk. On cautious items, a greater number of cautious arguments are generated (St. Jean, 1970; Clark, Crockett, and Archer, 1971; Silverthorne, 1971). In fact, the Silverthorne study found the ratio of risky- to cautious-arguments to be 12.5 to 1 in the discussion of items that shifted toward risk. The proportion was 6 to 1 for cautious arguments on items producing a cautious shift. This research suggests that it is the content of the group process which creates the shift, rather than the idea that riskiness is valued, or that one feels less responsible and is therefore more risky in a group.

3. *Utility Decision Theory.* Returning to our earlier position that the final choice or judgment is based on which alternative is seen as leading to the most valued outcomes (probability X utility), we find that risky shifts can be explained in the same manner (Vinokur, 1971; Burnstein, Miller, Vinokur, Katz, and Crowley, 1971). These studies show that group discussion changes the overall value (or utility) of the outcomes and, therefore, the shift really reflects a revision of the estimates of the best alternative.

All of these approaches suggest there is something about the content of the group process which changes individual behavior. Recent empirical findings are supportive of these ideas (Johnson and Davis, 1972; Roberts and Castore, 1972). For the decision maker, the type of information, its frequency, and its value are all modified by the group context. Besides the information he receives from external sources, we find that the individual is himself changed by the social condition. He is more motivated and attentive to the surrounding environment.

GROUP PROCESS

We have documented in some detail that individuals behave differently when they are in groups than when they are alone. The next step is to investigate how various characteristics of groups influence some major dimensions of decision making.

The individual decision maker needs information about the probabilities of certain consequences of his decisions. He must generate alternative actions. Consequences must be evaluated. For a good decision, "the things about which a person needs to know include not only the task and task states, but also his own responses and, of course, the response-state payoff contingencies. To solve a problem, he must know what state prevails at a given time, what his possible responses are, and what their effects are under different conditions. These are all facts, relevant to his success, and about which he strives to have a veridical view" (Kelley and Thibaut, 1969, p. 7). All of these aspects of the decision-making process may require interpersonal interaction and will, therefore, be influenced by certain group processes. Extracting from the many aspects of group processes, the rest of this chapter will be devoted to the following three topics:

1. *Personality Characteristics of the Individuals Participating in the Group Activity.* One of the most thoroughly researched variables in this area is that of cognitive complexity, and it is on this variable that our discussion will focus.
2. *Group Dynamics.* Here we will be concerned with how the homogeneity, cohesiveness, and cooperation dimensions affect the amount and kind of information exchanged in small groups.
3. *Communication Structure.* Finally, we will review some concepts of group structure and communication networks.

It is clear that there are numerous other components of the group process which influence decision making. We have tried, however, to cover only those topics which we believe have the greatest relevance to organizational decisions, and for which there is substantial empirical support.

Complexity Theory

In our earlier discussion of personality characteristics, we cited literature which indicated that an individual's cognitive complexity is related to information search, information processing, and performance. To briefly review, information can be considered as "anything that alters subjective (or objective) probabilities or utilities. Thus in this discussion, any environmental change which could cause a shift in expectations or evaluations will be termed information" (Driver and Streufert, 1969, p. 272). The research in this area has also been concerned with the interaction between the environment (e.g., amount, content, and complexity of information) and the complexity of the *group*. More specifically, do groups of complex individuals search for, process, and utilize information in systematically different ways than groups composed of individuals with simple cognitive structures?

A relatively recent article by Driver and Streufert (1969) reviews much of the research in this area. Figure 8-4 presents their model of integrative complexity.

There are a number of components of the model that warrant elaboration. First, overall environmental complexity is composed of three factors: (1) the rate of information input or information load, (2) the eucity or proportion of success content of the information, and (3) the noxity or proportion of failure content of the information. Second, the systems which process the information can be described in terms of: (1) the number of parts composing the system (e.g., ideas, roles, etc.), which is called *differentiation;* and (2) the degree of interconnection among these parts, called *integrative complexity.*

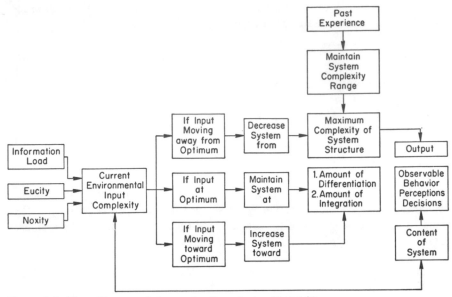

Figure 8-4 Flow Diagram of Integrative Complexity Model (*Source:* Driver and Streufert, 1969.)

Two other points need to be made before the results supporting the model are summarized. First, the model predicts that each of the three environmental input items is curvilinearly related to the performance of the system. Second, relationships are moderated by whether or not the groups are composed of complex or simple individuals. Figure 8-5 shows these relationships. In summary then, "a high degree of integrative complexity in a system implies that outputs such as decisions, verbalized perceptions, or performance will reflect extensive prior use of information and that therefore these outputs will be characterized by a high degree of relatedness among parts. Integrative complexity of output is often what is meant by the quality of the output" (Driver and Streufert, p. 274).

Empirical Findings. The results from numerous empirical investigations appear to support many of the predictions suggested by the model. First, there seems to be support for the idea that information load is curvilinearly related to *perceptual complexity,* and that complex groups do better than simple ones. A study by Streufert and Driver (1965) used a tactical war game involving two teams in a military negotiation. Half of the groups were composed of complex individuals and half of simple individuals. After the task, each team made perceptual judgments of the other team, and these judgments were rated for their complexity. Some components of these ratings were empathy, cause-effect patterns, three- (or more) step inferences, and imputation of intentions to others (see Schroder, Driver, and Streufert, 1967). As expected, both complex and simple groups showed curvilinear relationships with information load. However, at every comparable load position, the high complexity groups showed greater perceptual integration than did the low complexity groups. Eucity and noxity were held constant. In other investigations by Driver (1962, 1965, 1969), noxity or eucity has been varied and input load held constant. The task employed was Guetzkow's Internation Simulation (Guetzkow, Alger, Brody, Noel, and Snyder, 1963). Again, perceptions of the other team showed a curvilinear pattern between average perceptual complexity and noxity level. Also, the perceptions of the more complex subjects were more complex at all levels of input, except the most extreme. These findings support the idea that the perceptual complexity of the group is dependent on both the complexity of the environment and the complexity of the cognitive structures of the group participants. Since almost all later stages of the decision-making process are dependent upon the information perceived, these data are extremely important.

A second area of complexity research deals with information search. Driver and Streufert identify two types of search, the first being a simple request for more information. In the second and more complex strategy, the individual manipulates the environment to generate information. One study by Streufert and Driver (1965) used a tactical game in which groups representing different countries were involved in military, economic, intelligence, and negotiation decisions vis-a-vis other countries. Again, teams were composed of individuals with either complex or simple cognitive structures. Information load was varied systematically, and the results indicate a general decrease in search from very

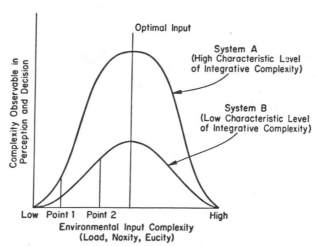

Figure 8-5 Information-Processing Systems with Low and High Levels of Integrative Complexity. (*Source:* Driver and Streufert, 1969.)

high to moderately high levels as load is increased. Complex players consistently use more complex search procedures (initiating reconnaissance-type missions) than non-complex players, especially at high input loads. A study by Driver (1966), with a simulated stock market, also showed that teams of simple subjects use and prefer simpler input sources.

A more recent investigation by Streufert and Castore (1971) varied information noxity for complex and non-complex groups working on the Tactical and Negotiations Game. Although no differences were found between complex and simple groups on self-initiated search, it was found that complex groups delegated less search and utilized information more efficiently than did simple groups across varying levels of noxity. The relationship between noxity level and information utilization and efficiency were also curvilinear, as predicted.

A third set of findings is related to the amount and type of communication that takes place in complex groups as compared to simple groups. In the study by Schroder, *et al.* (1967), cited earlier, it was found that greater numbers of communications (e.g., press releases) were sent out by complex groups than by simple ones, regardless of differences in input conditions. Also, in the study using Guetzkow's Internation Simulation, it was found that in most conditions complex groups engaged in more trade relations outside their natural alliance "blocs" than did less complex groups. These studies indicate that complex groups perceive, search for, and communicate more information than do simple groups. Studies by Streufert and Driver (1965) and Streufert, Suedfeld, and Driver (1965) also show that complex systems utilize this information in a more integrative fashion than do simple ones.

Implications for Decision Making. Two major generalizations seem appropriate. First, individuals should be placed in jobs which provide a match between their cognitive structure and the complexity of the environment. This requires measurement of both characteristics, and it requires that performance measures reflect dimensions of perceptual search or utilization complexity. Clearly, for jobs in which complexity is irrelevant, it would be a waste of time and other resources to attempt optimal matches. The second generalization is that input loads should be regulated according to the complexity of group members. In almost all investigations, perception, search, and communication were optimal under moderate input levels.

Group Dynamics

While the term "group dynamics" has been widely used in a variety of ways, we will use it to represent certain group processes which are related to some facets of decision making in group settings. More specifically, we are interested in the degree to which group heterogeneity, cohesiveness, and cooperation influence preception, information search and evaluation, communication, and performance.

Homogeneity/Heterogeneity. If we assume that the quality of a decision may depend upon various amounts of different skills from group members, then the homogeneity or heterogeneity of the group becomes important. The research in this area has generally followed one of two strategies. First, groups have been compared as to their homogeneity on one trait, such as sex or ability. The second strategy attempts to look at overall similarities (or profiles) of group members along several dimensions, and to observe the accompanying affects on group process.

Homogeneity of ability and sex are the two major traits that have been empirically researched. Studies by Goldman (1965) and Laughlin, Branch, and Johnson (1969) investigated the performance of teams that were homogeneous/ heterogeneous with respect to intelligence. Both studies report that heterogeneous groups composed of high, moderate, and low intelligence individuals did better on an intelligence-test task than homogeneous groups of either moderate or low intelligence.

Groups of mixed sex composition, compared to all male or female groups, have been shown to devote more of their time to social-emotional activities. Studies by Reitan and Shaw (1964) and Luchins and Luchins (1955) seem to support these findings. The usefulness of these findings is, of course, dependent upon the type of task involved. A job requiring more social-emotional activity would seem to be best suited to a mixed sex group.

The profile approach generally attempts to look at the similarity of personality profiles for a group. Studies by Hoffman (1959) and Hoffman and Maier (1961), for example, showed that heterogeneous groups (composed of people having different profiles on the Guilford-Zimmerman Temperament Survey) performed better on a number of different tasks requiring problem solving in which there were conflicts in values and personal conflicts. Also, a study by Triandis, Hall, and Ewen (1965) compared groups composed of people with similar attitudes about a large set of issues with groups of people having dissimilar attitudes. Groups with heterogeneous attitudes, but similar abilities, produced the most creative solutions. A study by Ghiselli and Lodahl (1958), with heterogeneous decision-making approaches of managers, found similar results. Shaw summarizes this literature by saying that "groups that are heterogeneous in terms of personality profile usually perform more effectively than groups that are homogeneous in this respect" (Shaw, 1971, pp. 227–28).

Before leaving this topic, some important qualifications should be made. Clearly, by having different types of people we increase the pool of potential information and skills available to the group. However, there are two major conditions under which this might not be helpful to the decision maker. First, under some circumstances a task may not require dissimilar skills and may, in fact, depend upon a unanimity of input and opinion. Secondly, while a group of different types of people may provide diversity of information, it may also have some disruptive consequences. In heterogeneous groups, people are less likely to be attracted to one another, less likely to be influenced by one another, and more conflict is likely to result. The group decision will probably take a longer time to reach. Again, one must attempt to match the decision demands with the types of people involved.

Cohesiveness.   A special case of homogeneity is the degree to which people are interpersonally attracted to one another. Although a variety of variables are known to increase attraction (see Lott and Lott, 1965), perhaps the most powerful dimension is similarity. Measures of similarity of attitudes (Newcomb, 1956; Byrne, 1961), personality (Griffitt, 1966; Izard, 1960a, 1960b), economic similarity (Byrne, Clore, and Worchel, 1966), and race (Smith, Williams, and Willis, 1967) have all been positively related to interpersonal attraction.

But what does cohesiveness gain for the group that would be important for decision making? One set of investigations has demonstrated that increased cohesiveness leads to more communication among group members. A study by Lott and Lott (1961), with dyads that differed in cohesiveness, found the correlation between communication and attraction was .42. A study by Moran (1966), with 233 dyads obtained from nine Dutch industrial training groups, also found greater communication in cohesive dyads. French (1941) investigated the quality of communication in cohesive groups and found them to be better. Finally, a study by Shaw and Shaw (1962) found that high cohesive groups were more friendly and cooperative, and that the members praised one another for their accomplishments. The reverse was found in low cohesive groups. So, in summary, cohesive groups have a greater quantity and quality of interaction, and they appear to be more friendly and cooperative.

Cohesiveness also appears to be related to other processes which may be peripherally related to decision making. Numerous studies show that cohesive groups have greater social influence over their members than do non-cohesive groups (French, 1941; Festinger, Schachter, and Back, 1950; Back, 1951; Schachter, Ellertson, McBride, and Gregory, 1951; Lott and Lott, 1961). It makes sense that the more attracted we are to the group and its members, the more likely we are to be influenced by group opinion. There are also investigations showing that cohesiveness is positively related to satisfaction on the job. Marquis, Guetzkow, and Heyns (1951) found in an investigation of seventy-two decision-making conferences in business and government that cohesiveness was positively related to members' satisfaction with the group and the meeting.

Research by Gross (1954), Exline (1957), and Van Zelst (1952) also reports similar results.

One should again be cautious in generalizing these results. Groups of similar individuals are more likely to communicate, be able to sway one another, and be satisfied. They may be less likely to produce a wide variety of alternatives or to be highly productive. If the decision maker is in need of integrative, agreed-upon strategies, then cohesive groups composed of similar people are appropriate. If diversity of opinion, and perhaps conflict, are needed to generate information, then a heterogeneous, non-cohesive group will be appropriate.

Cooperation-Competition.   One of the earliest investigations of cooperation and competition was conducted by Deutsch (1949). He saw a cooperative social situation as one in which the group members had similar interdependent goals. That is, the members wanted the same things and needed one another to obtain them. In a now classic study he found that cooperative groups showed greater coordination, greater acceptance of others' comments, had fewer communication difficulties, had more agreement with the ideas and suggestions of others, and had greater productivity. So, along with similarity of traits or liking, it seemed as if goal similarity also led to greater levels of communication, and more acceptance and efficient utilization of the information transmitted.

Later findings, however, were not so conclusive, as was pointed out in a summary by Miller and Hamblin (1963). In reviewing twenty-four studies on the topic, they found that fourteen pieces of research supported the contention that competitive groups were more productive, while ten studies found the reverse. In rethinking the concepts of cooperation and competition, these authors suggested that the two concepts are not pure types at opposite ends of a single dimension. They pointed out that these concepts could be more usefully broken down on two dimensions rather than one, and the dimensions they suggested were: (1) interdependence, and (2) differential reward. By interdependence is meant the degree to which the group members need each other to complete the task. Differential reward is the degree to which individual effort receives compensation. A high differential reward situation would be one in which, perhaps, the most efficient member receives twice as much as the least effective member from a somewhat fixed amount of resources. A low differential reward situation would be one in which everyone in the group receives the same compensation. Dividing these variables into highs and lows, one can produce a two-by-two table with four possible situations (Table 8-3).

Miller and Hamblin believe that productivity would be lower in situations 1 and 4 than in 2 and 3. In situation 1, people are highly dependent on each other, and yet to the extent that one person does well, another group member stands to lose. In situation 4, group members do not need one another to complete the job,

Table 8-3   Interdependence and Differential Reward

		INTERDEPENDENCE	
		High	Low
DIFFERENTIAL	High	1	3
REWARD	Low	2	4

yet everyone receives the same compensation. In both cases, there appears to be a mismatch between how success is achieved and how the rewards are distributed. Situations 2 and 3, on the other hand, show a consistent relationship between effort and reward. In situation 2, in which everyone is highly interdependent, rewards are distributed equally. In situation 3, in which people work independently, rewards are based upon one's individual contribution.

This theoretical conceptualization was tested by Miller and Hamblin and was generally supported. Also, in re-analyzing the twenty-four studies on the topic, they found that the results of twenty-three of them could be predicted from their formulation.

So, given that we are interdependent and have low differential reward, what sorts of communication patterns exist? A study by Ilgen and O'Brien (1968) shows that collaborative (interdependent) groups have greater amounts of communication. Two other investigations support the idea that interdependence is related to decision quality and communication. Bower (1965), for example, studied three-man financial committees making decisions about an investment project in terms of return on equity, sales, and variability of return. It was found that teams with similar goals gave better decisions, especially when they had to share information. The author concludes that conflict may "motivate superior search and analysis and obstruct group choice procedures" (p. 387). Finally, a study by Raven and Shaw (1970) indicated that on a cooperative task the greater the dependency on another group member, the greater the communication.

Two investigations have shown that when rewards are being shared, greater communication exists than when there is competition for rewards (a condition of low differential reward). Crawford and Haaland (1972) found that subjects working cooperatively on a probability learning task sought more information and communicated more than under competitive conditions. Tesser and Rosen (1972) investigated the reluctance to transmit negative information under different conditions of fate-similarity. These authors found that when individuals differ in terms of their fate, they are less likely to communicate bad news than they are if their fates are similar. They attribute these findings to guilt feelings on the part of the participants. So, not only the amount but also the type of information exchanged is influenced by interdependence and differential reward.

In considering the available empirical findings, it appears as if the following generalizations are appropriate:

1. Heterogeneous groups produce more ideas and, under certain conditions, are more productive.

2. Similarity of person characteristics leads to greater cohesiveness and attraction.

3. Cohesiveness is positively related to the amount of communication, social influence, and satisfaction.

4. Cooperative groups have greater within-group communication and are more likely to produce open and agreeable interaction processes.

There seems then to be an important trade-off. On one hand, similar people with similar goals may be more communicative and harmonious. However, where either numerous, unique, or contrary positions are needed, a heterogeneous collection of people may be advantageous. Since selection and assignment of personnel and task demands are all partially controlled by the organization, it becomes a matter of fitting the group to the task, a difficult but not impossible endeavor.

Communication Structure

The closing section of this chapter is concerned with the physical and communication structures that exist in an organization setting. Do these structures lead to more frequent or higher quality decisions? Do they enhance productivity or the morale of decision-making groups?

Physical Space. There is available a body of research which shows that how people are physically arranged in a setting is significantly related to their interaction patterns. Festinger, Schachter, and Back (1950) found that couples living next door to one another in university housing units were more likely to communicate with one another and to become friends than were those who live farther apart. These findings have been replicated by Buehler (1955) with college classes, and by Sommer (1959) with people in a cafeteria.

More interesting than the idea that proximity increases the likelihood of interaction is the notion that spatial arrangement with constant distances also influences interaction. Steinzor (1950) was the first to point out that people across from one another are more likely to communicate than people adjacent to one another. These findings were later replicated by Hearn (1957).

It has also been shown that the more distance there is between individuals seated around a table, the less friendly, acquainted, and talkative they are perceived to be. Thus, spatial arrangements seem to influence both the quantity and quality of communication.

Communication Networks. One of the areas that organizational planners are most interested in is how to optimally place group members such that information can be transmitted with maximum efficiency. It is not surprising, therefore, that the research on communication networks has been with us for many years, starting with the research of Bavelas (1948, 1950). These studies investigate the distribution of communication channels among members in an attempt to determine which patterns are most important for information exchange, accuracy of decisions, satisfaction, and system overloads. Most of the networks that have been tested are represented in Figure 8-6.

In most investigations the subjects have been placed in adjacent cubicles and communicate through slots in the walls. The tasks vary from simple mathematics or identification problems (e.g., identifying a missing symbol out of a whole set) to more complex discussion problems. Performance is typically measured by assessing the time to solve the problem, the number of errors, or the number of messages sent. Clearly, if the type of structure is related to the amount of information exchanged, its speed of exchange, and its degree of error, then these data could have major implications for structuring organizational decision units to obtain efficiency in handling various decision problems.

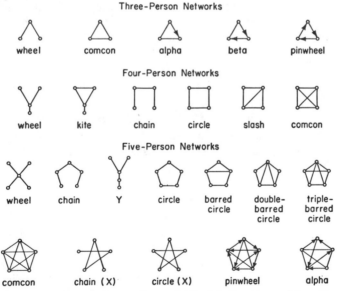

Figure 8-6 Communication Networks Used in Experimental Investigations. Dots Represent Positions, Lines Represent Communication Channels, and Arrows Indicate One-way Channels. (*Source:* Shaw, 1971, p. 139.)

Table 8-4 Number of Comparisons Showing Differences between Centralized (Wheel, Chain, Y) and Decentralized (Circle, Comcon) Networks as a Function of Task Complexity

	Simple Problems*	Complex Problems†	Total
Time			
Centralized faster	14	0	14
Decentralized faster	4	18	22
Messages			
Centralized sent more	0	1	1
Decentralized sent more	18	17	35
Errors			
Centralized made more	0	6	6
Decentralized made more	9	1	10
No difference	1	3	4
Satisfaction			
Centralized higher	1	1	2
Decentralized higher	7	10	17

*Simple problems: symbol-, letter-, number-, and color-identification tasks.
†Complex problems: arithmetic, work arrangement, sentence construction, and discussion problems. (*Source:* Shaw, 1971, p. 144).

The results over the years have produced a number of interesting findings (see Shaw, 1964, for a review). First, the person in the middle of the pattern, who has more channels, tends to receive more messages, be chosen more frequently as the leader, and has more social influence. Further, the type of structure greatly determines the pattern of interaction. For example, in patterns such as the wheel or the Y, it is much more likely that a central structure, in which one member is responsible for processing a lot of information, will develop. A more decentralized structure will tend to arise in patterns such as the circle or the slash.

The effectiveness of various networks seems to be dependent upon the complexity of the task. Table 8-4 shows performance data for centralized and decentralized networks as a function of task complexity. Shaw states that:

The interesting aspect of these findings is that they are contrary to the usual assumptions about the most effective arrangement of communication channels in a group. Since most of the problems that groups are faced with are more complex than the most complex task used in laboratory experiments, it is evident that a decentralized communication network is most likely to be effective in natural group situations (p. 144).

Finally, it has been shown that two other processes occur in centralized structures. First, when problems are relatively simple, the person in the central position is very satisfied with his job and position. Second, with increasing complexity comes increasing information load. Too much centralized information leads to errors and dissatisfaction on complex problems.

In summary, the kinds of communication *patterns* that exist are important for the amount of information exchanged, the errors made, the speed with which tasks are solved, and the felt satisfaction with the task. We now turn briefly to the content of the communications.

Communication Content and Direction. There is currently a body of research developing which discusses the direction of communication (upwards, downwards, etc.) and the content of the communication. Read (1962), for example, provides evidence that when executives are highly upwardly mobile they tend not to communicate frequently with their immediate supervisor. This relationship was modified by the degree of trust held for the superior. When the superior has influence and is trusted, then the subordinate will pass along information to him. Davis (1953) found difficulties in the amount of existing communication *across* organizational levels. He stresses the fact that management should attempt to provide liaison people to increase the communication between executives and supervisors. He also points out that informal networks develop which occasionally isolate important individuals. To remedy these problems it is suggested that the organization carry out an analysis of the communication links. These data can provide useful information about the gaps in information flows.

There are also some empirical studies showing that the type of information exchanged is important. Dahle (1954), for example, tested the following five conditions of communication: (1) oral only, (2) written only, (3) oral and written, (4) bulletin board, and (5) grapevine only. He selected a sample of eighty-four industrial employees working in production departments, and a sample of 1,030 students. In both cases it was found that the oral and written messages were most effective, followed by the oral only, written only, bulletin board, and grapevine. These data fit other principles of learning, which indicate that greater learning occurs with more sensory input.

A study by DeWhirst (1971) indicates that the choice of channels is partly determined by the existing norms in the organization, as well as by whether the message is meant for internal or external consumption. Earlier research by Allen and Cohen (1969) and Katz and Lazarsfeld (1955) showed there were key individuals or "gatekeepers" in organizations who were more aware of what was happening both inside and outside the company. The findings of DeWhirst indicate that when there are strong information-sharing norms inside an organization, personal, direct communication is likely to result. However, when this condition exists, it is also true that there is *less* personal communication outside the organization. External contacts are made through written messages. It is almost as if any given individual can only spend a certain amount of time in interpersonal exchanges. If they are internal (caused by strong sharing norms), then the external contacts are less personal. If there are few personal internal contacts, then more occur externally. In summary, not only the pattern but the type of messages that are sent are important for effective communication and, by inference, for effective decision making as well. Notice, however, that in these latter sections of the chapter we have mentioned concepts such as influence, leadership, and norms. All of these processes are concerned with aspects of control over others' behavior. It is to these topics that we turn our attention in the next chapter. We would further note that this chapter has considered some concepts that underlie group processes. The intent has been to introduce these concepts and to contrast individual decision processes with those that arise in the group context. These notions will be extended in Chapter 10 by discussing power and its implications for interpersonal and intrapersonal decision behavior. In Chapter 12 we will present some guidelines for managing group involvement, as it relates to organization design.

Chapter 9

Pressure to Change: Social Influence and Attitude Change

We are constantly interacting with a dynamic world. The decision maker finds that new conditions arise, that old ones change, and that his working relationships with others are modified. The likelihoods of various events change, as does one's evaluation of these events. Different social pressures arise. All of these areas emphasize the need to understand these change processes more thoroughly in order to act effectively in one's role as decision maker.

These concerns relate to our earlier discussions in two major ways. First, we have described attitudes and values as critical components of the decision-making process. Alternative courses of action have evaluations that are dependent upon the individual's attitudes and values. Thus, both in the process of deciding something for himself or in attempting to influence the decision made by someone else, attitudes play a crucial role. But secondly, we must concern ourselves with the social pressures around us, as described in the previous chapter. There are group norms to contend with, expectations which must be met, and people who must be relied upon, or even pressured, to implement decisions. It is these change processes which will concern us for the next two chapters.

One distinction that should be made immediately deals with the difference between attitudes and behavior. Changing attitudes is a matter of changing an individual or group's *evaluation* of some topic, outcome, person, concept or whatever. Changing behavior may only partly be a function of attitude change, since one's behavior is influenced by many different aspects (e.g., probabilities of events occurring, social pressure, etc.).

As a preliminary aid to understanding these *behavioral* change processes, we've developed the following conceptualizations. In any interpersonal exchange we can have either an individual or group persuader and an individual or group recipient. Combining these categories produces the relationships illustrated in Table 9-1.

In most of the research literature when one individual attempts to change the behavior of another individual, it is called social power. Thus, most of the theories of power are concerned with the likelihood that A can get B to do what he wants him to do. The relationship in which one individual attempts to direct or change the behavior of a group is frequently described as *leadership*. These two topics are reserved for the following two chapters.

But what about the situation in which the individual is the recipient of some group pressure? We typically describe this process as *social influence* or *conformity*. The final category, in which groups attempt to persuade groups, is usually included in the bargaining literature. Since our approach has been mainly an attempt to look at the individual decision maker, it makes sense to discuss processes in which the individual is either the persuader (power or leadership) or the recipient of social pressure (social influence). These topics will be described in more detail.

ATTITUDE CHANGE

In terms of Table 9-1, most of the attitude change research centers on either a group or an individual attempting to change the *feelings* of another individual. The emphasis has been on understanding the cognitive structures in which attitudes appear, and elaborating on how these structures change.

Table 9-1 Behavioral Change Relationships

		Persuader	
		One	Many
Recipient	One	[1] Power	[3] Social Influence
	Many	[2] Leadership	[4] Bargaining

Consistency Theories

You will recall from our earlier discussion that most theorists measure attitudes by seeing what the attitude object is related to and how one feels about those related objects. Thus, for example, Rosenberg (1965) and Fishbein (1967) agree that the affect attached to an attitude object will be highly related to (a) "the perceived instrumentality of the attitude object," that is, the judged probability that the attitude object would lead to, or block, the attainment of "valued states,"; and (b) the "value importance," that is, the intensity of affect expected from these "valued states." Our attitudes, then, are imbedded in a structure composed of other objects and our feelings toward these objects.

Most of the theories concerned with these cognitive structures are built around a principle of consistency. More specifically, it is suggested that the individual strives to hold consistent attitudes and beliefs. Thus, we want people that we like to feel the same way about things as we do. In terms of our decision processes, we would like a given decision to reach both personal and organizational goals. When inconsistency arises, the individual is supposedly uncomfortable and motivated to change. Note the similarity of these theoretical ideas to that of the TOTE concept described earlier.

Balance Theory

Fritz Heider (1946) was one of the first investigators to suggest a general theory of attitude organization (called balance theory). His specific interests were in the area of interpersonal attraction and he suggested that we like people who like the same things we do. When this situation does not exist (e.g., we perceive that a friend likes something we dislike), we feel uncomfortable and are motivated to change one of our attitudes.

The theory is presented in the form of the POX model. P stands for the perceiver or person, O for the other person, and X for a concept, object, or thing. Now, the link among these three parts can be either positive or negative. That is, P either likes or dislikes the object and the other person, and he has a perception or belief about the other's feelings toward the object in question. All possible combinations are presented in Figure 9-1. A plus stands for a positive feeling, a minus for a negative one.

Each triad represents a cognitive state: The state is positive (balanced) if by multiplying the three signs you generate a plus (triads 1, 5, 6, 7), and negative (unbalanced) if a minus sign is generated (triads 2, 3, 4, 8). For example, if you (P) like your supervisor (O) and you believe that both of you dislike the idea of close supervision (X), then you would have a balanced state (triad 6). On the other hand, if you believe your supervisor likes the idea of close supervision, situation 2 would exist—you perceive that someone you like is attracted to something you dislike. In this situation it is predicted that the individual will feel

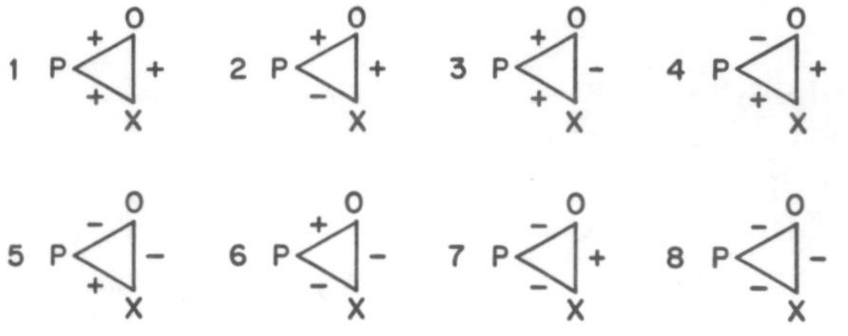

1 P∠+ (O+ / X+)   2 P∠+ (O+ / X−)   3 P∠+ (O+ / X−)   4 P∠− (O+ / X+)

5 P∠− (O− / X+)   6 P∠+ (O− / X−)   7 P∠− (O− / X+)   8 P∠− (O− / X−)

Figure 9-1 POX Combinations

uncomfortable and will be motivated to change one of his attitudes in order to return to a state of cognitive balance.

A number of studies have provided support for these ideas in organizational contexts or for decision making. However, the model has some major flaws which other researchers have sought to rectify. First, people have *degrees* of feeling about particular people or objects. Using just a plus or minus is too simplified. Second, Heider's theory failed to predict where changes would actually take place when confronted with inconsistency. For example, one could balance triad 2 in three separate ways: you could come to dislike your supervisor, you could come to like close supervision, or you could perceive that your supervisor was less favorable to close supervision techniques. A third problem was the fact that in reality one's attitude toward anything is a function of one's feelings toward many X's, not just one. A final issue was simply how all this cognitive activity related to behavior. (For reviews of this literature, see Triandis [1971] or McGuire [1966].)

Congruity Theory

One approach that was designed to deal with the first two suggestions was presented by Osgood and Tannenbaum (1955). Osgood was mainly concerned with how one evaluated and utilized information about some topic as a function of how one felt about the communicator and topic before they were linked together. Thus, you have an attitude toward one of your competitors and an attitude toward price fixing, and this competitor contacts you and suggests some sort of price-fixing arrangement. What happens? Well, first, Osgood argues that you have attitudes about both your competitor and price fixing before you receive the message. He typically measures these attitudes on by-polar scales, such as the ones presented below (Osgood, Suci, and Tannenbaum, 1957).

good _____ bad
        +3   +2   +1   0   −1   −2   −3

pleasant _____ unpleasant
          +3   +2   +1   0   −1   −2   −3

One could then take the average score over a set of scales and treat it as one's attitude toward the object in question. Let us assume, for example, that your attitude toward your competitor was +1, while your attitude toward price fixing was −2. In terms of Heider's model P → 0 = +1 and P → X = −2. You then receive the message from your competitor that he is in favor of some sort of price-fixing system. Thus, P is in favor of X, and someone you like is in favor of something you dislike. These attitudes are incongruous and Osgood argues that there will be pressure to move to a position of congruity. Since it is very hard to change the content of the message received, the individual will supposedly change his feelings toward his competitor, or price fixing, or both. Osgood presents a rather complex formula which predicts just how much change will take place. There are a number of other studies supporting his theory. In general he would suggest that we become less favorable toward our competitor and a little more favorably inclined toward price fixing. Our attitudes toward both the competition and price fixing would eventually be −1. See Figure 9-2 for a graphic representation.

The specific mechanics of the above approach are not highly important for our present purposes, but the underlying ideas should be discussed. First, we have a striving for consistency of attitudes. Osgood would argue that the individual can't have two separate attitudes toward the same bit of information at one time; thus, there is pressure to change. Secondly, he has quantified the components of the POX model and has predicted which attitudes will change, and how much they will change. Finally, he has built some assumptions into his theory such as the idea that more extreme attitudes are more difficult to change. Tannenbaum (1967) reviewed a number of studies testing the theory, and these results are generally supportive.

But other issues still remain. Surely our attitudes are more complex than either the Osgood or Heider models. And what about the relationship between our attitudes and our behavior?

Cognitive Dissonance

In an attempt to deal with these latter two problems, Festinger (1957) developed the theory of Cognitive Dissonance. According to Festinger, two cognitive elements are dissonant if the opposite of one follows from the other. These

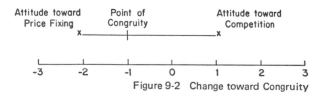

Figure 9-2   Change toward Congruity

cognitive elements, however, can be more than just attitudes; they can be beliefs or observations about one's own behavior. Thus, a belief, such as smoking causes cancer coupled with the act of smoking, would be expected to arouse feelings of discomfort (dissonance) and motivate the individual to change his behavior or his beliefs.

A number of qualifications should be discussed. First, Festinger argues that we must look at the proportion of dissonant elements to consonant elements in order to predict changes in behavior or attitudes. We must examine the overall cognitive structure to see how much dissonance exists. Thus, one dissonant belief in the midst of many consonant ones will probably not create enough discomfort to produce change. As a related issue, Festinger argues that these cognitions must be weighted by their importance. Thus, in some cases in which only a few elements are dissonant, if they are important enough the individual will be uncomfortable and motivated to change.

Another set of issues has to do with the idea that it is the individual's frame of reference that counts. If someone smokes and does not believe that smoking causes cancer (even though there is strong evidence to the contrary), he will not be dissonant. Finally, it should be pointed out that dissonance can be especially important when the individual is engaged in a free choice or decision process.

In summarizing the theory, Triandis (1971) states that "dissonance theory, as elaborated by Festinger and his students, involves four important variables: (a) the discrepancy between the cognitive elements, (b) the importance of the cognitive elements, (c) the subject's freedom of will (volition), and (d) the subject's commitment. Maximum dissonance occurs when the discrepancy is large, the elements are important, and when the subject has been free to exercise his volition and is committed to the outcome of his behavior" (p. 83).

How does one reduce dissonance? Festinger suggests three major strategies. First, one can reduce the importance of the dissonant elements. Second, one can add more consonant elements; or third, one can change the dissonant elements. Let's say, for example, that you're in an advertising firm that accepts the account of a pharmaceutical product which you believe might be harmful to peoples' health (including your own, perhaps). You must help make decisions about marketing, etc., but you feel uncomfortable doing so. One strategy to reduce the dissonance would be to simply say something to yourself like, "Well, any drug that we take probably does a little harm," and thereby reduce the importance of the dissonant element. You might, on the other hand, try to find out more about the positive effects of the product in an attempt to heavily outweigh the dissonant element. Finally, you might initiate some research to perhaps reduce the negative effects of the drug. A number of similar practical applications of dissonance theory are especially related to decision-making issues, three of which are discussed below.

Post-Decisional Dissonance

One particular situation that almost always produces dissonance is decision making. Whenever we are forced to choose one alternative from among a set of possible courses of action, we must usually forego the good aspects of the unchosen alternatives and live with the bad aspects of our choice. If, for example, you must choose between investing in firm A or B, and both seem attractive for a variety of reasons, once the choice is made, certain cognitive processes occur. First, there may be a brief stage of regret during which the unchosen alternative (let's say firm B) becomes more attractive. This period lasts only a brief time, during which dissonance begins to operate (i.e., you choose A and you must justify this behavior). Dissonance theory predicts that you will increase your positive attraction toward firm A and become more negative toward firm B.

A study by Brehm (1956) illustrates these points. College women rated eight products such as a toaster or a radio and then were asked to choose one of two products. After their choice was made, they again rated the products. Three separate experimental conditions were used. One group was presented with two products that were originally far apart in their evaluation; a second group had to choose between two items that were almost equally valued; and the third group was just given a gift. Table 9-2 shows the results. Thus, one can see that there is greater attitude change when the two were originally close together than when they were far apart.

A number of points should be discussed. First, note that we are talking about attitude change that occurs after the behavior. Choice is determining attitudes rather than the reverse. One of the major contributions of dissonance theory was its emphasis on this fact. A second related point is that the theory predicts that we shift our attitudes in line with our behavior which will then, in

Table 9-2   Post-Choice Attitude Change

Condition	Rating of Chosen Object	Rating of Unchosen Object	Total Reduction*
Low dissonance (objects initially rated far apart)	+.25	−.12	.37
High dissonance (objects initially rated close)	+.32	−.53	.85
No dissonance (gift— no choice)	.00	−	.00

*Figures are the increased evaluation of the chosen object plus the decrease in evaluation of the unchosen object. *Source:* Brehm, 1956.

turn, influence later choices. To the degree that choices are repetitive and between two fairly competitive alternatives, we will tend to bias our judgments because of dissonance reduction. In some objective sense, an alternative which was passed over may become the action that would maximize payoffs for the organization, but because of dissonance processes, it will have been devaluated further and will be overlooked.

Disconfirmed Expectancies

Another situation that occurs frequently in organizations is that some sort of expectation is disconfirmed or turns out to be incorrect. You decide that the route to success for your company is to buy out a number of small competitors. You spend many months and lots of money to reach your objective only to find that you were wrong, and company performance is down. Again we have dissonance directly related to some sort of decision activity.

The individual may attempt to reduce his discomfort in a variety of ways. He might argue that things are not so bad, and besides, the cause of the slump appears to be something other than his purchase of the small firms. He may believe that the basic idea was right even though the expectation was incorrect. Different positive outcomes may be substituted, such as, "Well, we're not making more money, but we're reaching a wider audience and we're better known."

A study by Aronson and Mills (1959) illustrates these points. Women were asked to join a group that was discussing various aspects of sexual activity. Before admittance, however, they were asked to go through a brief screening procedure to assure the experimenter and the other group members of their willingness to discuss these matters. One group was asked to read aloud obscene words and passages. A second group had to read some items mildly related to sexual activity, and the third group had no initiation. All the subjects then listened to a taped discussion of one of the group sessions as an introductory experience. The discussion presented on the tape was purposely dull, disorganized, and tedious. The subjects then rated the group in terms of attractiveness. As expected, the group that had a rather severe initiation liked the taped group more. A second experiment (Gerard and Mathewson, 1966), using severity of shock as the initiation, reported similar findings.

The ramifications of these points are important. It appears as if people change their attitudes and values to justify their behavior. For the decision-making process, it means that time and effort is spent in justifying a choice already made rather than trying to find out if a better choice could be made.

A third investigation tested these ideas in the field of marketing (Doob, Carlsmith, Freedman, Landauer, and Tom, 1969). The authors found that introducing a product at a low price (25¢), and then increasing the price (to 39¢), leads to fewer sales over a twenty-week period than if the product was sold at the "regular" price (39¢) all along. People have less commitment to the 25¢ product and have difficulty justifying the purchase when the price increases over fifty percent in cost. Dissonance, then, is important both for the understanding of the decision maker's cognitive processes, and also for an understanding of people who may be affected by the decision (in this case, those who might purchase your product).

Attitude-Discrepant Behavior

This third area of application is perhaps the most interesting, as well as the most controversial, topic of dissonance theory. Frequently we are pressured or asked to do something we find unpleasant. Decisions must be made about allocating resources, hiring and firing, etc. When we behave in a way which is discrepant with our underlying attitudes, we experience dissonance. The critical questions are, of course, how much pressure is needed to produce the discrepant behavior, and what are the implications for attitude change.

One set of predictions comes from the model of forced compliance, presented in Figure 9-3. This model attempts to predict an individual's attitude when pressured to do something against his wishes. If, for example, one wished to have a subordinate do an unpleasant job (some routine task), the theory predicts that just enough pressure to induce him to comply should be used (position 3). At this point he has done something he finds unpleasant, and he should be experiencing dissonance; that is, his behavior is not consistent with his attitude. He should, therefore, become more favorable toward the act he has just done in order to reduce the dissonance and to justify his behavior. If too much pressure is administered (a threat of dismissal perhaps), the employee would probably comply with his supervisor's wishes but still detest the task (position 4). He has little trouble justifying his behavior. If too little pressure is applied, the employee may refuse to do the job and may even become more unfavorable

Figure 9-3   The Forced Compliance Model

toward this type of work (position 2). This prediction is made due to the fact that the individual has said no to his supervisor and must justify his behavior in order to avoid feeling uncomfortable. He, therefore, becomes even more negative about the job involved (Festinger and Carlsmith, 1959). Clearly, in position 1 there is little need for change. The employee says no to a passing suggestion to do some unpleasant task. His behavior is consistent with his attitude, and he has not been made to feel uncomfortable in his refusal (as is the case for position 2). Festinger and his co-workers have presented data to support this model in a variety of studies and there are also critical reviews available (Chapanis and Chapanis, 1964). In general, the theory has increased our understanding of the ways in which attitudes are organized and changed.

A few recent studies have shed further light on these findings. One investigation by Sherman (1970) examined the importance of choice in the forced compliance model, in an attempt to reconcile two conflicting theories. Supposedly, reinforcement or learning theory would predict the greater the force (or reward), the greater the change. Thus, in terms of the model in Figure 9-3, situation 4 should produce the greatest change. Individuals were offered different amounts of money to take a public stand on an issue contrary to their personal beliefs. In the situation in which choice was possible, there was less attitude change when the reward was highest. However, in situations in which the subject had no choice, his greatest attitude change occurred with the greatest payoff. Finally, a study by Zimbardo and Ebbesen (1970) shows that the harder one works at doing something distasteful, the more he will come to like it.

These latter findings are of crucial importance for the execution of decisions. Obviously the decision maker does not want to have to constantly increase the pressure on his subordinates in order to obtain their compliance. He would also prefer situations in which they came to enjoy what they were doing, which would, in fact, lessen the pressure necessary for compliance. These questions also touch on the general relationship between attitudes and behavior.

Attitudes and Behavior

We have elaborated on how behavior causes attitudes, but what about the reverse? To what extent does an attitude cause behavior?

From 1930 to 1932, La Piere and a Chinese couple traveled around the United States by car. Of the 251 establishments which they approached for services, food, or lodging, only one refused them service. La Piere later sent out a questionnaire to these establishments to discover their attitudes toward Orientals and their willingness to serve them. Of the returned questionnaires, 95 percent of the respondents said *they would refuse service to Chinese.* Clearly there is a discrepancy between reported attitude and actual behavior (La Piere, 1934).

Theoretical Controversy

La Piere's research was not the only study that failed to find that behavior could be predicted from attitudes. Two general approaches have been taken in response to the problem. The first emphasizes a multi-dimensional definition of attitude. This argument suggests that if the one affective dimension (evaluation) does not predict behavior, then more information is needed. Attitude is defined as having three dimensions: affect, cognitions, and behavioral intentions. This new conceptualization of attitude prompted investigators to develop new measurement techniques to assess these additional dimensions (see Triandis, 1971). However, it appears that those new methods suffer from the same shortcomings as the old. The second response to the problem suggests why this is the case.

Most attitude measurement procedures assess feelings toward a rather general stimulus (e.g., Chinese). They generate this estimate by obtaining information about a number of objects to which the attitude object is tied. Fishbein and others have pointed out that perhaps we should be measuring more specific attitudes rather than general stimulus objects. If one wants to know whether a proprietor will serve a Chinese couple that is well dressed, speaks excellent English, and arrives in an automobile, then one should measure attitudes about that sort of couple rather than toward Chinese people in general. Measuring feelings toward a general stimulus provides one with little information about an individual's behavior in particular circumstances. Fishbein has reported correlations in the .50s and .60s between attitude and behavior using this approach (Fishbein and Raven, 1967).

A recent study by Rokeach and Kliejunas (1972) predicted the frequency of cutting class in five psychology courses by eighty-one students. Attitudes toward both the act and the situation were gathered and weighted by importance. The correlation between these two attitudes and classes cut was 0.61.

In summary, then, attitudinal consistency is an important factor for understanding both pre- and post-decision processes. Attitudes can cause changes in behavior, and behavior can cause changes in attitudes. It appears as if people strive toward cognitive consistency, and that this striving may inhibit the accuracy and judgment of the individual decision maker. But to understand the process of attitude change does not provide specifics as to how we can bring about inconsistencies that eventually result in changing people's attitudes.

MAJOR FACTORS IN ATTITUDE CHANGE

Since attitude change research has been one of the most intensively investigated topics in social psychology, we will not attempt to document a large number of specific investigations. Instead, we will cover the major areas of interest, mention an occasional representative study, and then summarize the results.

In most cases the process of attitude change is divided into four major topics: the source, the message, the audience, and the situation (e.g., the group or environment). We are concerned with who says what to whom, and with what impact.

The Source

Many people have realized for years that characteristics of the communicator are highly related to attitude change. Machiavelli, in his *Discourses,* pointed out that "Nothing is so apt to restrain an excited multitude as the reverence inspired by some grave and dignified man of authority who opposes them."

Perhaps the most frequently cited and well-known study on this topic was conducted by Hovland and Weiss (1952). These authors selected four topics and wrote position papers on each. These issues covered such things as whether antihistamines should be sold without a prescription, and whether the steel industry was to blame for the shortage of steel. Each message was placed in the cover of either a high-prestige or low-prestige source. For example, on the antihistamine issue, one cover was the *New England Journal of Biology and Medicine,* while the low-status source was a mass circulation, monthly pictorial magazine. Subjects' attitudes were assessed before, immediately after, and four weeks after they had read the booklets. As expected, the high credibility source produced greater attitude change, but this difference seemed to wear off over time. People tend to remember the communication and forget the source.

A second area of research indicates that more attractive sources are more persuasive. Studies by Mills (1966) and Mills and Aronson (1965) have shown that the communicator who is attractive can admit his intention to persuade and do better than without this admission. Also, mentioning that you like the audience seems to increase their willingness to change their attitude. Reminding the audience of how similar you are to them also increases the likelihood of change (Marsh, 1967; Simons, Berkowitz, and Moyer, 1970).

The sources' ability or expertise is also important. One recent investigation by Mills and Harvey (1972) compared expertise and attractiveness as source characteristics to determine which one produced more attitude change and under what conditions. Information was given to the subjects about the sources' expertise or attractiveness either before or after reading a speech advocating a broad general education for all college students. Attractiveness was manipulated by presenting an attractive or unattractive picture of the communicator. He was depicted as either a professor of education or as a student majoring in education. Table 9-3 shows their findings.

Thus, to be effective, information about the source's expertise should be presented before he communicates his message. Attractiveness, on the other hand, seems to be effective either before or after the message.

Table 9-3 Mean Values for the Measure of Agreement with the Communicator's Position

| Communicator | When information about communicator was received | |
	Before	After
Attractive	8.2	9.3
Expert	9.5	1.9

Note: The higher the scores, the greater the agreement with the communicator's position. N = 18 for each cell. *Source:* Mills and Harvey, 1972, p. 55.

Finally, a study by Stroebe, Thompson, Insko, and Reisman (1970) shows that people differentiate among various areas of expertise. They found that subjects changed their attitudes according to positive or negative information about the source in his area of expertise. Positive or negative information about the source in other areas (e.g., personal life) had less impact.

The Message

One can examine both the structure and the content of the message. The latter area is primarily concerned with emotional arousal. Hitler, in *Mein Kampf,* was aware of these principles when he stated, "An immense majority of the people are so feminine in nature and point of view that their thoughts and actions are governed more by feeling and sentiment than by reasoned consideration" (p. 78).

Janis and Feshbach (1953) conducted one of the better known pieces of research on this topic. They examined the effects of strong, moderate, or minimal fear-arousing communications. Subjects were exposed to one of these communications on the topic of tooth decay. The strong appeal emphasized pain and decay, and suggested that perhaps blindness and paralysis could follow in some cases. The minimal appeal showed only mildly disturbing pictures, and emphasized the positive effects of preventive care. The manipulation was clearly successful. The participants were more threatened, anxious, and worried by the strong appeal. However, the attitude change and eventual behavior change (e.g., visits to the dentist) was greatest for the minimal appeal. Janis and Terwilliger (1962) found similar results for smoking messages. However, Leventhal and Niles (1964) report high appeals to be most effective. Most investigators now believe that high appeal will only work when there is a clear way to reduce the fear, and to reduce it quickly. A recent study by Rogers and Thistlethwaite

(1970) shows that both high-fear and high-reassurance produced the greatest intention to quit for smokers presented with messages on the effects of smoking.

The structure of the message is also important, and a number of issues related to message structure have been investigated. Suppose, for example, you have an opportunity to speak either first or last in some conference at which important decisions will be made. Which should you choose? The critical elements are when the decision will be made and the time between the opposing viewpoints (Miller and Campbell, 1959). If there is a long time lapse between the two arguments, and the decision is to be made immediately after the last presentation, then choose to go last (a recency effect). If, on the other hand, both sides will be presented together, choose to go first. In general, an audience will use the first argument as a screen through which the second argument will be judged (called a primacy effect).

Should one present both sides of an argument or just one side? Should the weak points of your position be brought out? Secord and Backman (1964) summarize the literature as follows:

> One-sided communications are more effective for people who already agree with the communicator, but people who disagree with the communicator do not change their opinions in response to one-sided communications. Just the reverse is true for two-sided communications. Moreover, a two-sided communication is more effective than a one-sided communication in inoculating the audience against countercommunication. Whether the communicator draws the conclusion implied by his message or leaves it up to the audience does not seem to make a distinct difference in the audience's acceptance of it (p. 163).

As we can see, both the characteristics of the communicator and the way his message is constructed strongly influence its chance for acceptance.

Situation and Audience Characteristics

Two major research topics are concerned with characteristics of the situation or audience. The first is the idea of position discrepancy; that is, to what extent does the degree of distance between the communicator and the recipients' points of view influence the amount of change that will take place. In an important study, Hovland, Harvey, and Sherif (1957) attempted to change the attitudes of some people in two southern states on the topic of prohibition. In general, they found that on issues over which people are highly involved, a moderate discrepancy works best. People tend to use their own position as an anchor, and they judge others according to their distance (on either side) away from them. For communicators who had fairly similar views, their positions were seen as closer than they actually were (assimilation), and little change occurred. Communica-

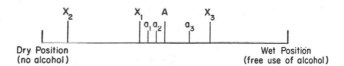

A = subject's position before communication

X_1 = communicator's position when assimilation occurs and A moves to a_1

X_2 = communicator's position when contrast occurs and A moves to a_2

X_3 = communicator's position on edge or range of acceptance and A moves to a_3

Figure 9-4 Effects of Degree of Distance Between Communicator and Recipient

tors who were fairly far away were judged as even more extreme (contrast), and little attitude change took place, presumably because the communicators were seen as extremists. Figure 9-4 diagrams these findings. The greatest amount of change took place when the communicator's position was on the outside edge of the subject's "range of acceptance." This range is the area in which the subject clearly perceives the communicator's position as different from his own (no assimilation), but does not perceive him as so extreme that he rejects the message (no contrast).

An important inference can be made from these results. It appears as if taking an extreme point of view is not likely to produce large changes of attitudes, especially on topics on which there is a lot of recipient involvement. One does find more change due to extreme positions on issues over which the recipient is not involved.

This introduces the second major area of interest under audience characteristics. A number of studies have shown that the recipient's ego involvement is highly related to the attitude change process. An investigation by Rhine and Severance (1970) examined three different degrees of position discrepancy, two levels of source credibility, and two levels of involvement. Both credibility and involvement seem to mediate acceptance and attitude change. More specifically, under low involvement conditions, the greater the discrepancy, the greater the change. However, when involvement was high, the extreme message did not produce greater change than the non-extreme message. These results are moderated by credibility. Thus, the recipient tends to reduce his range of acceptance if the communicator has low credibility. A later study by Rhine and Polowniak (1971) suggests that taking a stand on any issue increases involvement, making it more difficult to move a recipient a large increment from his original position.

Although there are other important aspects of the attitude change process, the main ones are covered above. A review by Zimbardo and Ebbesen (1969) summarizes most of the findings.

Summary of Social Psychological Findings[1]

A. THE PERSUADER
   1. There will be more opinion change in the desired direction if the communicator has high credibility than if he has low credibility. Credibility is:
      a. Expertise (ability to know correct stand on issue).
      b. Trustworthiness (motivation to communicate knowledge without bias).
   2. The credibility of the persuader is less of a factor in opinion change later on than it is immediately after exposure.
   3. A communicator's effectiveness is increased if he initially expresses some views that are also held by his audience.
   4. What an audience thinks of a persuader may be directly influenced by what they think of his message.
   5. The more extreme the opinion change that the communicator asks for, the more actual change he is likely to get, especially with low involvement.
      a. The greater the discrepancy (between the communication and the recipient's initial position), the greater the attitude change, up to extremely discrepant points.
      b. With extreme discrepancy, and with low-credibility sources, there is a falling off in attitude change.
   6. Communicator characteristics irrelevant to the topic of his message can influence acceptance of its conclusion.

B. HOW TO PRESENT THE ISSUES
   1. Present one side of the argument when the audience is generally friendly, or when your position is the only one that will be presented, or when you want immediate, though temporary, opinion change.
   2. Present both sides of the argument when the audience starts out disagreeing with you, or when it is probable that the audience will hear the other side from someone else.
   3. When opposite views are presented one after another, the one presented last will probably be more effective. Primacy effect is more predominant when the second side immediately follows the first, while recency effect is more predominant when the opinion measure comes immediately after the second side.
   4. There will probably be more opinion change in the direction you want if you explicitly state your conclusions than if you let the audience draw their own, except when they are rather intelligent. Then implicit conclusion drawing is better.

[1]Our organization and presentation of the material in this section is taken largely from Zimbardo and Ebbesen, 1969.

5. Sometimes emotional appeals are more influential, sometimes factual ones. It all depends on the kind of audience.

6. Fear appeals: The findings generally show a positive relationship between intensity of fear arousal and amount of attitude change, if recommendations for action are explicit and possible, but a negative reaction otherwise.

7. The fewer the extrinsic justifications provided in the communication for engaging in counter-norm behavior, the greater the attitude change after actual compliance.

8. No final conclusion can be drawn about whether the opening or closing parts of the communication should contain the more important material.

9. Cues which forewarn the audience of the manipulative intent of the communication increase resistance to it, while the presence of distractors simultaneously presented with the message decreases resistance.

C. THE AUDIENCE AS INDIVIDUALS

1. The people you may want most in your audience are often least likely to be there. There is evidence for selective seeking and exposure to information consonant with one's position, but not for selective avoidance of information dissonant with one's position.

2. The level of intelligence of an audience determines the effectiveness of some kinds of appeals.

3. Successful persuasion takes into account the reasons underlying attitudes as well as the attitudes themselves. That is, the techniques used must be tailored to the personal basis for developing the attitude.

4. The individual's personality traits affect his susceptibility to persuasions; he is more easily influenced when his self-esteem is low.

5. There are individuals who are highly persuasible and who will be easily changed by any influence attempt, but who are then equally susceptible to influence when faced with countercommunications.

6. Ego-involvement with the content of the communication (its relation to ideological values of the audience) decreases the acceptance of its conclusion. Involvement with the consequences of one's response increases the probability of change and does so more when source-audience discrepance is greater.

7. Actively role-playing a previously unacceptable position increases its acceptability.

D. THE PERSISTENCE OF OPINION CHANGE

1. In time, the effects of a persuasive communication tend to wear off.
   a. A communication from a positive source leads to more rapid decay of attitude change over time than one from a negative source.
   b. A complex or subtle message produces slower decay of attitude change.
   c. Attitude change is more persistent over time if the receiver actively participates in, rather than passively receives, the communication.

2. Repeating a communication tends to prolong its influence.
3. More of the desired opinion change may be found some time after exposure to the communication than right after exposure (sleeper effect).

To summarize, there are two major aspects of the decision process that are
dependent upon attitudes. First, to make a decision, one will include attitudes as
part of the overall judgment process. The attractiveness of alternative actions are
mostly a function of one's attitudes. Second, to have decisions executed correctly and enthusiastically (e.g., without surveillance) requires that those carry-
ing out the decision have attitudes which are similar to those of the decision
maker regarding relevant aspects of the decision. An awareness of how attitudes
are formed and changed is a valuable tool for understanding the effectiveness of
organizational decision processes.

SOCIAL INFLUENCE

We have described in some detail how the decision maker is not isolated from
others. He must depend on others for information and advice. The decisions that
he makes are frequently carried out by others. The degree to which others
change his beliefs or values or the degree to which he or his group can change the
behavior of others is frequently called conformity or social influence. Kiesler
and Kiesler (1969) define it as "a change in behavior or belief toward a group as
a result of real or imagined group pressure" (p. 2).

   In the decision-making case, we are mostly concerned with the use and value
of information presented by others. Freedman, Carlsmith, and Sears (1970) state
that in a conformity situation, the individual initially holds one view and
discovers that the group holds an opposing one. The individual wants to give the
correct response. Therefore, the more he trusts the group, or thinks of it as a
good source of information, the more likely he is to conform. At the extreme, if
he thinks that the group is infallible, he will always go along with it, even though
he might be quite certain of his own opinion. Similarly, if the group has vital
information he does not have, conformity would be high. In either case, the
individual is likely to decide that he is mistaken, and that the group is correct.
So, it becomes clear that: (1) we frequently need the information that others
provide us, and (2) we often decide to do what the group wants, even against our
own personal initial preference. The rest of this chapter concerns itself with this
process of social influence.

Norms

To state that group opinions influence our decisions begs the question. We must
know how this pressure is transmitted and received, what sorts of variables
increase the likelihood of its acceptance, and how can we control the phenom-

ena. Our ability to deal with these issues may be facilitated by a better understanding of social norms.

Whenever people interact in fairly consistent and persistent social settings (e.g., organizations), they tend to develop shared expectations about various things. Language, slogans, rules, communication patterns, and concepts of proper or improper behavior become agreed upon. These crystallized beliefs and expectations serve many purposes for the group members. They remove sources of vagueness or ambiguity, they decrease disagreement among group members, and they generally provide the group with a sense of cohesiveness or solidarity. Two of the foremost authors in this field, Sherif and Sherif (1969), summarize their definition of social norms in the following way.

1. Social norms does *not* necessarily refer to the average behavior by members of a social unit or even to what is typical. The concept has little in common with the terms "test norm" or "age norm" as used in psychology textbooks.
2. Social norms are standardized generalizations that epitomize events, behavior, objects, or persons in short-cut form. Like a verbal category or rule, a social norm applies to *classes* of objects (e.g., persons, behaviours, or events).
3. A social norm is *evaluative,* designating both what is valued and what is scorned, what is expected (even ideal) and what is degrading, what ought to be and what ought not to be, what is acceptable and what is objectionable.
4. Being generalizations, social norms typically define a range or *latitude* of what is permissible or acceptable, and a range of actions and beliefs that are objectionable. In other words, social norms take note of the universal facts of individual differences, of varying circumstances, and of novelty, by designating ranges of positive and negative evaluation, not absolutes (p. 141).

A social norm is an evaluative scale (e.g., yardstick) designating an acceptable latitude and an objectionable latitude for behavior, activity, events, beliefs, or any other object of concern to members of a social unit.

Norms, then, can be observed by watching behavior or inferred from responses to questionnaires. One can see the actions applied and the latitudes to which the punishments pertain. When one does what the group wants, especially against his previous beliefs or desires, he has been influenced or has conformed. The social norms, therefore, play a crucial part in the influence process.

Classic Studies of Influence

There are a number of empirical studies in the field of social influence that are well known and relevant to our discussion. The first was reported by Sherif and Sherif in 1935.

Sherif's Study on the Autokinetic Phenomena. Sherif (1935) was interested in the situation in which the task is ambiguous, and the individual making a decision needs information from others. He took advantage of a perceptual phenomena termed the autokinetic effect—a situation in which a stationary single point of light, if observed in the dark, appears to move. World War II pilots, when attempting to follow the plane ahead of them by observing its lights, often had difficulties, occasionally flying off course. Recently, in Vietnam, soldiers reported similar problems during night patrols, when they would look across large fields and see a light in the distance. In some cases, artillery strikes were called in on civilian homes instead of the moving vehicles which the soldiers believed they had observed.

In Sherif's study, a subject was taken into a dark room and shown a single point of light. He was told that the light might move, and that his task was to estimate the distance that it moved. Along with the naive subject there were one or more confederates, individuals who appeared to be naive subjects, but who were really working for the experimenter. The procedure demanded that each participant (the naive subject and the confederates) make repeated estimates of how far the light moved. The confederates could be instructed to answer in terms of feet or inches. The important finding was that the naive subject's response changed according to the estimates made by the confederates. In some cases the confederates would change the judgment of the naive subject by 10 feet. But this is a situation in which the naive subject was unsure of himself. He had little independent information on which to base his decision. The information provided by others would be expected to have a large effect on his behavior in such a situation. The confederate seemed sure of his responses, and in the absence of other inputs, it makes sense that so much influence could take place. Other research, however, has shown similar effects for non-ambiguous tasks.

Asch's Study. In 1951 Asch presented even more startling data from experiments on social influence. His research setting included a group of confederates and one naive subject. The task was to observe a set of lines presented on one card, and to estimate which of these lines was most similar in length to a line presented on a separate card. Figure 9-5 presents an example. One can clearly see that the task is unambiguous and the correct answer is obvious. In a series of trials (each trial consisting of a new card) each participant would indicate aloud which line was most similar. In each case the naive subject would make the last judgment. For the first few trials all went well. Then, on the third or fourth trial, all of the confederates would give an agreed-upon incorrect answer. For our example, shown in Figure 9-5, they might say that line C was most like the line on the other card.

The naive subject was faced with a real dilemma. Here was a group of supposedly normal people just like himself. But they all agreed upon some

Key: Confederates say that line C
is most like line x.

Figure 9-5   Stimulus Objects Used in Asch Experiment

judgment that appeared to be incorrect according to the information provided by his senses. The pressure was unanimously exerted by all group members. It was current; he had to decide immediately.

The results astounded Asch and numerous other social scientists. Over many trials, in many different experiments, subjects conformed over one-third of the time on the critical trials (e.g., those trials in which the confederates clearly choose the incorrect response). Thus, many individuals were willing to conform to the group, even when the judgment was clearly opposite of the information provided by their senses. Some subjects, of course, never conformed, while others conformed on every trial. However, over all trials and subjects, conformity occurred about 35 percent of the time.

Numerous modifications of the Asch-type study have been conducted, and we will discuss some of these experiments later in the chapter. However, another well-known study illustrated the effects of social influence and normative pressure on specific work-related activities.

The Hawthorne Studies at Western Electric.   Although the major impact of the work reported by Roethlisberger and Dickson (1939, 1961) was on the human relations movement, they also provided interesting information on the social influence process within the Hawthorne plant. Interviews of men in the Bank Wiring Room revealed rather clear expectations about "a fair day's work." Those who worked too slow were called "chiselers" and those who worked too quickly were known as "rate busters." Thus, there were clear expectations about how much effort one should exert, and what to do if these expectations were not met. Some data gathered by Dalton (1955) on eighty-four workers in a machine shop also indicates the effects of expectations on worker output. All but 10 percent of the men indicated they systematically tried to maintain their work rate at a pace agreed upon as a "good honest day's work."

The implications of these findings are interesting. It was reported, both in the Hawthorne and Dalton studies, that almost everyone could bust the rate if he wanted to. Greater productivity and greater rewards were *possible* for everyone. Also, each individual had to decide for himself how much to produce. So, almost everyone could exceed the norm, and yet 90 percent choose not to do so. This is a clear indication of the power of social influence. While in the

Asch and Sherif studies the subjects were faced with possible rejection by a group of unfamiliar peers, in the industrial setting, rate busting is followed by physical harassment or social isolation.

All of these studies point out rather clearly the following inferences: (1) we use the information that others provide when making decisions; (2) we will bow to group pressure, even when it is not necessarily in our best interests; and (3) this effect is more powerful than most people believe.

Factors Producing Social Influence

Since decision makers constantly evaluate information from others and are constantly the recipients of various group pressures, it becomes important to describe those conditions which are most likely to lead to increases in conformity. Two preliminary points need to be made. First, like other topics we have reviewed, the situation is complex. We must take into account the task, the group setting, and the sorts of people involved. Second, we must distinguish between compliance and acceptance. We frequently see cases in which someone will do something that the group wants although his underlying attitude remains unchanged. This process is called compliance, and the Asch-type setting is a good example. On the other hand, people frequently change their behavior as a response to group pressure, and then come to believe in what they are doing (e.g., non-rate-busters). This latter process includes both behavioral and attitude change. Our concern here will be with those variables that are most likely to lead to changes in behavior, since the attitude change research has been dealt with earlier (see Allen, 1965, for a review).

Characteristics of the Task. A number of factors having to do with the task, or the individual's relationship to the task, are important for producing conformity. Several aspects are listed below with a brief summary of the supporting research.

1. Task Ambiguity. We mentioned that in the more ambiguous situation, as presented by Sherif (1935), more conformity was obtained (almost 80 percent of the subjects conformed) than in the Asch-type setting (33 percent conformed). A study by Shaw, Rothschild, and Strickland (1957) had subjects count the number of metronome clicks, again using confederates to exert pressure on a naive subject. They report that about six out of ten subjects conform to the group norm, and they argue that this task is somewhat more ambiguous than the Asch-type setting. An experiment by Nickols (1964) had subjects judge the relative areas of circles, squares, triangles, and other geometric figures. Again, we have a study of moderate ambiguity, and Nickols reports that about half of his naive subjects yielded to group pressure. Finally, it appears as if the more the subject must depend upon his memory, the more ambiguous the task becomes. A study by Deutsch and Gerard (1955) compared Asch line-judg-ments when the cards were still present to when they had been removed fifteen seconds prior to the subject's response. There was an average of thirty-four percent conformity after the cards were removed, compared to 25 percent in the visual trials. A study by Haaland (1968), with subjects working on decision-making tasks of differing degrees of ambiguity, also found that more conformity occurred on ambiguous tasks.

2. Anonymity of Response. A number of investigations have shown that the more public one's response is, the more he is likely to conform. In most of the settings described earlier (except for Sherif's work), all the participants, both naive subjects and confederates, worked together and could see one another. Other conditions have been examined where the subject either makes a private judgment, or he makes a judgment that can be known to the other group members even though he is physically isolated from them. An example of the latter approach was tested by Deutsch and Gerard (1955). These authors had subjects work in either a face-to-face condition or in separate booths with electronic display boards indicating the responses made by the other members. Less conformity was found in the conditions of private responding. Similarly, Mouton, Blake, and Olmstead (1956) found that if the subject announced his name first (even when alone in a booth) he conformed more than when he was completely anonymous. Findings by Levy (1960), Raven (1959), and Jellison and Mills (1969) report similar results.

Asch (1956) ran one study in which subjects could write their responses instead of answering publicly. He reported fewer yielding responses in this more private condition. Argyle (1957), having people turn in their decisions in a sealed envelope, obtained similar results. Clearly, the more public the response, the greater the effect of group pressure.

3. Confidence and Competence. People differ in their ability to do a job, as well as in their confidence in this ability. Both of these factors are related to conformity. In a number of studies the individual's perceived competence has been manipulated. Samelson (1957), in a study in which subjects identified nonsense syllables flashed on a screen, told some subjects they had better vision than the other group members. The conformity was less for those who believed they had expert vision. Hochbaum (1954) found that people who failed on previous trials of a task tended to yield more on subsequent trials than did subjects who had experienced success. Similar findings have been reported for opinion items (Di Vesta, 1959), objective stimuli (Rosenberg, 1963), and the autokinetic effect (Kelman, 1950). Fagen (1963) also reported that both real and supposed ability decrease conformity. Individuals who were randomly told that they had task-relevant skills, as well as those who actually had ability, yielded less. Experiments using feedback of results during the experiment report the same results (Crutchfield, 1955).

Thus, people's real abilities influence their confidence and their conformity. When Coleman, Blake, and Mouton (1958) varied the actual difficulty of the task, they found that conformity also increased. Finally, Krech and Crutchfield

(1967) had subjects indicate their confidence in different task items. They reported significantly more conformity on the uncertain items than on the confident ones (36 to 15 percent conformity). The greater the confidence and competence, the lower the conformity.

Characteristics of the Group. Some aspects of the group itself increase the likelihood that one will conform to group norms. Some of these are discussed below.

1. Group size. One would expect that if conformity is partially a function of the information provided by others, increasing size would lead to greater conformity. Table 9-4 presents the findings from studies by Asch (1951) and Gerard, Wilhelmy, and Connolley (1968). One can see that increasing size over and above four or five members does not appear to lead to great increments in conformity. An investigation by Rosenberg (1961) reported an even greater drop-off in groups containing more than three confederates.

2. Unanimity. In most of the situations we've described, the individual is confronted with a unanimous opinion about what should be the correct response. In most realistic settings, however, one might not expect such a clear, agreed-upon norm. In some of Asch's early studies (1951, 1955), this variable was experimentally controlled. In one condition, the naive subject had what was termed a "true partner." One of the confederates gave the correct answer, rather than the false one, on the critical trials. Conformity dropped from 35 to 5 percent. A second condition had a confederate, at first, join with the naive

Table 9-4   Group Size and Conformity

Size of Unanimous Majority	Percentage of Conforming Responses		
	Asch Study (Males)	Gerard Study (Males)	Gerard Study (Females)
1	2.8	12.6	
2	12.8		
3	33.3	25.9	
4	35.0		33.6
5		24.1	
6			34.6
7		30.1	
8	32.0		
16	31.3		

Source: Adapted from Asch (1956) and Gerard, Wilhelmy, and Connolley (1968).

subject on the first few critical trials, and then on the rest of the critical trials he agreed with the other confederates. On these latter trials, conformity went back to about 30 percent. A third condition included a confederate who gave neither the correct response nor the other confederates' response. This was known as the "compromise partner" condition. Here, conformity decreased, but not as much as in the true partner condition. A study by Malof and Lott (1962) found it made no difference whether the "true partner" was black or white, even for prejudiced subjects. Conformity decreased significantly when the unanimity was broken. A recent study combined unanimity with anonymity to look at decisions about product evaluation (Cohen and Golden, 1972). The authors presented conditions of high or low uniformity of pressure in the form of group judgments about product preference, and they varied subjects' beliefs as to whether their decisions would be visable to others. The greatest amount of influence came under the high uniformity–visibility condition, as we would predict.

3. Attractiveness of the Group. Many groups are characterized by high interpersonal attraction and friendliness, and it appears as if these conditions place strong pressure on individuals to conform to group norms. In a study of university housing units, Festinger, Schachter, and Back (1950) found that groups whose members were highly attracted to one another had significantly more conformity than groups without the high attraction. In a study having more direct relevance for organizational settings, Schachter, Ellertson, McBride, and Gregory (1951) manipulated cohesiveness and the kinds of influence attempts that were made. Individuals worked in triads on an assembly line task. Some were told they would be working with similar others (high cohesiveness), and the remainder were matched with dissimilar others (low cohesiveness). Half of each of these groups received messages indicating they should work hard on the task, while the other half was told to slow down. These messages were supposedly from other group members, but were, in reality, sent by the experimenter. The high cohesive-work hard groups produced most, while the high cohesive-work slow group produced least. Thus, conformity was greatest for the high cohesive groups whether the message was to speed up or slow down. Berkowitz (1954) reported similar results.

The relationship between group attraction and conformity has been found in laboratory settings as well as field settings. Sherif and Sherif (1969) reported that liked members have greater influence in the autokinetic-type experiment, while Harper (1961) found no differences in the Asch-type setting. A study by Lott and Lott (1961) reported that conformity was significantly related to attraction in fifteen natural friendship groups. Here, the subjects got together, discussed an important issue, and then made independent judgments about where they stood on the issue. The experimenter then gave them bogus information about what the rest of the group felt, and gave the individual a chance to change his decision. The greater the attraction, the greater the change in the direction of the supposed group decision. Shaw (1971) summarizes all these findings by saying, " . . . there is good evidence that group cohesiveness is related to social influence in the group. When group members are attracted to the group, they are motivated to behave in accordance with the wishes of other group members and in ways that facilitate group functioning. These motivations are reflected in greater responsiveness to group inductions and in greater conformity to group norms and standards" (p. 200).

4. Interdependence and Participation. Most of the studies cited so far have dealt with situations in which the individual, making a judgment or decision, had to choose whether or not to rely on information provided by others. Deutsch and Gerard call this process informational influence. They also argue the existence of a process called normative influence, which has to do with group members holding similar goals. In their 1955 experiment, they manipulated the degree to which group members were dependent upon one another to reach their goal. Half the groups were told that prizes would be given to the five groups making the fewest errors. There was greater conformity under the interdependent condition.

A study by Crutchfield (cited in Krech, Crutchfield, and Ballachey, 1962) used financial reward as an incentive to increase interdependence. Ten dollars was offered to the best group, as opposed to ten dollars being offered for the best individual performance. Greater conformity was found under the group reward condition. Other investigations by Julian and Steiner (1961) and Thibaut and Strickland (1956) support these ideas, using different types of rewards.

Individual Characteristics. We've documented a number of group and task parameters which increase the likelihood that conformity will appear. The personal and personality traits of the people involved are also related to conformity. The major relationships are reviewed below.

1. Age. We can probably assume that people learn to conform to group norms as they grow older and participate more in group settings (Berg and Bass, 1961). One must learn group norms as part of the socialization process. We must expect, therefore, some general increase in conformity with increasing age. Piaget (1954) argues, however, that at younger ages (from let's say seven to twenty-one) we would see, at first, an increase in conformity, and then a slight decrease. The youngster first learns the "rules of the game" and tends to follow them. Later on he learns that "rules" are mostly made for the group's convenience and can be broken if necessary, or under certain prescribed conditions.

Earlier studies by Marple (1933) and Patel and Gordon (1960) had provided conflicting results, so Costanzo and Shaw (1966) tested the hypothesis by observing the conformity behavior of individuals from age seven to twenty-one. They were tested with a Crutchfield-type apparatus (whereby the subjects are isolated in booths with display panels), using the Asch-type line-judgment tasks. The results of the study are shown in Figure 9-6. One can see the increase, and then the decrease, as predicted by Piaget. These findings can also explain results reported by Marple (1933) in which high school students conformed more than college students, and the findings by Patel and Gordon (1960) in which conformity decreased from the tenth to the twelfth grade. Iscoe, Williams, and Harvey

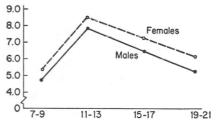

Figure 9-6 Mean Conformity as a Function of Age (*Source:* Costanzo and Shaw, 1966.)

(1963) also found a general increase in conformity up to age twelve, and then a decrease to age fifteen. So, in general, it looks as if conformity decreases as a function of age from age twelve to age twenty-one. Whether it continues to decrease is debatable.

2. Sex. There is a general stereotype of the American female that includes the idea that women play a relatively submissive role compared to men (see Reitan and Shaw, 1964). These notions would suggest that women tend to conform more than men, and experimental evidence seems to support these ideas. Investigations by Julian, Regula, and Hollander (1967); Julian, Ryckman, and Hollander (1966); and Gerard *et al.* (1968) report data with seven to fourteen percentage points difference, with women conforming more frequently than men. The results reported in Figure 9-6 also support this notion.

These sex differences may be due to cultural sex roles, or they may be due to different motivations on the part of males and females. It does appear as if males are more task oriented, while women may be more socially oriented. Tuddenham, MacBridge, and Zahn (1958) report that men conform more when concerned about completing a task quickly, while women conform more when they are concerned about how their responses would appear to others. Berg and Bass (1961) report that college men were more task oriented, while college women were more concerned with harmonious relations.

3. Personality Variables. The most consistent findings relating personality variables to conformity are concerned with cognitive or intellectual characteristics. Crutchfield (1955) conducted one investigation in which a large battery of personality variables was correlated with conformity; that is, the higher the intelligence, the lower the conformity. The connections between measures of conformity and intellectual competence (−.63) and concept mastery (a measure of abstract mental functioning) (−.51) support these ideas.

Data also support the idea that people who are better able to stand on their own and live with a little ambiguity tend to conform less. The correlation between ego strength and conformity was −.33, between tolerance and conformity it was −.41, between dominance and conformity anywhere from −.23 to −.50 (McDavid and Sistrunk, 1964). On the other side are the findings that those who tend to be inflexible, more extreme, and rigid will conform more. Correlations between authoritarianism and conformity have been reported as high as +.39 (Crutchfield, 1955).

Two other characteristics showing positive relationships with conformity are test anxiety and self-blame. Subjects high in test anxiety tend to conform more (Meunier and Rule, 1967). Costanzo (1970) reported that across different age groups (seven to twenty) high self-blame subjects conformed significantly more than low self-blame subjects. One may conclude, then, that individual and personality characteristics are noticeably related to conformity.

Social Influence and Decisions

We have suggested that social influence is a major determinant of one's behavior in an organization. We would expect, therefore, that influence would be related to various factors important in the decision-making process. From our previous discussions, it would clearly be important for the execution and implementation of decisions. But there is also some literature showing that influence is important in the information search and choice phases as well. Crawford and Haaland (1972) studied situations in which "information seeking and subsequent conforming behavior were related to the effects of motivational orientation (cooperative or competitive), task uncertainty, and the reinforcement value of information" (p. 112). Both conformity and information seeking were viewed as behaviors instrumental for ordering the decision alternatives. Their research revealed that cooperative groups displayed greater information seeking and conformity than did competitive groups. They explain that "if each group member perceives that group goal attainment is facilitated by uniformity, then conformity becomes reinforcing. Any response instrumental to achieving conformity, namely, information seeking, is strengthened and increases in its probability of occurrence. Thus, conformity is the reinforcement for search behavior" (p. 117). Thus, information seeking is instrumental for conformity, and the latter leads to consensus and goal achievement.

Several recent theories of decision making and choice behavior have attempted to explicitly include social influence. Fishbein (1967), Dulany (1968), Graen (1969), and Mitchell and Biglan (1971) all include the meeting of the expectations of one's peers as an integral part of their theoretical models of behavioral choice. In a recent study, Mitchell and Knudsen (1973) attempted to predict the attitudes toward, and actual choice of, occupations by students about to leave the university. Using an instrumentality approach, they ascertained the degree to which various occupations were likely to lead to organizational outcomes (beliefs), and the importance of these outcomes (values). Two of the outcomes were defined as meeting the expectations of one's friends and family. While these latter aspects of social influence were only slightly related to the students' attitudes toward the occupation, they were significantly related to their choice behavior. By combining attitudes and social influence to predict choice, the results indicated that a substantial amount of the variability in oc-cupational choice was predictable. Other investigations of job effort and satisfac-tion have produced similar findings (see Mitchell and Biglan [1971] or Heneman and Schwab [1972] for reviews), lending support to the idea that social influ-ence is an important aspect of the choice process in decision making.

SUMMARY

The major thrust of this chapter was to describe the areas of attitude change and social influence, with special reference to aspects of decision making. Both of these areas are important for different stages of human decision processes. First, attitudes are important in that they partially determine the values that are placed on various outcomes prior to choice. Thus, one way to examine or modify the decision process is to understand how attitudes are formed, orga-nized, and changed. A second major component of the decision process is execution and implementation. Decisions must be carried out by others in the organization, and the more positive their attitudes are toward the decision, the more efficient the execution (e.g., surveillance may not be needed). Our review of these topics suggested the following principles:

1. Attitudes are formed as a function of the degree to which the attitude object is related to other positively or negatively valued objects.
2. People tend to hold consistent attitudes, and when this is not true, they are upset and motivated to return to a state of consistency.
3. Behavior and attitudes are frequently inconsistent when we do things which we would prefer not to do. In these cases attitude change often follows behavior, rather than preceding it.
4. Changing another's attitudes implies that we change the individual's behavior toward, or beliefs or values about, objects or concepts that he perceives to be related to the attitude object in question.
5. Using high status or using credible or attractive communicators (e.g., to announce a decision) increases the likelihood of attitude change in the desired direction.
6. Trying to change others' attitudes and behavior by the use of fear arousal (e.g., threats of pay cuts, firing, etc.) is a poor way to change the underlying attitude, unless the pressure is mild or it is clear how the fear can be dissipated.
7. Taking extreme positions on an issue is unlikely to change people's attitudes, unless it is on an issue of little importance. Moderate positions lead to greater change.

In looking at the area of social influence, we can draw similar conclusions. It appears that search and choice processes in decision making are highly related to social norms and expectations. The execution of decisions is also dependent upon the normative pressure exerted on the group and individuals. General principles can also be generated for this topic.

1. The more ambiguous or uncertain the situation, the greater is the role played by norms and influence.
2. The more anonymous the information exchanged, the less influence is exerted.
3. The more confident and competent the decision maker, the less he is likely to be influenced.
4. Increasing pressure by increasing the number of people exerting the pressure does not seem very effective past groups of five.
5. The more unanimous the pressure, the greater the influence.
6. The more cohesive and interdependent the group members, the greater the likelihood of conformity.
7. Certain persons can be selected who will conform less than others (e.g., flexible, bright, independent individuals).

Note that many of these aspects are under the control of the organization. They can select the types of people they want and place them in positions in which their characteristics will be helpful. The reward and communication structures are major determinants of the degree of interdependence or attractiveness of the group. Manipulating the size of the group is also feasible. Thus, the major issue is whether the organization wants, desires, and needs social influence to be an integral part of the decision process. If participation, consensus, and similar attitudes are necessary, then appropriate steps are available. If independence, heterogeneity, and to some extent creativity are demanded, then other strategies are applicable. In the final analysis the organization must choose according to its needs.

Individual Clout:
Organizational Power

In Chapter 2 we identified certain organizational and social forces that impinge on the individual as he makes decisions in the organization. These forces arise from various behavioral and environmental phenomena, one of which is power, the topic of this chapter. Our purposes are to show how this phenomenon arises and persists, to develop an understanding of what it is, and to identify where and how it impacts on organizational decision processes.

As we shall see, power significantly affects the relevant stimulus set, the set of evoked memory, the structure of plans, and finally the overt decision behavior of the individual. Conversely, this same phenomenon, power, provides one means by which the individual affects the decision processes of others. He thereby has a hand in determining organizational direction by reshaping the forces operating in his decision environment.

Our discussion of power proceeds in three steps. First, we present a theoretical overview of the concepts of power that have been developed in the behavioral disciplines, concepts which are not restricted in application to the organization but are meant for application in any social setting. We next present a general concept of social power which reconciles several points of disagreement and inconsistency among the previously presented theories. Finally, the theories and concepts of the first and second sections are presented in an organizational context with emphasis on their implications for organizational decision processes. Research results from several sources are used to amplify the discussion.

BACKGROUND

The concept of social power has interested and intrigued numerous social scientists and social philosophers. "That some people have more power than others is one of the most palpable facts of human existence," wrote Dahl (1957, p. 201) in his discussion of social power. "Because of this," he continued, "the concept of power is as ancient and ubiquitous as any that social theory can boast" (p. 201). Other writers have viewed the concept of power as occupying a central position in the social sciences. Bertrand Russell (1938) wrote, "I shall be concerned to prove that the fundamental concept in social science is Power, in the same sense in which Energy is the fundamental concept in physics" (p. 9). Social psychologists Dorwin Cartwright and Kenneth Clark have both argued that the study of power should be a central concern of social psychology (Cartwright, 1959a, p. 13; Clark, 1965, p. 16), and Clark, like Russell, stated that "A theory of power could serve not only as a unifying principle for social psychology, but as a unifying principle for social science as a whole" (p. 16).

Despite this interest in the topic and its pervasiveness in organizational decision processes, power has yet to occupy the central position in the social sciences as envisioned by the above writers. Part of the explanation lies in the lack of accord among those who have studied and developed this subject. Cartwright (1965), Kornberg and Perry (1966), Riker (1964), and Schopler (1965) have all pointed out the disagreement and disunity that exists in the power literature. There are a number of theories of social power that differ in emphasis and in scope, and the relationship of these different views to one another is not entirely clear.

THEORETICAL OVERVIEW

Kornberg and Perry (1966) suggested that theories of power can be arranged along an ends-means continuum. Theories are classified according to the aspect of the power relationship that is dealt with in most detail. On one end of the

actor attempting   recipient of power
to exert power   attempts

Figure 10-1   Power Actors

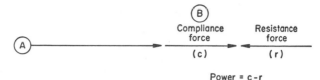

Power = c - r

Figure 10-2   Power as a Resultant Force

continuum are those theories that focus on the *means or process* by which power is exercised, while on the other end are those that focus on the *end state or outcome* of the power relationship. Of course, most writers discuss both process and outcome; but there does appear to be a real difference in emphasis. Of the theories discussed here, the field theories and the exchange theories are process oriented, whereas the political science decision-making theories are outcome oriented.

Throughout the current discussion power is conceptualized as a process involving dyadic interaction of individuals, groups, or other collectives. Relationships which consider more than two parties are treated elsewhere under the topics of social influence and leadership. In the following remarks the actor attempting to exert power is represented as A, and the other actor as B (Figure 10-1). In some cases the notation of other authors has been modified in accordance with this convention to avoid confusion.

Field Theory

This approach to the study of power is based on Lewin's field theory (1951) in which behavior is seen as a function of needs or tensions, conceptualized as force vectors. Our interest is on the forces that the two actors may bring to bear on one another in a power relationship. Although Lewin himself did not discuss power in great detail, his approach was extensively researched. We will focus on Cartwright's analysis, which has been described in the most detail (Cartwright, 1959b; Cartwright and Zander, 1968).

Cartwright (1959b) defined power as follows: "The power of A over B with respect to a given change at a specified time equals the maximum strength of the resultant force which A can set up in that direction at that time" (p. 193). As represented in Figure 10-2, A's act is seen as creating in B both a force to comply and a force to resist. The resultant force (power) is given by the *difference* between these two. Cartwright pointed out that in Lewin's definition the force A can "induce" on B and the "resistance" that B can offer are terms that can be interpreted in a number of different ways. Nonetheless, it should be noted that power is viewed here as a *possibility* for inducing forces—it refers to the maximum effect A could have if he actually decided to use his power.

Whether some change in B actually occurs is a function of *all* the forces

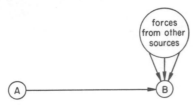

Figure 10-3   All Forces Operating on B

operating on B at the time, not just the forces exerted by A (Figure 10-3). The outcome depends on whether the force set up by A is large enough to overcome opposition forces. A is said to have *control* over B's behavior when the desired change actually occurs. For this to happen A must overcome B's resistance forces *and* the opposition forces as well.

Two important factors that determine A's power are the resources he controls and the needs or "motive bases" of B. The idea is that "an act of A must 'tap' **a** motive base in order for it to activate a force" (Cartwright, 1959b, p. 205). In other words, A can create a force in B by using resources that affect B's need satisfaction. French and Raven (1959) provided a detailed discussion of some of the different motive bases involved and we will examine them in greater detail later in this chapter.

Exchange Theory

The exchange theories provide an economic-like analysis of the interaction between two individuals (groups, collectives, etc.). This interaction is viewed in terms of the outcomes the actors mediate for each other, outcomes that are measured by the rewards and costs accruing to each individual. In these terms A has power and can influence behavior to the extent that he can determine the rewards and costs B experiences.

The general assumption is that an individual behaves so as to maximize the rewards and minimize the costs he obtains. As presented by Thibaut and Kelley (1959), each actor has a repertoire of behaviors from which to select. The outcome of the power relationship is not known until both parties have selected and performed some behavior. It is the combined behaviors of the actors that determine the outcomes for both. In Thibaut and Kelley's conception the rewards and costs are seen as an *objective* statement of the outcome-con-sequences. In other words, these consequences represent what the actors will *actually* experience and not necessarily what they perceive or anticipate they will experience.

Certain outcomes will usually be of greater value than others to an actor. It is possible that a highly desired outcome cannot be obtained by B unless the other actor chooses certain behaviors from his repertoire that will provide that outcome. A, then, has the ability to determine the outcomes B experiences, and this ability is defined as power by Thibaut and Kelley. In contrast, if B values all outcomes equally, A has no power, for his choice of behavior can have no effect on the outcome-value B will experience. The *extent* of A's power is a function of the range of outcome-values he can determine for B. The upper limit of this range is the best outcome B can obtain in interacting with A; however, the lower limit depends on the value of outcomes B can obtain in some other relationship. If the outcomes provided by A are poorer than he can get elsewhere, B is likely to leave his relationship with A. This sets the lower limit, or minimum outcome, that A must give B to maintain power over him. Thibaut and Kelley also point out that A may not be able to use the full extent of his power since the performance of certain necessary behaviors may be quite costly to him. Thus, power is usable only to the degree that it does not excessively penalize its possessor.

Emerson's theory is similar in that "power resides implicitly in the other's dependency" (1962, p. 194). The *dependence* of B upon A is positively related to his motivational investment in the goals mediated by A, and negatively related to the availability of these goals outside the A-B relationship. If B is not dependent on A, then A has no power over B. *Power* is defined as "the amount of resistance on the part of B which can be potentially overcome by A" (p. 194).

Emerson argued that there is a tendency for power relationships to move toward a state of balance at which power is equal. He provided a detailed discussion of the processes involved and analyzed norms, roles, authority, and status in these terms. In later papers, Emerson (1973a and 1973b) has expressed these ideas in reinforcement theory terms and has gone into the analysis of group processes in more detail.

Although these theories use different terms and have somewhat different emphasis, they are generally similar in arguing that A has power to influence behavior by manipulating the rewards and costs, or positive and negative values, that B experiences in exchange for the desired behavior on the part of B. Blau (1964), Karlsson (1962), and Kuhn (1963) have provided similar analyses of social power. These theories emphasize the processes that operate in the power relationship. We now briefly highlight some theories which emphasize the outcome of the relationship.

Political Science Decision-Making Theory

The study of power by political scientists has emerged under the headings of "decision-making theory." This label should not be confused with "decision theory" as discussed in our succeeding sections, for although the early work appeared to be going in the same direction, the two theories have since diverged.

March (1955) argued that power (he used the term "influence") should be studied in the context of decision making. He stated that "influence is to the study of decision making what force is to the study of motion—a generic explanation of the basic observable phenomena" (p. 432). In other words, the power of an actor can be examined in terms of *the effects he has on the decisions or choices of other actors.* He then defined influence as "that which induces behavior on the part of the individual at time t_1 different from that which might be predicted on the basis of a knowledge of the individual organism at time t_0" (p. 438), where behavior means any change in the state of the organism. Thus, "if the individual deviates from the predicted path of behavior, influence has occurred and, specifically . . . it is influence which has induced the change" (p. 435). March provided some discussion of power in terms of changes in the values and expectations of actor B and the consequent effect on his decision. However, in later papers by him and others in this area, this psychological aspect of the theory is de-emphasized and the major emphasis is placed on the assessment of power in terms of his definition.

Dahl (1957) elaborated on March's definition. He started with an intuitive definition of power, which is "A has power over B to the extent that he can get B to do something B would not otherwise do" (p. 202–03).

He worked from this idea to his view that the power of A over B is a function of the difference between (1) the probability of B performing a given behavior after A has made some intervention, and (2) the probability of B performing this behavior without A's intervention. The amount of power is expressed as the difference between these two probabilities (Table 10-1).

These brief descriptions show that the emphasis of Dahl and March is on the outcome of the power relationship. In contrast, the concepts underlying exchange- and field-theories of power emphasize the process by which power is exercised. In the following section a decision-theory approach to power is presented, an approach that links the process and outcome theories.

A Decision-Theory Model of Power

Our ultimate interest in analyzing power relationships is to understand how and why they impact organizational decisions. We wish to understand the origins

Table 10-1   Dahl's View of Power

The probability, before A's intervention, that B will perform the specific behavior	$= P_1$
The probability, after A's intervention, that B will perform the specific behavior	$= P_2$
$P_2 - P_1$ = the amount of A's power	

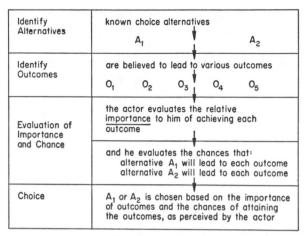

Identify Alternatives	known choice alternatives A_1 $\qquad\downarrow\qquad$ A_2
Identify Outcomes	are believed to lead to various outcomes O_1 $\quad$ O_2 $\quad$ O_3 $\downarrow$ O_4 $\quad$ O_5
Evaluation of Importance and Chance	the actor evaluates the relative importance to him of achieving each outcome $\qquad\downarrow$
	and he evaluates the chances that: alternative A_1 will lead to each outcome alternative A_2 will lead to each outcome $\downarrow$
Choice	A_1 or A_2 is chosen based on the importance of outcomes and the chances of attaining the outcomes, as perceived by the actor

Figure 10-4   The Decision-Theory Logic

(bases) of power, the conditions under which power can and will be exercised, and the various forms it can assume. This cannot be accomplished by focusing on either process or outcome to the exclusion of the other. Instead, we will presently consider elements of both. The purpose of this section is to suggest an approach to the study of power based on decision theory. The essential idea is that power processes can be studied in terms of the decisions people make in exerting power and in responding to the exertion of power. Decisions made in response to power will be examined in the most detail since this has been the major focus of work in this area. This approach may be useful for integrating various theories of power with one another and with more general theories of behavior and decision making. It will be necessary for us to review some concepts of decision theory, to consider the notion of "goal attainment," and then detail the components of actor B's cognitive processes. Having done this, we will suggest which of the subcomponents of his processes can be affected by actor A to achieve various forms of power.

Decision Theory

In our earlier discussions, it was suggested that individual decisions are made as a function of the expected payoffs of various alternatives. More specifically, the individual decision maker generates a set of alternative choices and estimates the degree to which each alternative is likely to lead to various outcomes. These estimates are then weighted to reflect the importances of the outcomes. He then chooses the alternative which he believes will lead to the greatest expected payoff (Figure 10-4).

These ideas have been recently generalized to cover the area of social power (Pollard and Mitchell, 1973). More specifically, B's action with regard to A's exertion of power is like any other of B's decisions in that this same conceptual framework can be applied to analyze his behavior. The concept of subjective expected utility (SEU) is important here. The actor's SEU for an alternative is found by multiplying the actor's utility (importance) for each of the outcomes of the alternatives by the probability (chances) the actor associates with their occurrence, and summing across outcomes. Suppose actor B has identified two behavior alternatives, B_1 and B_2. For action-alternative B_1,

$$\text{SEU (for } B_1) = \sum_{i=1}^{n} p_i u_i$$

with

$$\sum_{i=1}^{n} p_i = 1.0$$

where n is the number of possible outcomes of this action, p_i is the actor's subjective probability that the behavior (action B_1) will lead to the outcome i, and u_i is the utility or importance the actor attaches to the outcome i. Therefore, the decision involves actor B comparing the expected payoff (SEU) for action B_1 with the expected payoff of alternative B_2 and selecting the course of action with the largest SEU.

One should note three points regarding this analysis. First, we are dealing with the actor's perception of the situation—the focus is on the actor's subjective identification of possible outcomes of an action, his subjective evaluations of utilities of the outcomes, and his subjective probability estimates regarding the chances of occurrence of the outcomes. Thus, the actor may hold socially or organizationally deviant utilities (values) or objectively inaccurate probabilities (beliefs) and yet perform as the SEU analysis would predict, given his utilities and subjective probabilities. Second, this type of analysis is often criticized for allegedly portraying man as an avaricious miser out to maximize his satisfaction at everyone else's expense. Actually, there is nothing in our analysis to prevent the individual from attaching positive utility to the welfare and happiness of others and behaving accordingly. Third, the components of this theory are similar to some of the ideas suggested by the field, exchange, and political science theorists. One can see that concepts such as costs and rewards or resources and motive bases are appropriate considerations in evaluating the utilities of outcomes. The process of comparing rewards and costs, suggested by exchange theorists, is somewhat like the idea of comparing the SEU's for various alternatives. The major differences are the explicit inclusion of subjective probabilities and suggestions about how probabilities are combined multiplicatively with utilities and are summed over outcomes. Thus, the decision-theory analysis provides a description of the underlying cognitive process involved in choosing to comply or to not comply with the wishes of another person. A more detailed analysis will point out the important distinctions incorporated in this approach.

Figure 10-5   Effective Forces and Goal Attainment

Refinements of Decision Theory: Goal Attainment of A

Our starting point here is Kuhn's (1963, p. 317) general notion of power as the ability to satisfy wants or obtain goals. These goals may be social or non-social. Heider's analysis of an actor's goal attainment is useful to consider in this context (1958, pp. 82–83). He views the ability of an actor (A) to obtain a goal (X) as a function of the effective force of the actor (ff actor) and the effective force of the environment (ff environment). Whether or not actor A obtains his goal depends on whether or not his effective force is great enough to overcome any opposing effective force of the environment (Figure 10-5). Heider argued that the effective force of A (ff actor) can be analyzed into a power factor and a motivational factor called *trying* (Figure 10-6). The power factor is a function of a number of things such as the actor's power bases or ability. The motivational factor refers to A's intentions and the effort he exerts.

Several components in Heider's analysis are generally similar to concepts labeled "possible," "realized," and "effective" power by several authors (Dahlstrom, 1966, p. 238; Nagel, 1968, pp. 133–35; Wrong, 1968, pp. 677–81). Distinctions among these types of power and their similarities to the components of goal attainment are summarized in Table 10-2.

The meanings of these different concepts of power are clarified by substituting them into Heider's framework, as shown in Figure 10-7. A's *possible power* refers to the abilities and resources he could use to obtain a goal. It refers to the effects A *could* have in a given situation, but not necessarily to the effects he will actually have in that situation. Possible power is an objective assessment of what A could do, and this is not necessarily the same as his perceptions or other actors' perceptions of what he could do. A's *decision* involves the choice to actually use some of this possible power in a specific way to obtain some goal. This decision is a function of his SEU for taking some goal-oriented action, in comparison to his SEUs for alternative actions. A's decision requires prior consideration of his positive utilities associated with the goal, negative utilities associated with the expenditure of various resources (time, effort, etc.), and his

Figure 10-6   Components of Goal Attainment (*Source:* Heider, 1958.)

Table 10-2   Types of Power and Components of Goal Attainment

Type of Power	Characteristics	Heider Analysis
Possible	The force that *could be* exerted to obtain a goal	Power
Realized	The force that *is* exerted (as perceived by B), at the discretion of actor A, to obtain a goal	ff actor
Effective	The extent to which actor A's goal is attained	Attainment of X

probability estimates regarding the occurrence of these outcomes given that the effort is expended. *Possible power* plus the *decision* to use some of it in a specific way to obtain a goal contributes to A's *realized power*. This is the force (as perceived by B) that will actually be exerted by A in an effort to obtain the goal. A's *effective power* or his ability to actually obtain the goal is determined by his realized power and by situational factors. These situational factors might be negative or opposing forces; however, they can also be forces that facilitate or support goal attainment.

Decision Theory and Goal Attainment in Social Power[1]

Social power can be seen as a special case of this general conception of goal attainment—it refers to the situation in which A's goal is to obtain certain behavior from another actor (B). Thus, A provides incentives, information, promises, threats, etc., in order to influence B's willful choice of actions or behaviors. A's power can be examined in terms of his effect on various elements in B's decision process.

In the situation represented by Figure 10-8, B has two discrete behaviors from which to choose. Suppose the behavior desired by A is represented by B_1. There are a number of possible outcomes for each of the behaviors. B's overall payoffs (SEUs) for each of the behaviors can be determined by multiplying B's

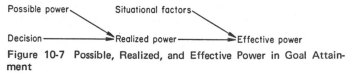

Figure 10-7   Possible, Realized, and Effective Power in Goal Attainment

[1] For the development and assumptions of this model see Pollard and Mitchell, 1972.

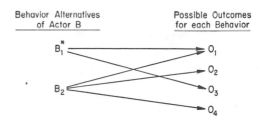

Behavior Alternatives
of Actor B

Possible Outcomes
for each Behavior

*B_1 is the behavior of B that is desired by A

Figure 10-8   Outcome-Alternative Relationships for B

subjective probabilities that the behavior will lead to each of these outcomes times the utility B attaches to each of the outcomes. Thus, we can obtain SEU_{B1} as well as SEU_{B2}, where the latter is some possible behavior that is different from the one desired by A.

The outcomes that B will experience are partially determined by A since he controls certain resources that may be allocated at his discretion. However, the outcomes are not totally under the control of A, but are partly determined by situational factors such as other people, the impersonal environment, intrinsic satisfactions or dissatisfactions that B experiences from performing certain types of behavior, etc. Thus, B's SEUs are determined partly by A's manipulation of the outcomes and partly by the effects of situational factors. These two subcomponents of SEU for behavior B1 are shown in Figure 10-9. Similarly, B's SEU for each behavior alternative can be broken down into two parts—one reflecting A's effects and the other representing the effects of the situational (S) factors.

In this example, A's goal is to get B to perform B_1 and to not perform B_2. Consequently, A's influence-attempt would involve manipulating the outcomes in such a way that the SEU for the preferred alternative (B_1) is greater than the SEU for the other alternative (B_2). However, A can effect only one portion of B's total SEU for each alternative, as shown in Figure 10-10 (column 2). The extent to which A contributes to the difference between the SEUs of the desired and the not-desired behavior alternatives,

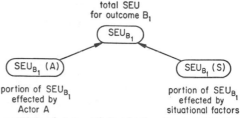

Figure 10-9   Decomposition of Actor B's Subjective Expected Utility for One Outcome (B_1)

(1)	(2)	(3)	(4)
Behavior Alternative	Portion of SEU effected by Actor A	Portion of SEU effected by situational factors	Actor B's total SEU for the alternative
B_1	$SEU_{B_1}(A)$ +	$SEU_{B_1}(S)$ =	SEU_{B_1}
B_2	$SEU_{B_2}(A)$ +	$SEU_{B_2}(S)$ =	SEU_{B_2}

Figure 10-10 Decomposition of SEUs for Alternatives B_1 and B_2

$$SEU_{B_1}(A) \quad - \quad SEU_{B_2}(A) \tag{1}$$

measures his *realized power* over B. This measure indicates the effect that A has on B's choice.

Although A may be able to effect favorable directions in the difference in expression [1], B still may choose B_2 because of situational factors. The choice will be made not only on the basis of A's effects, but on the combined effects of A and all other environmental considerations that B perceives to be relevant. These combined effects are summarized in B's *total* SEU for each alternative (column 4, Figure 10-10). The components leading to B's choice are symbolized in expressions [2] and [3].

$$\left(\begin{array}{c}\text{the effects}\\ \text{of A}\end{array}\right) \quad + \quad \left(\begin{array}{c}\text{the effects of}\\ \text{all other factors}\end{array}\right) \longrightarrow \begin{array}{c}\text{determines}\\ \text{choice}\end{array} \tag{2}$$

$$\left(SEU_{B_1}(A) - SEU_{B_2}(A)\right) + \left(SEU_{B_1}(S) - SEU_{B_2}(S)\right) \begin{array}{c}+ \nearrow B_1 \\ - \searrow B_2\end{array} \tag{3}$$

The terms in the left parentheses represent the effects of A on the outcomes, A's *realized power* over B. The second parentheses represent the effects stemming from additional factors such as other actors, the impersonal environment, intrinsic satisfactions, etc. The combination of the two is A's *effective power* over B which determines whether or not B will perform B_1. Referring back to Figure 10-7, one can see that realized power is the force A exerts on B's perceptions whereas effective power is indicated by A's realized power compared with other forces on B.

According to this conception of social power, A can exert power over B and have some effect on B's decision and still not obtain B's compliance, for B's ultimate decision and behavior is determined by situational factors in addition to A's realized power. We could, of course, focus solely on A's effective power and measure power only in terms of B's behavior. However, as Nagel (1968) pointed out, this can lead to confusion, for the statement "A has no power to affect B's behavior" can be erroneously interpreted as meaning A is totally impotent and exerts no force at all. Furthermore, such an approach would fail to reveal, and not allow us to understand, the number and complexity of many forces that impinge on the decision maker.

Implicit in our analysis is the idea that power refers to, in Bertrand Russell's words, "the production of intended effects," for the analysis is centered around the behavior that A desires or intends to affect. The central question in our analysis is whether or not A is able to affect B's decision making regarding some behavior A desires. Thus, the assessment of power here requires the determination of *both* A's intentions and the effects A has on B's decision making.

It should be pointed out that it is not necessary for A to act in order to make B aware of A's intentions. B can anticipate A's decisions and intentions on the basis of general cultural knowledge, experiences with others similar to A, communication from other actors regarding A, past experiences with A, certain features of the organization structure, and other factors. Friedrich (1941) referred to this process as the "rule of anticipated reactions," and in his discussion of power in organizations, Simon (1957) wrote: "an organization member is seldom presented with an ultimatum 'to do so and so or suffer the consequences.' Rather, he anticipates the consequences of continual insubordination or failure to please the person or persons who have the ability to apply sanctions to him, and this anticipation acts as a constant motivation without expressed threats from any person" (p. 196). Nagel (1968) has pointed out that this "rule of anticipated reactions" is a problem for a number of theories of power, for power is often defined in terms of B's response to some act of A. Consequently, situations in which A does not act fall outside these definitions of power. The effects of anticipated reactions are included in our analysis, for we do not require that B's consideration of A's intentions necessarily results from some overt influence attempt or command by A.

Consideration of the effects of anticipated reactions helps to clarify the distinction between actual and potential power. Specifically, actual power stems from an *act* or influence attempt whereas potential power is derived from the effects of *anticipated* reactions. Both actual and potential power are included in our concept of realized power since both are based on B's perceptions rather than on objective reality.[2]

Finally, it should be noted that the decision-theory analysis of power may be extended to deal with other issues that have appeared in the power literature. First, the term in expression [3] which represents the effects of situational factors can be broken into separate components representing the realized power of several other actors. Thus, the analysis may be applied to situations in which a number of actors are trying to influence B. Second, as indicated earlier, the basic

---

[2]Wrong (1968) has provided further discussion of these distinctions.

ideas of this approach are related to a number of theories of motivation (Vroom, 1964), attitudes, and attitude change (Fishbein, 1963, 1967; Peak, 1955; Rosenberg, 1956). Consequently, it should be possible to tie in notions of influence, attitude change, and motivation with this analysis. Third, we have focused on B's decision-making process in the most detail since this corresponds with the major focus of the other theories of social power. However, A's and B's decisions are interrelated in that each of the actors is influenced in making his decisions by his perceptions and expectations regarding the other's decision-making process and behavior. A more detailed analysis of this interaction between the decisions of A and B may be useful in clarifying various topics such as bargaining and the effects of counterpower. Fourth, one can also analyze the non-social components of the process. For example, one individual may decide to not follow another's instructions because of inaccessibility of a suitable technology upon which he would have to depend given the suggested course of action. Also, one can examine other sources of outcomes. Thus, the analysis could be extended to include the force on the individual attributed to his peers (social influence); his supervisor (realized power); the organization (authority); and the physical environment (technology). We turn now to a brief review of the empirical support for these ideas.

POWER CONCEPTS IN THE ORGANIZATION SETTING

The idea underlying the above analysis is that if a decision maker is dependent upon others to accept and execute his decisions, he can effect this acceptance and execution in a formal sense by the use of rewards and perhaps punishments. However, he must use the proper rewards (ones for which B has a high utility) and he must make clear and consistent the contingencies between the expected behavior and the outcomes (subjective probabilities must be high). As we shall see, some additional means exist, other than rewards and punishment, for effecting acceptance and execution of one's decisions.

Bases of Power

Perhaps the most well-known classification of power sources was presented by French and Raven (1959). These authors suggest that B will perceive A as possessing, or having control over, six major factors affecting outcomes. These are: (1) rewards; (2) punishments; (3) information; (4) expertise; (5) social approval; (6) personal guidance. These last two are called legitimate power and referent power by French and Raven and are defined as: (a) power such that B sees A's request as within legitimate norms and expectations; and (b) power such that B wishes to be like A or to use him as a referent. Most of the empirical research seems to follow these six categories fairly well.

Reward and Punishment Power

The early psychological research in this area focused on basic reinforcement theory in which rewards and punishments consisted of fines, shocks, threats of dismissal, physical punishment, etc. Studies of relatively limited aspects of human activity such as verbal conditioning show that rewards and punishments are powerful determinants of an individual's behavior (Greenspoon, 1955; Taffel, 1955). These basic concepts of reward and punishment have been studied in organizational contexts. Supervisory power was found to be greater when the appropriate reward was being controlled and when the supervisor accurately perceived the subordinate reward system (Bennis, Berkowitz, Affinito, and Malone, 1958). In a similar vein, Cohen (1959) found that greater anxiety was experienced by the subordinate when he was not sure which behaviors were to be rewarded or punished.

The exercise of power requires an interesting choice between the use of reward and punishment. An investigation by Zipf (1960) found no difference in overall compliance in the use of reward vs. punishment power, but individuals felt greater resistance for the supervisor when they were under coercive or punishment conditions. A study by Ring and Kelley (1963) showed reward power to be more effective than punishment. However, a study by Wahba (1971) produced the opposite results. He found that coercive power can produce greater cooperation than reward power, but may eventually lead to conflict. Further work on this issue indicates the effectiveness of the mode of sanction depends on its legitimacy as perceived by the recipient of the influence attempt (Kipnis, 1958).

It appears that reward or coercive power is used only under certain conditions. Goodstadt and Kipnis (1970) found that when problems of discipline occurred supervisors tended to use coercive power. When problems of ineptness occurred, other bases of power such as information and expertise were used. Later studies show that reward power rather than coercive power is used when subordinates resort to flattery or ingratiation (Jones, 1964; Kipnis and Vanderveer, 1971).

In summary, it appears that rewards and punishments provided by a superior (a) are perceived as important outcomes by subordinates, and (b) influence subordinate behavior in predictable directions. Further, the outcomes must be made clear and they must be perceived as appropriate to result in maximum effectiveness.

Information Power

The control over useful information is an important basis of power. One would predict that supervisors with greater power would do more communicating and receive more communications if they were using information power to change subordinate behavior. Many studies of communication flows, in both laboratory and organization settings, show that the person who communicates more is seen as having more power (Shaw, 1964; Hurwitz, Zander, and Hymovitch, 1953; Lippitt, Polansky, Redl, and Rosen, 1952). In the Hurwitz study, for example, groups of mental hygiene workers with varying degrees of power were observed. It was found that high power members communicated more frequently and received more communications than low power members. Studies by Watson (1965) and Watson and Bromberg (1965) have also found that more powerful members communicate more extensively. A recent study (Watson, 1971) found that individuals who were both powerful and high on dominance-personality measures showed the greatest amount of communication. The content of these communications indicated that the dominant, high power individuals tended to give "suggestions and direction" more frequently than did the other group members. So, one's ability to control useful information is clearly related to power and is used to control the behavior of others.

Expert Power

The number of studies showing the influence of expert power in a *group* setting are too numerous to document here (see Collins and Raven, 1969, or Schopler, 1964, for reviews). In general, when one group member clearly has the expertise to do the job his power is markedly greater than the power of the other members (with other outcomes held constant). This effect seems to operate even more readily when the task is complex, ambiguous, or difficult (Coleman, Blake, and Mouton, 1958; Luchins, 1945).

Other investigators have examined conditions under which expert power may be advantageously used. For example, Mulder and Wilke (1970) found that expert judges working on a town planning problem had considerably more power than non-expert judges, especially under more participative conditions. The study by Goodstadt and Kipnis (1970), mentioned previously, found that supervisors used expert power more than other power bases when confronted with the problem of an inept subordinate. Conversely, Evan and Zelditch (1961) found that supervisors were disobeyed more frequently when they were perceived as having inadequate knowledge about the job.

There has been some discussion as to the degree to which an individual's expert power is transferable to situations in which he has less expertise. Brim (1954), for example, reports that physicians have power in areas other than their speciality and French and Snyder (1959) report similar findings for military officers. However, if the expert judge strays too far afield he is likely to be a victim of the "boomerang effect" in which the subordinate believes he is being misled and behaves in a way contrary to the desires of the person attempting to influence him (Hovland, Lumsdaine, and Sheffield, 1949; Kelman and Hovland, 1953). Expertise, then, appears to be an important basis of power in that the possessor of such expertise can increase his chances of attaining desired outcomes.

Legitimate Power

Conformance to the social norm of legitimacy is also an important outcome as perceived by a subordinate. He views compliance as a way of "obeying the rules," or meeting the reasonable expectations of those around him, and this is important to most people. Certain organizational positions have accompanying "rights" to demand various behaviors from others. To the extent that these "rights" are generally recognized by others, they provide an effective base of power called legitimacy. An extreme example in which the issue of legitimacy has become very important is the role of the research experimenter. Studies by Frank (1944), Block and Block (1952), and Orne (1962) have found that subjects will do almost anything that the experimenter asks. Orne's research, for example, had subjects computing long lists of addition tasks and then destroying their answers or plunging their hands into a bowl presumed to contain acid (Orne and Evans, 1965). Milgram (1963), in a now famous study, found that subjects would administer high levels of electric shock to another individual when asked to do so by the experimenter. Legitimate power of the experimenter, in many of these studies, was the only basis that could logically account for the observed behaviors since the reward, punishment, information, and expertise bases were not applicable.

Some investigations have manipulated legitimacy (Raven and French, 1958) and found that those people with legitimacy (perhaps a leadership title) are more powerful. In a recent study, Shiflett and Nealey (1972) manipulated legitimate power and found that it influenced not only the performance of the group, but also the leader's behavior. More specifically, the high power leaders engaged in more structuring of the task than did leaders with less legitimacy. Again, the perceived legitimacy of the leader's influence attempts is a powerful determinant of a subordinate's behavior and performance.

Referent Power

The referent power base suggests that an individual who wishes to be like another person, or looks up to him as someone to model, will be more easily influenced by that person. One study by Zander and Curtis (1962) indicated that subjects worked harder to meet the expectations of those possessing referent power than they did when confronted with coercive or punishment power. Many of the social influence studies described earlier (e.g., Asch, 1956) suggest that people behave in ways contrary to their own experience because of the desire to meet the expectations of others. People will make greater contributions for a gift for another (Blake and Mouton, 1957), sign a petition, volunteer for an experiment (Rosenbaum and Blake, 1955) or cross the street against a traffic signal (Lefkowitz, Blake, and Mouton, 1955) if they see this behavior encouraged, expected, or carried out by a referent person.

In comparative investigations, it appears as if legitimate, referent, and expert power have the greatest effect. A study by Kelman (1958) found that referent and expert power controlled more behavior than reward-coercive power when the participants were sure that the communicator would not see their responses. An extensive investigation by Ivancevich (1970), with 228 insurance agents in thirty-nine different agencies, had subjects rate their reasons for compliance with the agency manager's directives. Table 10-3 summarizes these findings.

Again, one can see that legitimate, expert, and referent power seem to be more important than just reward and coercive power.

The implications of these results should be clear by now. First, it appears as if an individual's power can be conceptualized as a function of the types of outcomes he mediates. Second, there is a wide variety of effective outcomes other than traditional rewards and punishments that comprise the bases of power. Third, high power individuals are frequently liked, communicated with, listened to, and modeled. In summary, then, a decision maker who needs the compliance of others for the effective implementation of his decisions, or to influence the decisions of others, has a large variety of outcomes at his disposal. When the outcomes are clear and appropriate, the subordinate is likely to see compliance as offering a high probability of obtaining rewards he values highly. Given that other factors from the environment and the social group are not working at cross purposes with the decision maker's goals, the decisions should be more effectively executed.

Table 10-3   Bases of Power

Power bases	Rating
Referent	2.98
Expert	3.38
Reward	2.91
Coercive	2.17
Legitimate	3.72

Source: Adapted from *Academy of Management Journal,* December 1970, p. 434.

Informal Power

A peculiar characteristic of organizations is the complexity arising from a multitude of reciprocal role relationships, and the need for coordinated efforts among them. Organization structures are established to give desired direction to the influence-relationships among role occupants, to create " . . . a pattern of coordinated and effective behavior" (Simon, 1965, pp. 2–3). Formal systems of authority and channels of communication are established to assure the orderly conduct of organizational operations. The organization's work is subdivided and formal authority relationships are established between organization units. Standard practices prescribe the ways in which certain activities are conducted. The exercise of individual discretion is limited by decision criteria which are passed down from superordinate levels of the organization (pp. 102–03). All of these factors contribute to the location and extent of power relationships that exist in the organization. However, as organizations increase in size, and as their decision problems become more complex, all of these formal mechanisms are less capable of providing communication networks adequate for making good decisions. It is in this context that the role and scope of informal aspects of organization are of crucial importance.

> The term "informal organization" refers to interpersonal relations in the organization that affect decisions within it but either are omitted from the formal scheme or are not consistent with that scheme (p. 148).

The informal organization gives rise to informal power relationships which play a significant role in decision making. Our emphasis to date has been on one side of the power relationship, the superior's power over the subordinate. Subordinates do, however, exert power upward and laterally in the organization.

> . . . lower participants in organizations can often assume and wield considerable power which is not associated with their positions as formally defined within these organizations (Mechanic, 1964, p. 137).

On what bases does such power rest? How pervasive is informal power? The answers to these questions reside, partly, in the superior's dependence upon the lower participant for providing access to information, persons, and resources (Mechanic, 1964). The subordinate may be relied upon for his knowledge of other persons, rules, procedures, techniques, or relationships among various organization units. He may control access to persons upon whom the superior is dependent or to elements of the physical plant and financial resources. By obtaining, maintaining and controlling " . . . access to persons, information, and instrumentalities" lower participants effectively achieve power (p. 142).

To the extent that this can be accomplished, lower participants make higher-ranking participants dependent upon them. Thus, dependence together with the manipulation of the dependency relationship is the key to the power of lower participants (p. 142).

The general bases of informal power arise primarily from unique personal characteristics of the individual or from his location (physical and social) in the organization. These variables are not controlled by the formal organization structure. A number of specific factors affecting the power of lower participants are detailed in Table 10-4.

Table 10-4   Mechanic's "Factors Affecting Power"

Factor	Affect
1. expertise	Delegation of responsibility and specialization results in expert knowledge with respect to specific areas of operation. Thus, the specialist becomes an important source of information upon whom the higher participant is dependent.
2. effort and interest	The lower participant may exert effort in areas in which higher participants are reluctant to act. The extent of effort exerted is related to his level of interest.
3. attractiveness	"Personality" or "attractiveness" of the lower participant increases the likelihood of his obtaining access to other persons and of succeeding in "promoting a cause."
4. location and position	"Location in physical space and position in social space" determine one's access to persons, information, and instrumentalities.
5. coalitions	Informal coalitions enable the lower participant to provide services upon which the higher-level participant is dependent. Provision of these services permits the lower participant to bargain on other issues of importance to him.
6. rules	Lower participants can justify their point of view, and refuse to comply with higher-level requests, by using their knowledge of organization rules.

Source: Mechanic, 1964.

By employing these factors the subordinate can indeed bring forces to bear on the decision processes of the superior. The superior, when evaluating his various behavior alternatives, must consider the effects of these factors on the desirability of outcomes and on the chances of attaining the outcomes.

Information and Power

The possessor of useful information is an important element in the organizational information search process and in the organization's communication network. We have noted that one's possession of useful information or his control of access to such information increases others' dependence on him. Such individuals will be sought out by decision makers to provide needed information and, subsequently, they are in a position to place demands on the decision maker. Their power rests on two factors: (a) the absence of alternative information sources and (b) the reliability of their information (their ability to "deliver"). With regard to the first point, if the decision maker must bargain to obtain needed information, then its acquisition is more "costly" than comparable information he could obtain from sources which do not require bargaining. This notion has led to the proposition, " ... information which can be obtained without bargaining will be preferred to that which requires bargaining" (Ference, 1970, p. B-92). If alternative sources do not exist, then the power position of the information holder is strengthened. The extent to which needed information is relatively concentrated or diffused determines, in part, the power structure in the organization, and this effects the direction and amount of information search activity.

Regarding the second factor, reliability of the information source, it is clear that as the accuracy and timeliness of information diminishes, so does its usefulness. The deterioration of information-reliability reduces the decision maker's dependence on the source, whose power position is subsequently weakened.

In their everyday organizational lives decision makers maintain an awareness of the reliability of various information sources. Through surveillance and experience, they learn to assess source reliability and they selectively use information from various sources in resolving decision problems. This differentiation among sources as to reliability, and the selectivity in the use of information, are exemplified in Ference's (1970) proposition:

> The more reliable a source has been, or the more power a source has, the less likely it is that the information it provides will be rejected even if inconsistent with information acquired earlier in the problem-solving process (p. B-93).

The assessment of source reliability is a specific example of the judgment processes we discussed in Chapter 6. Recall that judgments and inferences resulted from the assimilation of various informational cues, and the judge learned to differentiate cue-relevance through his experiences with the sources of those cues. Furthermore, predominant weight was placed on relatively few such cues in formulating the judgment. Ference's foregoing statement suggests to us that differences in power and reliability among information sources will be strongly related to the weightings of cues which enter into the judgmental processes of organizational participants.

As a final point in the discussion of information and power, we reiterate the notion of "uncertainty absorption" which takes place " . . . when inferences are drawn from a body of evidence and the inferences, instead of the evidence itself, are then communicated" (March and Simon, 1965, p. 165).

Uncertainty absorption is a common practice in organizational communication systems. It is an important means of controlling information and thereby is a basis of individual power.

> Both the amount and the *locus of uncertainty absorption* affect the *influence structure of the organization*. . . . Because of this, uncertainty absorption is frequently used, consciously and unconsciously, as a technique for acquiring and exercising power (March and Simon, pp. 165–66).

For decision-making purposes it is important to be cognizant of the pervasiveness and potential impact of uncertainty absorption in the organization. It results in the transmission of information that includes biases of the editor. This same information provides the premises for subsequent organizational action.

Voluntary Power Allocation

One of the "occasions for decision," discussed previously, arises when an individual refers a decision problem to another person. The act of referral may occur for a variety of reasons but its relevance to the current discussion resides in the accompanying power-relationships that are formed. When person A refers a decision problem to B, then B has power over A if the resulting decision has future implications for A. If the stymied decision maker, A, has a choice of referring the problem to several possible decision makers, who does he seek out and to whom does he allocate such power? On what basis? A preliminary study, by Filley and Grimes (1967), indicates that these power allocations are made not only on formally prescribed bases, but are related to leadership style, perceptions of expected fairness of the decision, perceptions of the expectations of getting a desirable judgment, perceived expertise, on the basis of friendship, etc. This is of significance in two respects: first, it identifies a number of bases for one's voluntary granting of power to another in the organization; and second, relating back to the occasion for decision, it identifies some variables which may determine the likelihood, frequency, and patterns of decision-problem referral to an organizational decision maker.

At a different level of analysis it has been argued by Lammers (1967) that the voluntary allocation of power within an organization can result in power increases throughout the organization. This argument contends that power in an organization, rather than being a fixed quantity, is variable. The voluntary allocation of more power to subordinates (through participation in decision making) may lead to more effective implementation of decisions, ultimately resulting in overall power gains for the organization. It is here that our level of analysis shifts, for these overall power gains cannot be explained without reference to *external* institutions. In Lammers' theory the organization's ability to allocate power among various internal factions is limited by the amount of power, prestige, etc., granted to it by external institutions. In the section below, we consider the decision-making implications arising from the organization's relationships with others in the larger environment.

Boundary-Related Power

The characteristics of intraorganizational power relationships are not the whole story insofar as pointing out the role and impact of power on organizational decision making. The kinds of power relationships that exist and their importance to decision processes vary across levels of the organization. Recall our earlier distinction among the technical, institutional, and managerial levels. Differences in the crucial dependency relationships at these levels are reflected in different kinds of decision problems and operating strategies. For instance, boundary-spanning positions at the institutional and managerial levels involve negotiation with elements in the outer environment. This results in interorganizational power relationships which are typically not based on formal authority, whereas in many intraorganizational relationships formal authority is an important basis of power. Without the capability of resorting to authority and formal control to attain compliance in the dependency relationship, different strategies and skills must be adopted. In discussing the management of interdependence among organizations, Thompson (1967) suggests various strategies for maintaining the organization's viability. The premises of these strategies are derived from Emerson's power-dependence concepts, and they assume the organization seeks to reduce uncertainty.

a. The organization is dependent on elements of its task environment.
   (1.) Its dependency is proportional to its need for the resources or performance (support) that can be supplied by an element.

(2.) Its dependency is inversely proportional to the ability of other elements to supply the same resources or performance.
b. This dependency poses contingencies and constraints for the organization.
c. Organizations seek to reduce uncertainty (contingencies).

Therefore, to reduce uncertainty, organizations attempt to maintain alternative sources of support, thereby reducing the power of other organizations over them. If they must compete with others for support from an element of the task environment, they will seek to increase their prestige as an inexpensive way of gaining that support. If " . . . support capacity is concentrated in one or a few elements of the task environment," the organization will attempt to find ways of increasing its power relative to those elements (p. 34). These activities constitute one strategy for managing power to reduce uncertainty for the organization. As the number of interdependencies with the task environment increases, the organization may respond by attempting to increase its power over other elements. Failure in these attempts may lead to organization efforts to change the composition of its task environment.

Cooperative strategies are also adopted to acquire power:

Using cooperation to gain power with respect to some element of the task environment, the organization must demonstrate its *capacity to reduce uncertainty* for that element, and *must make a commitment* to exchange that capacity (p. 34).

Contracting, coopting, and coalescing are alternative forms of cooperative strategy that may be employed, and they involve different degrees of cooperation and commitment. Whereas contracting refers to negotiated agreement of future performances between the parties, coopting is a more binding and constraining form of cooperation in which new elements of the task environment are brought in to participate in the leadership and policy making of the organization. Coalescing involves joint venture among organizations in which they act as one with regard to decision making, and is the more binding form of cooperation. Propositions have been postulated about the conditions under which these alternative forms of cooperation will be employed.[3]

The point we wish to make is that a decision maker functioning at the institutional level is confronted with the need for dealing with some difficult issues. Such a position requires an individual who possesses unique skills and orientation. He must recognize crucial elements of the organization's task environment and be sensitive to the established dependencies and critical contingencies that they pose. He must be aware of various strategies for acquiring and

[3] For an elaboration of these situations see Thompson (1967).

maintaining power. In managing power relationships he must recognize differences in the degrees of commitment that accompany these alternative strategies. Furthermore, he must seek out, and be aware of, common interests of his organization and others in the task environment so as to foster and maintain the interdependency relationships upon which organizational viability rests.

Within an organization, boundary-spanning positions may differ as to the demands they place on individuals occupying such roles. In positions in which the occupant faces a relatively stable and homogeneous task environment, his relationships with environmental elements may be routinized and structured, resulting in little opportunity for individual discretion. The ability of the organization to gain relative power over elements of its task environment reduces its dependency on individuals in boundary-spanning positions. In contrast, a dynamic, heterogeneous task environment may require that the individual be afforded considerable discretion in negotiating dependency relationships for the organization. In this case the individual has relatively more power since the organization is dependent upon him for its viability. His power rests on his ability to successfully maneuver in this role. The individual's success in mediating crucial contingencies in the boundary-spanning role enables him to extend his participation into other decision-making matters in the organization. We see, then, that the distribution of power within the organization is related to the organization's power in its task environment; *inter*organizational power cannot be divorced from *intra*organizational power. The ability to reduce organizational uncertainty is an important basis of intraorganizational power. The exercise of discretion in reducing this uncertainty is the mechanism by which individual power is acquired. Thompson (1967) proposes that individuals in highly discretionary positions will attempt to maintain power at least as great as their dependence upon others in the organization. Failure to do so will lead to their seeking coalitions with others in the organization or with vital elements of the task environment. As changes occur in organizational dependencies and uncertainties, coalitions will crumble and others will rise. The demands that an individual can place on others, and on the organization, depend upon his sustained ability to mediate crucial contingencies. Such persons are most likely to have the greatest involvement and influence in the organization's key decision-making activities. The number of such "influentials" can be expected to vary with the number of crucial contingencies confronting the organization. It would include a member(s) of the core technology to the extent that technology is highly imperfect. It would be expected to include larger numbers of boundary-spanning positions when the task environment is highly heterogeneous. We see then that the group of "dominant influentials," making key decisions for organizational direction, can vary in size and composition across organizations and time. As the size of this group increases, power is more widely distributed, and Thompson's work suggests that the central power figure will be one who can manage the diverse interests of the "dominant coalition." What is significant here is the massive set of complex constraints imposed on this individual. His actions may not be unilateral but must meet with the approval of the diverse interests and demands of the dominant coalition. The decision problems faced by such an individual are qualitatively distinct from those in other positions, requiring astute judgmental skills as well as abilities for resolving conflict.

SUMMARY

Seeking, acquiring, and maintaining power is an organizational fact of life. Power resides not only in individuals but also in groups, coalitions, other organizations, etc., and the maintenance of a coalition and its power may require (induce) the organization member to make decisions in a different manner than he might otherwise do as an individual. Because of this, the decision maker cannot viably function in isolation, but must consider others. These complexities have led to the statement that " . . . almost no decision made in an organization is the task of a single individual." It is, instead, more accurately described as a "composite process" of the effort and influences of many (Simon, 1965, p. 221).

We have presented concepts and theories of power from the behavioral sciences and a decision-theory model of power focusing on the individual's cognitive processes. These efforts provided the basic building-blocks for examining power relationships in the organization. We were then able to identify various ways that power enters into organizational decision processes. The bases of intraorganizational power relationships were identified. We then showed how external considerations may intrude on the internal power structure.

Chapter 11

Leaders and Leadership

The process of leadership is distinct from the ideas of social power in a number of ways. Recall from Chapter 9 that power relationships are dyadic; both the persuader and the recipient are regarded as distinct entities acting one-on-one in the relationship. In contrast, the process of leadership involves one persuader acting on many recipients. Furthermore, we see leadership as more than just getting someone to do something. It includes the idea of acceptance as well as compliance. In this sense, the process of leadership is broader than the concept of power, for it suggests that the recipients will not only do something but will come to feel that what they are doing is desirable. Another major factor is that leaders are in charge of *groups* and their effectiveness is primarily determined by an analysis of the group's performance. Therefore, to the degree that a decision maker has to depend upon both the compliance with and acceptance of his decisions in order for them to be carried out, leadership becomes an important topic to review and understand. As discussed below, leadership is one means by which the individual affects the decision process of others. It is another of the major phenomena which create forces that impinge on organizational decisions.

THEORETICAL OVERVIEW

Simon (1965) has noted that authority can arise informally in the organization if one accepts the leadership of another. Under what conditions will this occur? A number of approaches have been used in attempting to answer this question. The early research in the area of leadership contained an underlying bias that the individual was the origin of his actions (Cartwright and Zander, 1968). Leadership was a function of the personal qualities of the individual, not of the situation, the technology, or the supporting cast.

THE TRAIT APPROACH

Research attempting to discover the traits that are possessed by great leaders can be traced back to historians of ancient Greece or Rome such as Herodotus or Tacitus. The belief is that the man makes the times, that great successes can be attributed to the personal characteristics of the person in charge. The research that has utilized this approach has investigated two major questions: What distinguishes leaders from followers and what makes certain leaders more effective than others?

Although hundreds of studies have been conducted on the topic, very little agreement or support for specific leader characteristics has resulted. Critical reviews of these studies by Stogdill (1948), Gibb (1954), and Mann (1959), effectively discouraged this trait approach. Their assessments, similar for both of the above questions, are summarized below.

Physical Characteristics

Historical traditions would lead one to believe that effective leaders would be tall, strong, physically dominating types of individuals, and the reviews by Stogdill and Mann generally support this notion but with severe qualifications. They report that a majority of the studies analyzing these variables did find leaders to be slightly heavier, taller, and neater in appearance. However, the differences that are reported are very small and were not consistent over different situations. The findings for physique and health were even more confusing. In general, it appears that physical characteristics will be helpful only when they are demanded by the job. Therefore, the usefulness of these characteristics as methods for differentiating leadership skills is limited.

Intellectual Factors

Intellectual factors are perhaps the most well documented as contributing to leadership status and effectiveness. Reviews of the research show that intelligence is positively correlated with these characteristics and that the relationship is fairly consistent, although not very strong. The average correlation across studies is in the low 20s. One possible interpretation of these results is that leaders are usually somewhat, but not too much, brighter than other group members.

Personality Traits

The list of personality measures that have been related to leadership effectiveness and status is very long, and for the sake of brevity will be broken down into three categories: responsibility, sociability, and dominance. The research has generally supported the idea that leaders should be responsible, sociable, and somewhat dominant. Again, however, the findings across settings are inconsistent and those results that are reported are generally weak.

Criticisms of the Trait Approach

Clearly, the above results leave much to be desired. The trait approach has been highly criticized for the following reasons:

1. The trait approach dominated leadership studies prior to World War II and paralleled to some extent the methodology of the instinct theories which characterized sociology and psychology at the turn of the century. Whenever distinctive behaviors occurred that were not explained by existing traits, a new trait was posited, until it became apparent that the inclusion of everything discriminated nothing. Traits became mere hypotheses due to the fact that no independent measures of the traits were available.

2. The strategy then turned to developing better measures of these traits or personality characteristics, but this also presented problems. The reliability and validity coefficients of most personality tests are uniformly low (.25–.50). Also, the concepts which are supposedly being measured are often poorly conceptualized and therefore mean different things to different people. As our knowledge about the nature of personality improves and as our techniques of measurement become more dependable, it is possible that traits will be specified which regularly distinguish leaders from followers or good leaders from poor ones. However, any empirical results supporting this approach will always be limited since situational demands are not considered.

3. It has become apparent that the variance in performance due to leadership traits is only a very small percentage of the total variance. Many other factors, such as technological equipment and facilities, along with member characteristics and situational demands, are important. These variables are often situationally determined and different in different circumstances. It would also seem logical that different traits are more effective in different situations than are other traits.

A related fact is that the attainment of leadership status is often a function of sociological, political, or economic factors such as age, financial status, social class, or chance circumstances. More specifically, it appears that the attainment of a leadership position is influenced by personality variables to a small degree and probably much less than is believed by most laymen (Warner and Abegglen, 1955).

In summary, then, the trait approach was confronted with many theoretical, methodological, and practical problems. And in general, across a number of situations, traits do not consistently distinguish the leaders from the followers or the good leaders from the poor ones.

THE BEHAVIOR APPROACH

Dissatisfaction with the trait approach to leadership led to a new tactic which focused on leadership behavior. The methodological and theoretical emphases were on reliable observation of leader behavior rather than on his internal states or traits. *Leadership was viewed as the performance of those acts which helped the group achieve its preferred outcomes* (e.g., improving the quality of inter-actions, building cohesiveness, making resources available to the group, increasing effectiveness). Three main schools of research have been identified with this theoretical orientation.

Bales' research at Harvard has emphasized that leadership behavior may be performed by any group member; yet, early in the life of a group, certain persons engage in such behavior to a greater degree than others (Bales and Slater, 1955). By means of a detailed observation system, Bales recorded the behavior of newly formed laboratory groups and discovered what he felt were three distinct facets of leadership behavior: *activity*, *task-ability*, and *likeability*. In a number of studies, Bales' findings indicated that the individual who is both the best idea-man and the best-liked member is the *best* leader, i.e., has better performance.

A distinctly different approach was directed by Shartle and his co-workers at Ohio State University (Shartle, 1952; Stogdill and Coons, 1957). Their source of data on leader behavior comes from the Leader Behavior Description Question-naire (LBDQ), a questionnaire which is distributed to group members and on which they rate how often their leader uses particular behaviors. The two main facets of leadership behavior are labeled *consideration* and *initiation* of struc-ture, which account for about eighty percent of the common variance. The work has typically been done in organizational settings and leaders who are high on both factors are generally seen as more effective than those who are regarded as deficient in one or both of these behavior factors.

The third line of research includes the work of Likert and his colleagues at Michigan and is similar to that of the Ohio State group (Likert, 1961; Kahn and

Katz, 1953). Here, however, the information about behavior is frequently gathered from a questionnaire distributed to group *leaders*. In this approach, two main categories of leader behaviors are identified, *job centered* and *employee centered*, and in general the employee-centered supervisors and managers tend to have higher productivity.

Evaluation of the Behavior Approach

The finding which seems to be most agreed upon in these three approaches is that there are two styles of leadership: task oriented and interpersonal oriented. Although the three groups of researchers might have minor disagreements about specific behaviors, they would probably concur on the conceptual similarities of the styles. Further research by these groups has attempted to specify more clearly the styles which appear to mix the two extremes (i.e., pure task orientation vs. pure interpersonal orientation), but very little has been suggested in the way of *new* and *different* styles.

There are two major problems with the behavior approach. First, the various schools of thought have used different sources to assess the leader's behavior: leaders, members, and observers. Some investigators have found that there is little agreement among different raters of an individual's behavior. Therefore, it becomes difficult to assess what the leader is actually doing. More specifically, it is hard to tell whether it is more important to know what the leader thinks he is doing, how his members perceive his behavior, or how nonparticipating observers categorize his acts (Mitchell, 1970).

A second shortcoming is the lack of agreement about what sort of style is more effective. Reviews of the empirical findings show that in some cases the interpersonal orientation is related to effectiveness, while other instances support a task-oriented style, and still other cases indicate that the leader who is high on both dimensions is best (Korman, 1966). None of the approaches takes into account the fact that varying situations require different behavior from the leader in order for him to be effective.

In summary, then, it appears that the behavior approach pointed out some important aspects of leadership. A combination of the behavior or trait approaches in conjunction with an emphasis on task and situational demands was tried next.

THE SITUATIONAL APPROACH

There are two major theories of leadership which try to combine information about the leader *and* the situation in which he finds himself. One of these theories is Fiedler's, which was mentioned earlier and will be discussed in more detail shortly. The other theory is known as the "open-systems" approach.

This latter theory begins by identifying and mapping the repeated cycles of input, transformation, output, and renewed input which compose the organizational pattern. Organizations are seen as being closely entwined with the environment, and as being constantly capable of change through feedback and other mechanisms (Katz and Kahn, 1966).

Leadership is defined as any act of influence on a matter of organizational relevance which goes beyond the routinely utilized bases of decreed power. These acts are seen to differ across organizational levels and situations, and each requires for successful use a different cognitive style, different kinds of knowledge, and different personal characteristics.

The theory, then, is rather broad and to date very little empirical evidence has been presented either for or against its position. The evidence that does exist seems to suggest that skills in the interpersonal area are more important at higher levels of management, while a more task-oriented approach may be more applicable at lower levels. A somewhat different approach was taken by Fiedler.

THE CONTINGENCY MODEL

An extensive research program by Fiedler since 1951 resulted in the development of "The Contingency Model of Leadership Effectiveness." This model suggests that an effective leader must match his "style" with the demands of the situation. To provide support for this model it was necessary to define effectiveness, leadership style, and the situational demands. The following pages describe the model, the data on which it was based, validation evidence, and the implications of using such a model (Fiedler, 1967).

Effectiveness

By *effective* leadership it is meant that the leader's group has performed well, or that it has succeeded in comparison with other groups. In other words, leadership effectiveness, as the term is defined here, is measured on the basis of group performance.

Leadership Style

Relationship-oriented vs. task-oriented leadership styles are measured by means of the Least Preferred Co-worker Scores (LPC). The individual is asked to think of all the people with whom he has ever worked and to then describe his Least Preferred Co-worker (or LPC) on seventeen biopolar scales in the form of Osgood's Semantic Differential (Osgood, Suci, and Tannenbaum, 1957). A favorable description of the least preferred co-worker indicates a relationship-oriented style; an unfavorable description indicates a task-oriented style of leadership.

This leadership style measure, or variants of it, has been used in a wide variety of interacting groups, ranging from high school basketball teams and surveying parties to military combat crews, research and management teams, and boards of directors. The results, however, have failed to indicate that one type of leader is consistently better than another. To interpret the results it is necessary to have some sort of assessment of the situation.

Factors Determining Situational Favorableness

Fiedler has argued that the basic component of leadership is the leader's ability to get his subordinates to do what he wants them to do. *That is, leadership is defined as a relationship in which one person tries to affect others in the performance of a common task.* Therefore, his situational assessment consists of one underlying dimension—the degree to which the leader can affect the behavior of his members.

Fiedler argues that this dimension is composed of three major factors. The first and most important variable which contributes to the leader's impact is defined as the leader-member relations. In situations in which these relationships are positive, the leader is believed to have greater impact than in those in which he is disliked. The second factor is the leader's formal power (the formal portion of possible power, as discussed in Chapter 10). The more positive and negative sanctions that he can use, the more impact he will have. The final factor is defined by the degree to which the task is structured or unstructured. The greater the structure, the easier it is for the leader to tell his people what to do. Specifying these three factors leads to the classification of group situations shown in Table 11-1.

Table 11-1   Fiedler's Classification System

Classification of Group Task Situations on the Basis of Three Factors

	Leader-Member Relations	Task Structure	Position Power
I	Good	High	Strong
II	Good	High	Weak
III	Good	Weak	Strong
IV	Good	Weak	Weak
V	Moderately poor	High	Strong
VI	Moderately poor	High	Weak
VII	Moderately poor	Weak	Strong
VIII	Moderately poor	Weak	Weak

Source: Fiedler, 1967.

Note that this says nothing about how intrinsically difficult the task itself may be. A structured task, such as building an electronic computer, may be much more difficult than an unstructured job of preparing an entertainment program. But the leader's problem of influencing the group will be greater in the volunteer committee than in the task of building a computer. It will obviously be easier to lead if you are the liked and trusted sergeant of a rifle squad (cell 1) than if you are the informal leader of a recreational basketball team (cell 2), and it will be very difficult indeed to be the disliked and distrusted leader of a volunteer group which is asked to plan the program of an annual meeting (cell 8). In other words, the cells can be ordered on the basis of how favorable or unfavorable the situation will be for the leader.

Empirical Results

Fiedler then asked what kind of leadership styles various situations required. To answer this question, the leadership-style score was correlated with performance of the leader's group in a variety of situations (Figure 11-1).

The correlation between the leadership-style score and group performance is shown on the vertical axis of this graph. The difficulty of the situation is shown on the horizontal axis. There are over five hundred different groups represented on this plot.

What does this figure show? Positive correlations, represented by points falling above the midline of the graph, indicate instances in which relationship-oriented leaders performed better than did task-oriented leaders. Negative correlations, represented by points falling below the midline of the graph, indicate situations in which the task-oriented leaders performed better than did the relationship-oriented leaders.

Taken as a whole, the plot shows that the task-oriented leaders are more effective in situations in which the leader has very little or very much influence. The relationship-oriented person is most effective in situations which are only moderately favorable for the leader. Fiedler argues that in the very easy or very difficult situations, strong task-oriented leadership is needed to be effective. In situations of moderate difficulty, the leader who spends time being concerned about the interpersonal relationships in the group will be most effective.

Criticisms of the model have also appeared (Mitchell, Biglan, Oncken, and Fiedler, 1970; Fiedler, 1971; Graen, Alvares, Orris, and Martella, 1970). These critiques have suggested the use of other personality characteristics (Bass, Fiedler, and Krueger, 1964; Fishbein, Landy, and Hatch, 1965) or cognitive variables (Mitchell, 1970) and proposed various ways to match these characteristics with the situation (Foa, Mitchell, and Fiedler, 1971). Other problems have dealt with methodological concerns (Posthuma, 1970) and alternative interpretations of the favorability dimension (O'Brien, 1969). Clearly, more research is needed, but as

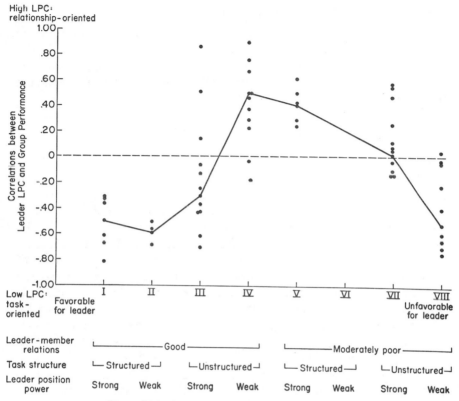

Figure 11-1 Leadership Style and Group Performance in Various Situations (*Source:* Fiedler, 1967.)

a first step the model has been a valuable contribution to our understanding of leadership. More specifically, it has been pointed out that both the individual and the setting are important for determining how well a leader will perform. With this background we are prepared to examine relationships between leadership variables and decision-making variables.

LEADERSHIP AND DECISION MAKING: EMPIRICAL FINDINGS

There are few studies that specifically relate decision-making variables, such as information search and decision-problem uncertainty, to leadership traits or situational demands. Those studies that can be found indicate that leadership is an important consideration in understanding organizational decision making.

Leader Characteristics and Decisions

Two studies have been conducted that tie the leader's LPC score to important dimensions of decision making. First, a study by Mitchell (1972) found that high and low LPC leaders utilized different kinds and amounts of *information* when making judgments about a set of hypothetical task situations. The situations were varied along the three situational favorability dimensions (i.e., interpersonal relations, task structure, and position power). The subject made judgments about: (1) how much influence he would have as leader, (2) how much he would like the situation, (3) how well he thought he could perform, and (4) what sorts of behaviors he would use in each of the different situations.

The analysis was similar to those described in Chapter 6, on judgment. The degree to which leaders used information from the three cues in a linear fashion was determined, as well as how much total information they used and which specific cues were most important for different types of people. Low LPC leaders tended to use less information overall and to use it in a more linear fashion than did high LPC leaders. Secondly, high LPC leaders tended to use all three cues systematically, whereas low LPC leaders were inclined to use only one. The pattern was clear: high LPC leaders appeared to be more cognitively complex in their information utilization than were low LPC leaders. This result fits well with a second experiment (Mitchell, 1972) in which LPC scores were found to be positively correlated with cognitive complexity for two separate samples of subjects; high LPC subjects were more cognitively complex.

When Fiedler's favorability dimension is thought of as a situational complexity dimension, it appears that the extremes would be classified as simple while the middle is more complex (Foa, Mitchell, and Fiedler, 1972). Situations in which everything is either all good or all bad are cognitively simple, whereas situations with some good and bad aspects require greater differentiation. The results of the previous studies, therefore, fit Fiedler's model very nicely, with low LPC (cognitively simple) leaders performing best in very favorable or unfavorable situations, while high LPC (cognitively complex) leaders perform best in situations of moderate favorability.

These results are preliminary attempts to integrate leadership theory with the conceptual level (cognitive complexity) theories that were discussed in Chapter 5. The findings suggest that both the leadership and cognitive styles of the individual decision maker must be matched with the demands of the situation. While there is some reason to believe that a cognitively complex individual will be better at many aspects of the decision-making process (see Chapters 5 and 8), it does not appear as if this is true for the whole range of situations in which he might find himself.

Finally, Jones and Johnson (1972) found relationships between LPC and communication variables in a study involving managers of a large service-oriented organization. In general, their study showed that "The high LPC managers appeared primarily to differentiate themselves from their low LPC counterparts by their ability to communicate with subordinates and by their trust and confidence shown subordinates" (p. 193). Thus, the high LPC leader was seen in these situations as a better communicator with his subordinates. This suggests that the flow of decision-related information depends, in part, on leadership style.

Situational Demands and Leadership

Not only are leader characteristics related to decision variables but so are the situational demands. Both the organization level and the type of problem are important for the behavior employed by the leader. One study by Shrode and Brown (1970), for example, involved interviews of fifty-one managers at three different levels of a major U.S. chemical firm. Their findings are summarized as follows: (1) people-oriented decisions are the most difficult, while money-oriented decisions are the least difficult to make; (2) task-oriented and people-oriented decisions are about equally important, but task-oriented decisions are more preferable to work on; (3) higher-level managers spend more time making decisions than do lower-level managers; and (4) time spent on different types of decisions varies with the level of supervision, as follows: (a) higher levels spend less time on task-oriented decisions than do lower levels; (b) higher levels spend more time on people-oriented decisions than do lower levels; (c) higher levels spend more time on money-oriented decisions than do lower levels; and (d) higher levels spend less time on information-oriented decisions than do lower levels. Their data also indicate that different types of decisions also vary on the dimensions of difficulty and importance as a function of the organizational level. Again, one would conclude that situational level is important for determining which type of leader will be optimally effective.

As discussed in Chapter 7, a decision problem may include various types and amounts of uncertainty. At the same time, Figure 11-1 and Table 11-1 indicate that Fiedler's "situational favorability" measure varies from highly favorable to highly unfavorable for various task situations. A recent study attempted to determine if situational favorability is related to the degree of uncertainty posed by the characteristics of the task situation (Nebeker, 1973). For a given behavior that could be employed by the leader in a specific situation, he must decide upon the amount or intensity to be used by him in affecting the behaviors of others. Consider, for example, his use of one kind of behavior—coercion. He may choose to use a relatively high, medium, or low amount of coercion in a situation. If his payoffs (subjective expected utility—SEU) among these three amounts are approximately equal, then he faces a relatively high degree of uncertainty among his alternatives. If his expected utility of using, say, a high amount of coercion is noticeably higher than the expected utilities of using moderate or low amounts, then less uncertainty exists regarding his choice. Nebeker measured this uncertainty for eight different behaviors across eight different settings and found that the less favorable the situation (as defined by Fiedler) the greater the uncertainty. In unfavorable situations, it was less clear to the leader how he should behave than in favorable situations. In this respect, uncertainty was found to be negatively related to situational favorability; that is, greater uncertainty was associated with decreasing situational favorability.

Recently, research by Vroom and Yetton (1973) has shown that leaders use different decision processes depending upon the situational variables. Thirty cases describing an important decision were developed in which the following seven variables could assume different values: (a) the importance of decision quality; (b) the extent to which the leader has the necessary information/ expertise to make a high-quality decision by himself; (c) the extent to which the problem is structured; (d) the extent to which acceptance or commitment on the part of subordinates is critical to the effective implementation of the decision; (e) the prior probability that the leader's autocratic decision will receive acceptance by his subordinates; (f) the extent to which subordinates are motivated to attain organizational goals presented as explicit objectives in the statement of the problem; and (g) the extent to which subordinates are likely to be in conflict over preferred solutions. One may note that many of these variables correspond closely to Fiedler's definition of situational favorability.

These thirty cases were then administered to over five hundred managers in eight industrial organizations. Each manager chose one of five decision strategies that differed in the amount of subordinate participation he would allow in resolving the case problem. A number of individual difference variables were also obtained dealing with biographical and personal characteristic differences. Thus, the authors could determine the extent to which diversified individual character- istics or dissimilar situational characteristics caused differences in the chosen decision strategies. Table 11-2 shows the findings for the eight samples.

Combining these data shows that individual differences account for about 8.2 percent of the variance in decision strategies, while about 29.8 percent of variance in choice is attributable to situational differences. The following is a summary of the authors' substantive findings:

   1. Managers use decision processes providing greater opportunities for participation when the quality of the decision is important rather than when the quality of the decision is irrelevant.
   2. Managers use decision processes providing less opportunity for partici- pation when they possess all the necessary information to generate a high-quality decision rather than when they lack some of the needed information.
   3. Managers use decision processes providing less opportunity for parti- cipation when the problem which they face is well structured rather than when it is unstructured.

Table 11-2   Variations in Choice of Decision Strategies

The Proportion of the Variance in Behavior across the Eight
Populations which is accounted for by Individual and Situational
Differences

	POPULATION (ORGANIZATION)							
	P_1 n = 92	P_2 n = 73	P_3 n = 32	P_4 n = 153	P_5 n = 27	P_6 n = 64	P_7 n = 35	P_8 n = 75
Individual Main Effect	10.0%	9.4%	7.9%	7.8%	3.8%	11.6%	8.1%	7.2%
Problem Main Effect	30.1%	26.8%	35.8%	31.0%	33.4%	27.1%	26.9%	27.2%

Source: Vroom and Yetton, 1973.

4. Managers use decision processes providing more opportunity for participation when both the subordinates' acceptance of the decision is critical for its
effective implementation and when the prior probability of acceptance of an
autocratic decision is low rather than when either or both of these conditions are
not satisfied.

5. Managers use decision processes providing a greater opportunity for
participation when the subordinates' acceptance of the decision is critical for its
effective implementation, when the manager trusts his subordinates to pay
attention to organizational rather than personal goals, and when conflict among
subordinates is absent, rather than when one or more of these conditions are not
satisfied.

So, individual leadership styles for decisions are contingent upon (1) the
leader's characteristics, (2) the level of the organization, and (3) the situational
demands. It is clear from Vroom and Yetton's results that "participative"
leadership is perceived as being desirable only under certain conditions. Since
this is a topic of current importance we will briefly elaborate on the use of
participative leadership styles.

PARTICIPATION AND MOTIVATION

The controversy over the effectiveness of participative-management approaches
is a current issue in the literature on organization behavior and theory. In a
recent article Alutto and Belasco (1972, p. 117) describe the issue this way:

In reviewing the literature on individual participation, at least three distinct themes emerge. The first concerns the importance of decisional participation by employees in determining the acceptance of organizational change. Following the original work of Coch and French (1948), most investigators have concluded that by encouraging participation in decision making, organizations can increase both the probability that change will be accepted and the overall effectiveness of that change. It has also been suggested that allowing participation in decisions over which participants exercise no control may be just as damaging as no participation at all (Lammers, 1967).

The second major area of research concentrates on interactions between the decisional participation rates of subordinates and the perceived relative influence of administrative superiors. Gouldner (1954), Tannenbaum and his colleagues (1968), and Mulder (1971) have argued that by allowing subordinates to participate in decision making, superiors gain influence over the actions of individual role performers. As a participation franchise is extended and superiors relinquish complete control over decisions, they gain both increased certainty concerning the actions of their subordinates (encouraging commitment through involvement) and increased influence over a widespread set of decisional issues (gaining in the legitimate exercise of authority). It is suggested that one clear consequence of shared decision making is increased administrative control.

Thus, we have somewhat of a paradox—by decreasing control we are in some sense increasing control. That is, by the use of participation a supervisor may actually have more power or influence than without participation.

We have already stated conditions under which participation does not seem to be an effective decision-making strategy. Vroom and Yetton's (1973) research indicated that the importance of the decision, its structure, and the amount of information available from the group were important considerations. That is, when acceptance is important, when a high-quality decision is needed, and when the necessary information is possessed by several individuals, then participation is seen as a viable strategy.

Alutto and Belasco (1972) present results of teacher participation in two New York school districts that differed in the characteristics most related to effective participation. If enough or too much information is already available, participation may be harmful. Also, studies by Berkowitz (1953) and Maier and Maier (1957) suggest that people expect the leader to structure the task to some extent and to use his influence when necessary. To be effective, then, participation must be matched with certain conditions of the environment, such as the need for new information, different points of view, and group acceptance.

It is clear, however, that in many cases participation does increase the motivation and satisfaction of people working in organizational settings. Vroom (1964) in his review of all of this research states, "When the entire pattern of results is considered we find substantial basis for the belief that participation in decision making increases productivity" (p. 226).

The critical question is why does participation help when it does? Recent work by Mitchell (1973) attempts to answer this question. If we agree that one's behavior is influenced by the outcomes that are controlled by others (a supervisor, one's peers, or by the environment), and the perceived probabilities of obtaining these outcomes, then participation plays an important part in at least four ways.

First, organizational contingencies are clearer with participation. Studies by Cohen (1957) and Raven and Rietsema (1957) support this view. Leavitt (1967) also presented data indicating that feedback and information exchange "increases the accuracy with which information is transmitted" (p. 483).

Second, participation increases the likelihood that employees will work for outcomes they value. The research by French (1950) and Lawler (1971) suggests that the individual will work harder when he is working for goals he values. Thus, if you know what must be done to obtain valued outcomes, you are more likely to behave in a way which will facilitate the attainment of these outcomes.

Third, participation increases the effects of social influence on behavior. With increased participation comes increased attraction and influence (see Lott and Lott, 1964, for a review). Vroom's review states that participation increases "the strength of group norms regarding execution of the decisions and the 'ego involvement' in the decisions" (p. 229). Recent investigations by Wood (1972), Mitchell and Nebeker (1973), and Mitchell and Knudsen (1973) also point out the importance of these social expectations.

Fourth, participation increases the amount of control that one has over his behavior. With increased responsibility, the individual is able to carry out those behaviors which he intends to utilize and over which he has expertise. In this sense, decisions are made at the appropriate level. Studies by Mitchell and Nebeker (1973) and Mitchell and Pollard (1973) support these ideas.

SUMMARY AND CONCLUSIONS

Two major ideas have been presented in this chapter. First, leadership is an important process which determines how decisions will be carried out and accepted. Different personal characteristics and leadership styles facilitate effectiveness when they are matched with the appropriate setting and group composition. We presented a number of ways in which this match can be achieved.

The second major point is that the process of leadership can be explained in terms of beliefs and values. People tend to obey their supervisor or attend to group pressures depending upon the kinds of payoffs they see to be likely consequences of compliance. It also appears that under certain conditions, a participative style on the part of a leader, or management in general, may increase the effort, motivation, and compliance of group members. We turn now to the topic of organization design in an attempt to discuss the practical implications of findings presented in previous chapters.

Part Four

Chapter 12

Issues for
Action and Design

The primary orientation of the preceding chapters has been to analyze various aspects of decision making in an attempt to bring together theories and research from diverse disciplines. This was done for the ultimate purpose of providing a foundation that would permit (a) an understanding (clearer picture) of what is known about organizational decision processes, and (b) a better understanding of what are the most promising directions for further study and development of organizational decision making.

Ideally, we would like to conclude with specific recommendations for designing decision environments, recommendations which would conclusively and unequivocally assist the organization designer in attaining maximum decision-making effectiveness. Unfortunately our concluding picture is not so bright and promising. At best our analysis suggests a number of important issues and problems for organization designers. These issues and problems are identified below, along with several general design guidelines. Satisfactory solutions to these penetrating issues are not presently available. Nonetheless, the issues exist and are dealt with daily, consciously or not, in organizations. Most are handled

267

by experienced judgment, probably at a relatively high cost in terms of organizational and individual resources.

ORGANIZATION VARIABLES AND CONSTRAINTS

Decision quality is jointly determined by many factors. Some of these are controllable by the organization, others are not. Major categories which are controllable are referred to as design variables. Uncontrollable factors are treated as constraints.

Design Variables

Selection of Stimuli
  Goal setting processes
  Criteria selection
  Performance measurement
Definition and Position of Decision Units
  Allocation of decision responsibility
  Determination of formal power distribution
Staffing of Decision Units
Definition of Formal Information System

Constraints

Character of Extra-organizational Environment
Character of Core Technology
Informal Systems
  Power distribution
  Information systems

Of course, several factors fail to fall neatly into either of these two categories. The factors treated here have been forced into one or the other category according to their primary character. Note, for instance, that the core technology is identified as a constraint. This, of course, is not strictly true. It can be modified. However, in many organizations it must be taken as a "given." Frequently it is subject to only minor modification while its basic character remains fundamentally unchanged over long periods of time.

These variables and constraints are the principal determinants of the decision environment. A wide variety of "mixtures" or configurations of these variables is possible and must be made in relation to the nature of constraints facing the organization. The resulting decision environment is assumed to determine decision quality.

Note that the design variables are not independent of the constraints. For example, informal systems (power and information) are identified as constraints, not directly controllable. However, changes in any of the design variables, such as redefining and repositioning decision units, can result in subsequent reactions (adjustments) in the informal systems. Thus, the designer has a direct *influence*

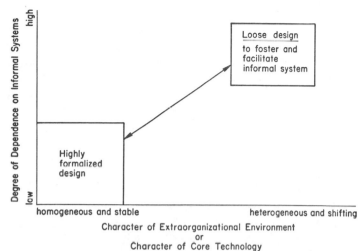

Figure 12-1   General Design Strategies for Mixtures of Constraints

on the constraints, but not substantial *control* over them. Herein lies an imposing design issue. Intended changes in design variables may result in unintended constraint responses. The direction and magnitude of these responses cannot be fully anticipated, yet their ultimate impact on the decision environment can be substantial. In the process of response and counter-response between variables and constraints, a tendency toward stability emerges. As this occurs, organizations can be expected to differ in degree of dependence on informal systems in their decision environments. This might be pictured as in Figure 12-1. Different sets of these relationships may exist for the technical, managerial, and institutional levels of an organization.

These constraint relationships suggest two general strategies for the manipulation of design variables. For organizations with a low dependence on informal systems, a strategy directed toward a relatively high degree of formalization is suggested to achieve control. If a high degree of dependence exists, the design strategy is one of fostering and facilitating informalization (or, if formalized, to do so in very general terms). Within a single organization it may be appropriate to facilitate formalization at one level (e.g., the technical core), while at the same time facilitating informalization at another level.

INTRAORGANIZATIONAL DESIGN FACTORS

The handling of design variables is a complex process. We know they can be manipulated in many ways, but our knowledge of when and to what extent is meager. By way of illustration several issues and problems are summarized below.

Stimuli in the Decision Environment

Attempts can be made to control the "attention directing" elements that are active in the environment of the decision unit in a number of ways. First, we know that what one perceives is influenced by his beliefs and values. Hence, we may attempt to staff decision units with individuals whose value systems are compatible with role requirements. The organization also can influence some values of the individual upon entry into the organization. Ongoing attempts may be made to effect changes in his beliefs and values by structuring his role requirements in relation to those of other decision units. In these ways organizational and social forces may be directed toward channeling individual perceptions.

The organization can define and control goal-setting processes, decision criteria, and performance measurement, all of which determine what stimuli will be regarded as relevant. Doing so, however, often poses difficulties. Frequently, organizations are unable to explicate suitable criteria and goal statements. Goal conflict and criterion conflict are common problems awaiting resolution, both theoretically and operationally. Measurement of decision performance is an important variable which is inadequately developed and understood. To what extent should it be based on the processes used, rather than on outcome? Extensive work is needed to resolve such issues if effective control of environmental stimuli is to be achieved.

Defining the Formal Information System

Several poignant issues exist for designing organizational information systems to facilitate decision making.

1. There is a need for designing information filters. Irrelevant information can detract from effective decision performance. However, it is difficult, and in many cases impossible, to identify the degree of relevance of information a priori.

2. The mere standardization and formalization of information flows can negatively, as well as positively, affect the decision environment. Formalization can lead to modified power structures and may, in some instances, impede informal information flows. Also, standardization can lead to inappropriate and/or inadequate entry of stimuli into the decision environment. Furthermore, standardization and formalization require consideration of the appropriate degree of information redundancy for various decision units. To date, these issues have been addressed at a very crude level only.

3. Available evidence suggests that a redistribution of emphasis is needed among the types of information provided by information systems. Decision makers are currently provided inadequate information about their decision-making styles. Rather than providing "outcome feedback" alone, we need to

consider how to give decision makers indications of relationships between environmental variables they believe to be of importance in their environment. Ways are needed to help the decision maker assess beliefs independently of values. New methods must be devised to help him constructively simplify his environment on other than an intuitive basis. Increased efficiency of information search is surely possible, as is greater accuracy of judgmental conclusions, if ways can be found to accurately revise beliefs.

4. Previous studies imply that a formal focus on non-standardized, flexible elements in the information system is warranted. To some extent information search activities and information flows should be permitted to be flexible, i.e., compatable with the decision maker's cognitive style. Rather than universal standardized systems we need selectively standardized systems to avoid imposing a decision environment that is either too complex or too simple relative to the individual's level of cognitive complexity. Some minimal portion should be standardized to facilitate coordination among units and to control the "attention directing" stimuli in the unit's decision environment. Beyond this level, the system should be geared to the unique characteristics of the decision unit. Where this point lies has been the subject of little study.

5. Some cue redundancy seems to be helpful in increasing judgmental consistency. Just how much redundancy is optimal is not known. Nonetheless, it remains an important issue, since Bowman's work shows that inconsistency is often a costly phenomenon, particularly in programmed decision making.

6. The research on human judgment suggests a number of issues pertaining to information systems. First, it indicates the desirability of "early warning systems" to notify the decision maker of anticipated changes in critical environmental variables. With such foreknowledge, if it can be obtained, the chances are increased for more rapid adaptations by him. The decision maker can further benefit from information regarding environmental validities of cues he uses. Expenditures of resources toward this end may be worthwhile because judgmental accuracy stands to be improved. As a starting point, various models (correlational, etc.) may be used to provide such information.

Matching Individual Attributes with Role Requirements

Our previous analysis has shown that many individual attributes are related to decision performance. However, the relative importance of these characteristics for various organizational roles is insufficiently understood. Disposition toward risk, level of cognitive complexity, tolerance for ambiguity, etc., are variables studied by behavioral scientists. They are defined in terms that are not directly compatible with and translatable into terms used by designers to specify and define decision-making roles in the organization. We need a measurable profile of task attributes to which can be matched a compatible, or potentially compatible, role occupant. This will require development of measurement capabilities on two sides—the individual and the role.

Defining and Positioning Decision Units

Due to its size and complexity the organization must be subdivided into decision-making units. By so doing, phases of the decision process may be split apart and allocated to specialized subunits. The appropriate basis for these allocations is difficult to specify. Nonetheless, these actions determine the distribution of power and influence in the organization. Power and influence distributions are further affected by specifying the number, size, and relationships of subunits. The structure and authority relationships that emerge from these manipulations will largely delineate the limits of the decision unit's sphere of action discretion. Below is a sampling of perplexing considerations facing the designer of decision units.

Size.   A crucial issue is the determination of the size of each decision unit. Should it consist of one or many individuals? Our analysis shows that substantial differences in decision behavior can be expected. In situations in which groups must contribute to or make decisions, numerous problems occur. One individual may dominate interaction. Social factors such as attraction, status, or power influence what is said. People feel more comfortable in smaller groups (e.g., four to eight members) than in larger groups. Discussion in these groups flows more freely. Communication links are relatively uncomplicated and the individual's opportunity to make contributions is enhanced. When groups become much larger, it becomes difficult both to maintain good group interpersonal relations and communication. It is physically more difficult to make contributions because there are more people competing for time.

There are exceptions to the above statement. First, on tasks to which each new individual contributes a new substantive amount of knowledge, labor, or productivity, the communication and interpersonal problems may be offset by increased output. Another exception is when groups are too small. With only two or three members, people become overconcerned with maintaining good interpersonal ties at the expense of being candid. This causes discomfort and dissatisfaction.

Similarity.   Through the processes of selection and placement, groups can be composed of individuals who are more or less similar in personality, background characteristics, attitudes, and abilities. Thus, it is fairly easy to obtain value consensus. People tend to like one another more, communicate more, and have more influence over their fellow workers in groups high in similarity.

Again, however, one must match these group characteristics with the task. What is gained in harmony may be lost in creativity. If new, different ideas are needed, a more heterogeneous group composition may be desirable.

Reward Structure. One of the major group characteristics that can be manipulated by the use of different compensation systems is group interdependence. Clearly, if rewards are distributed on a group basis (bonuses, raises, prizes, etc.), people will be more concerned with the contributions of other group members. If people are rewarded individually, they will be less concerned about their peers. The task is again a moderator. If the task demands individual skills and contributions, there should be individual compensation. If group cooperation and coordination is necessary, group incentives may play an important role.

The compensation system also helps to ensure commitment. A flexible system, which allows individuals or groups to choose their reward package, increases both commitment and motivation. For settings such as the craft strategy suggested by Shull *et al.* (discussed below), a flexible compensation system will help to facilitate needed decision processes.

Communication Channels. Finally, through both the distribution of information and the physical location of personnel, there can be some control over who talks to whom. By increasing communication links between parties, we can increase the chances for interpersonal attraction and consensus. We can also increase or decrease the perceived importance of individuals through information distribution.

The same process can be used to match the cognitive complexity of group members with their information load. Thus, groups with a large information processing capacity can be given inputs that match their abilities.

The Imposition of Process. A critical question is how to generate and elicit important information that is available in the group and, then, how to combine it to arrive at a good decision. Should formal processes be imposed on groups? When no formal process is imposed, a somewhat equalitarian system of interpersonal relations tends to emerge (Davis, Hornik, and Hornseth, 1970). While this process may contribute to member satisfaction, it does not necessarily produce the best decision. But when interaction processes are to be imposed on the group, the question turns to which process is most effective. There are indications that reaching a consensus after having taken a majority vote results in decisions that are superior (1) to the average of individual decisions made alone without interaction, (2) to an appointed leader making the decision, (3) to a selected committee (two people) arriving at a decision, (4) to a majority vote by itself, or (5) to a consensus by itself. The majority plus consensus seems both to clarify how most of the contributors feel, as well as to incorporate minority opinions (Holloman and Hendrick, 1972). However, other studies show that high-quality decisions also result from combining *independent* judgments *following* group discussion (Huber and Delbecq, 1972). Furthermore, the expected error of judgment decreases with larger group size (up to groups of ten) and type of aggregation rule.

In other cases, in which an individual is responsible for making a decision, inputs from others may vary in quality. Clearly, in those instances, some sort of weighting of expertise must be incorporated into the final overall estimate. Perhaps, as we discussed earlier, the only guide is past experience. As long as some reliable estimate of past expertise is available for a specific source (such as past performance in predicting some event), then weightings seem appropriate and possible with a fair degree of accuracy. As of yet, no formal system exists for generating these weightings.

Under what circumstances is a group preferable to an individual as the decision unit? What is the appropriate group size? Which of several procedures should be used to aggregate group judgment into a single decision? Satisfactory answers to these questions do not exist. Our normative understanding of how to structure role relationships is relatively meager. There are, however, directions that offer some promise of gaining better insights. One approach is to consider additional elements of the organizational environment.

DECISION STRATEGIES
UNDER DIFFERENT ENVIRONMENTS

Different approaches to decision making are carried out under different circumstances. To optimize effectiveness, we must ascertain and integrate characteristics of the decision process with characteristics of the environment. The literature in this area is somewhat sparse, but some interesting attempts have been made to match up these two areas.

Thompson and Tuden's (1959) typology considers characteristics of the environment and the decision process to suggest a structure for decision making. Using beliefs and values, they argued that we can generate four possible decision strategies (Table 12-1).

Computation is described as a decision situation in which group members agree both on the valued outcomes and the correct alternative to obtain the outcomes. In its extreme form, of course, the decision is self-evident. However, in most cases the information must be gathered, reviewed, distributed, evaluated, etc.

The authors argue that under these conditions it is specialists who are needed most. Since everyone agrees about means and ends, the crucial thing is to get the correct information to the proper people. To some extent this type of organization closely represents the "pure type" of Weberian bureaucracy. Decisions are delegated to the proper source, and conflict is nonexistent.

When people agree on ultimate goals but not on the way to attain them, we have a situation which requires a "decision by majority *judgment*." The authors

Table 12-1   Decision Strategies and Structures

		Preferences About Possible Outcomes	
		Agreement	Non-Agreement
Beliefs About Causation	Agreement	Computation in Bureaucratic Structure	Bargaining in Representative Structure
	Non-Agreement	Majority Judgment in Collegial Structure	Inspiration in "Anomic Structure"

Source: Thompson and Tuden, 1959.

describe a situation in which proof of the worth of a specific alternative is lacking, but in which differential perception and interpretation exist. Structurally, each member should be afforded access to all available information and should have equal participation and influence in the decision process. The argument is for some sort of weighted average or majority decision. Many voluntary organizations, trade unions, and universities frequently face this type of decision modality.

In some situations, participants may agree about the consequences of various alternatives but disagree in their preferences for them. In these cases, it is clear that some people will be satisfied with the decision, while others will not. In such situations, Thompson and Tuden argue for a group process which facilitates *compromise.* While computation requires a small number of decision makers, and judgment a large number, compromise requires a decision unit of intermediate size. The viewpoints of all factions should be heard, but not necessarily the viewpoints of all individuals. Thus, they argue for a representative structure of which the United Nations Security Council is an example.

The fourth cell of the typology calls for *inspiration* as the mode of decision making. Here there is disagreement about both beliefs and values. In general, this is a fairly precarious situation for an organization. Thompson and Tuden suggest that organizations which seem to have difficulty responding appropriately, or even at all, to a problem situation are likely to be facing this type of decision problem. It is suggested that charisma is the correct leadership style. Participants should be interdependent, faced with a high information load, and factions should have access to communication channels in case inspiration strikes.

Many organizations will find themselves with mixed types of the above situations. In some areas there will be agreement, while in others there will be disagreement. These situations call for an administrative procedure that allows a mixture of decision strategies. But this leaves us with two problems. One, we must have an organizational design that is flexible enough to incorporate different decision strategies and, second, we must know how to change various group properties in order to obtain the best fit.

A second and somewhat similar typology has been presented by Delbecq (1967) and elaborated on by Shull, Delbecq, and Cummings (1970). These authors attempt to categorize decision processes according to the task characteristics and personnel characteristics of the individual participants (Figure 12-2). They state that " ... the model assumes that an increase in task complexity normally results in the organization recruiting more highly trained or professional personnel as well as personnel with differentiated skills and interests. Thus the model deals with organizational situations where 'qualified' personnel, neither underemployed nor overemployed, are available to or present within the system" (p. 194). The features of the four subunit structures are summarized below.

Routine Strategy.   Repetitive solutions and implementations are the central task demands. The recommended decision unit consists of a technical staff with an appointed leader. The group process is characterized by specifying quantity and quality objectives, along with critical control points and sequencing. Econ-

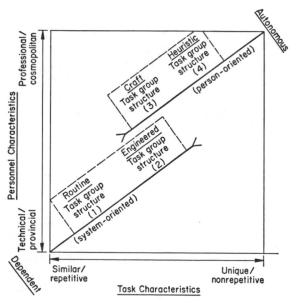

Figure 12-2 Structures of Organizational Units (*Source:* Shull, Delbecq, and Cummings, 1970, p. 192.)

omy and efficiency are the group norms. The administrative system specifies ends and clarifies contingencies. Control is specified through control points and individual responsibility. This closely parallels the computation strategy of Thompson.

Engineered Strategy. Here the tasks are nonrepetitive, but again specialists are required with a designated project leader. The group process is characterized by control points, periodic review, and specific quantity and quality objectives. There is more independent planning and individual responsibility, with a heavy emphasis on economy and efficiency. While ends are again specified by the administrative system, there is more negotiation about the inputs and outputs with the project unit. Critical control points are available, as are feedback mechanisms about the adequacy of performance.

Craft Strategy. For the previous strategies, the task was rather well specified and clear check points were available. For the craft strategy, however, the definition and solution of problems reside with skilled personnel. The task may still be fairly repetitive, but craftsmen or professionals are dealing with the problem rather than engineering or machine systems. Independent action diagnosis and consultation represent the group process, with peer review and administration consultations used for planning and control. Professionalism is the norm.

Heuristic Strategy. In this final situation, there are both a nonrepetitive task and highly trained professional personnel. It features independent analysis and solution with full participation and majority rule. The unit environment is relaxed and non-stressful, with open support or disagreement. Time constraints are minimal and eccentricity is allowed. Creativity is the norm. The administrative system seldom intrudes in planning, and control is usually group centered.

While Schull *et al.* (1970) realize that these "pure types" are actually mixed and appear in gradations in real organizations, they believe they have isolated significant representative styles of decision making based on the people and tasks that exist. They have attempted to match a group process and administrative structure with each of these "types" to produce maximum performance. Both Thompson and Tuden (1959) and Shull, *et al.* (1970) base their predictions on numerous studies that had been done earlier. However, to date there are few independent empirical tests of their typologies.

A third typology, which is not quite as specific as the preceding two, was suggested by McWhinney (1968). The environments are described in terms of their uncertainty and interdependence (see Emery and Trist, 1963). We have *placid, randomized environments* in which organizations exist as single, independent small units with known goals. Next, there are *placid, clustered environments* in which strategies and tactics become important. One can identify less environmental causality, but still make predictions about future events. Third, there are *disturbed, reactive environments*. Here there are competitive systems with interdependent environments. One must be cognizant of the environment, including both causal relationships and the intent of competitors in order to function correctly. Finally, there are *turbulent fields*. Here, both the environment and the competition are dynamic, and the turbulence comes from the complexity of the causal relationships.

McWhinney classifies different decision problems as certainty, risk, uncertainty, and domain problems. Under certainty, we know the causal relationships with a probability of 1.00. Under risk, the probability is known but is less than 1.00, while uncertainty means that the probabilities are unknown. With domain problems the decision maker has to determine what aspects of the environment are of concern. One can readily see how these decision strategies fit with the above environmental descriptions. What we do not have, however, is a description of the group process that matches these environments and decision modalities.

A number of things should be clear from reviewing these typologies. First, the uncertainty or certainty of causal beliefs and agreement about goals (interdependence) are critical components of all of them. Throughout the book, we have dealt with the idea of individual and group uncertainty, as well as value consensus. Thus, our two major dimensions of beliefs and values are a recurring theme both for individual and group processes.

A second major point is evident. Not all groups are striving for or placed in environments in which certainty and value consensus exist. Thus, the problem for organizational design is not so much to attain certainty and agreement, but to structure the organization in a fashion that will allow it to have appropriate adaptability to the kind of environment it faces.

AN OVERVIEW OF STRUCTURES AND FORMS

This final section carries our analysis to the broadest conceptual framework—the total organization. We will discuss first the overall relationships between structural characteristics and decision-related behavior. This is followed by a discussion of organizational forms, which generally seem to modify the effectiveness of decision making across numerous settings.

Structural Characteristics and Behavior

At the most general level, one may ask about the effects of organizational structure on behavior. By structural characteristics is meant those physical

characteristics which are readily observed. Examples are organizat
ber of hierarchical levels, average number of subordinates per supe
control), etc. Organizational behavior at the broadest level inc.
such as job satisfaction, or critical behaviors such as absenteeism or turn.
The empirical findings clearly show that these aspects of organizational life are
highly interrelated. A summary of these relationships was presented by Porter
and Lawler (1965):

Independent Variables	*Dependent Variables*
Suborganization Properties	Job Attitudes
1. Organizational levels	Satisfaction
2. Line and staff hierarchies	Need fulfillment
3. Span of control	Role perceptions
4. Size: subunits	Leader attitudes
Total organization properties	Job Behavior
5. Size: total organizations	Absenteeism
6. Shape: tall or flat	Turnover
7. Shape: centralized/	Output
decentralized	Accidents
	Grievances

Without overdue repetition we have attempted to review their findings
below.

1. Organizational levels. Managers at higher levels appear to have greater
satisfaction and need fulfillment, attach greater importance to "higher-level
needs," and are clearly aware of their increased responsibility. Higher-level
managers are better informed than lower-level managers and tend to have less
downward communication. Also, a study by Martin (1959) indicated that
decisions were more risky and abstract for higher-level positions.

2. Line and staff hierarchies. Turnover seems to be higher for staff
personnel and they appear to be better informed and have greater mobility.

3. Span of control. Very little data exist on this topic, but those studies
which are available appear to indicate that no one span of control is ideal.

4. Size: Subunits. Job satisfaction and cohesiveness seem to be higher for
small groups. Absenteeism, labor disputes, and turnover are lower than for large
groups. The relationship with productivity is complex and dependent upon the
task. Groups which are too small (e.g., two or three members) may produce
discomfort. Communication is relatively poor in larger groups.

5. Size: Total organization. Again, managers appear to be less satisfied and
have greater turnover in larger organizations.

6. Shape: Tall or flat. Little difference has been reported in job attitudes
or behavior for tall vs. flat structures.

7. Shape: Centralized/Decentralized. No differences in job attitudes have been consistently reported. Decentralized executives appear to spend less time giving orders and making decisions and there are some tentative findings that turnover, grievances, and absenteeism are less than in centralized organizations.

The structural character of the organization obviously has a major impact on the attitudes and behaviors of its members. Recent studies have generally replicated the above findings and have examined decision-making activities more directly. For example, the investigation by Shrode and Brown (1970) reported that higher-level managers spend more time on decisions, and that these decisions are more related to interpersonal and financial issues than to task-oriented or information-oriented decisions. The study by Vroom and Yetton (1973) suggested that a participative decision strategy was less likely to be used under highly structured task conditions.

An investigation by Blankenship and Miles (1968) had managers indicate their decision behavior with respect to five different types of decisions. The summary measures are shown in Table 12-2. Eight organizations ranging from 2,000 to 112 employees were sampled. Organization level, size, and span of

Table 12-2   Decision Behaviors and Response Measures

Summary measures of decision behavior	Response items included in measures
Personal initiation	Manager initiates action on decision for himself
Autonomy from superior	Manager must consult his superior before taking action on decisions
	Manager's superior initiates action for the manager on decisions
Perceived influence on superior	Manager is consulted by his superior on decisions
	Manager's advice is followed by his superior
Reliance on subordinates (consultation downwards)	Manager consults his subordinates on decisions Manager's subordinates initiate action on decisions
Final choice	Manager exercises ultimate right of choice on decisions

Source: Yukl and Wexley, *Readings in Organizational and Industrial Psychology,* (Oxford University Press, 1971) p. 145.

control were then related to these decision-related behaviors. Managers at upper levels of organizations made more final choices, had high influence and autonomy, and did not rely heavily on their subordinates. Lower-level managers showed the reverse pattern. Size had an interesting moderating effect. For top-level managers, size was positively related to greater autonomy and freedom of action. For span of control, it was found that the more subordinates one has, the more likely they are to initiate action for him. The authors summarize their findings by saying:

> The dominant point emerging from the analysis is the overriding importance of hierarchical position. Although organizational size, span of control, and a manager's perceptions of whether or not he enjoys the right of final choice modify its effects somewhat, hierarchical level is still strongly and consistently associated with a manager's decision-making style.
>
> Upper-level managers not only claim greater freedom from their superiors in decisions of the type used in this study, they also show a stronger pattern of reliance on their own subordinates in the decision-making process to a greater degree than managers at lower levels. Lower-level managers, on the other hand, tend to have decisions initiated for them by their superiors and are required or expected to consult with their superiors before proceeding on most issues. In turn, these managers tend not to involve their subordinates in the decision-making process, even though their subordinates are themselves managers in their own right (Blankenship and Miles, as quoted in Yukl and Wexley).

Finally, a recent interpretation of organizational structure by Rice and Mitchell (1973) shows interrelationships between structural and decision-related variables. People with high status and influence communicate more directly with co-workers and are chosen more frequently by co-workers as important colleagues. Also, people who are central in the communication structure have more reciprocal choices of liking, intense activity, and are seen as instrumental for goal attainment. Central people are more satisfied, have better performance, and spend more time on attractive activities.

In summary, then, structural characteristics of both the subunit and the total organization modify the perceptions, attitudes, and behavior of decision makers.

Organizational Forms

A major dilemma is to create an organization structure that is flexible enough to deal with different issues in different ways, and yet is also facilitative of efficiently handling specific types of problems. When the demands of the environment are multifaceted, an overall flexible structure seems appropriate. When problems are more specific, well defined, and repetitive, a more highly specified design seems more suitable.

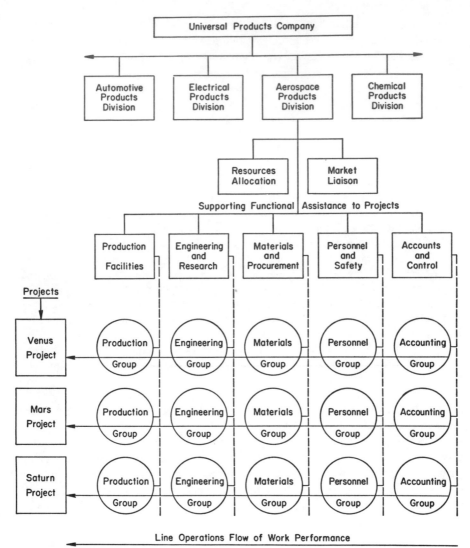

Figure 12-3 Portrayal of a Matrix Organization (*Source:* Hampton, 1969, p. 94.)

The most currently discussed approaches to an overall design have their roots in systems theory. Scott and Mitchell (1972) describe it as an:

... aspect of organization analysis which is devoted to discovering organizational universals. The aim of general system theory is the creation of a science of organizational universals—or, if you will, a universal science—using the elements and processes common to all systems as a starting point. Needless to say, this synthesis, if accomplished (and it has yet to be) will be at a very high level of abstraction. Even though general system theory is still in a tentative phase there is much to be learned from it (p. 53).

The thrust of the theory is to investigate (1) the strategic parts of the system, (2) the nature of their interdependency, (3) the main processes which link the parts, and (4) the goals sought by the system. The overall organizational setting requires that such an analysis considers individuals, the formal and informal organizations, the structure of status and role-expectancy systems, and the physical environment. Thus, inputs, process, output, and the cyclical nature of organizational life become an integral part of systems design. The recent literature of Burns and Stalker (1961), Lawrence and Lorsch (1967), and Woodward (1965) all emphasize attempts to understand and match the task and group process for overall organizational design.

Recent years have witnessed the evolution of various organizational forms created in response to the demands placed on organizations. These forms reflect different degrees of tradeoff between control and flexibility. One of the more contemporary forms is the matrix or project organization. It has apparently been found appropriate for organizations faced with completing specified tasks on schedule with certain cost and project guidelines. The organizational form depicted in Figure 12-3 departs substantially from traditional designs.

A summary of differences between this form and more traditional structures is given in Table 12-3.

Table 12-3 Cleland's Comparison of Functional and Project Forms

A Comparison of Functional and Project Viewpoints

Phenomenon	Project viewpoint	Functional viewpoint
Line-staff organizational dichotomy	Vestiges of the hierarchal model remain, but line functions are placed in a support position. A web of authority and responsibility relationships exists.	Line functions have direct responsibility for accomplishing the objectives; the line commands, staff advises.
Scalar principle	Elements of the vertical chain exist, but prime emphasis is placed on horizontal and diagonal work flow. Important business is conducted as the legitimacy of the task requires.	The chain of authority relationships is from superior to subordinate throughout the organization. Central, crucial, and important business is conducted up and down the vertical hierarchy.

Table 12-3 *(continued)*

Phenomenon	Project viewpoint	Functional viewpoint
Superior-subordinate relationship	Peer to peer, manager to technical expert, associate to associate relationships are used to conduct much of the salient business.	This is the most important relationship; if kept healthy, success will follow. All important business is conducted through a pyramiding structure of superiors-subordinates.
Organizational objectives	Management of a project becomes a joint venture of many relatively independent organizations. Thus, the objective becomes multilateral.	Organizational objectives are sought by the parent unit (as assembly of suborganizations) working within its environment. The objective is unilateral.
Unity of direction	The project manager manages across functional and organizational lines to accomplish a common interorganizational objective.	The general manager acts as the head for a group of activities having the same plan.
Parity of authority and resonsibility	Considerable opportunity exists for the project manager's responsibility to exceed his authority. Support people are often responsible to other managers (functional) for pay, performance reports, promotions, and so forth.	Consistent with functional management; the integrity of the superior-subordinate relationship is maintained through functional authority and advisory staff services.
Time duration	The project (and hence the organization) is finite in duration.	Tends to perpetuate itself to provide continuing facilitative support.

Source: David I. Cleland, "Understanding Project Authority," *Business Horizons,* Spring 1967, pp. 63–70.

The advantages suggested for this design include better control of the project, more flexibility and control over the program, lower costs and higher profit margins, better customer relations, and shorter development time (Middleton, 1967). Although some problems of increased complexity and inconsistency arise, this form appears to be well suited for adapting to a broad category of problems.

Other forms have been created and are discussed in the management and organization literature. Filley and House (1969) review a few of these:

Dual Hierarchies. Dual hierarchies are to be found in some research and development divisions, and are used in a more general way in some European countries. It involves a clear distinction between the operating hierarchy and the technical hierarchy. Programs and standards are developed in the technical segment, and fed to parallel operating units for performance. We would expect this form to work best for straight-line manufacture and mass production.

Matrix Structures. The matrix structure minimizes the role of hierarchy, and is usually based on highly technical functional departmentation, receiving technical direction from within the department and administrative direction from project leaders. Project leaders are relatively independent, perhaps reporting to project coordinators who allocate resources to various projects. The result is dual supervision (administrative and technical) and little job mobility within the firm. We would expect this form to be most important for unit and small batch production, as in aerospace industries.

Functional Organizations. The functional structure provides a means for operating departments to draw information and other resources from a variety of technical departments. This form is occasionally found in continuous processing firms where goals are fixed and methods are not highly adaptable. It would seem to be a natural development where methods are capital-intensive, where there are multiple goal-oriented units controlled by technical process departments, or where profit centers are the basis for control.

Tactical Units. Whether existing as separate organizations or as affiliates of larger structures, it is likely that a better picture of the exploitative, tactical structure under the direction of an entrepreneur will emerge. Where an established firm wishes to exploit an innovation, for example, an autonomous division can be created under the direction of a leader selected because of certain well-defined personality traits. The exploitative unit draws resources as needed from the parent firm, but is allowed to operate with minimum of structure and indirect labor under the tactical direction of the entrepreneur. This form seems to be most suitable where operations are labor-intensive but not highly technical (p. 488).

It is no surprise that great effort has been expended in recent years on studying structural characteristics such as size, span of control, centralization, etc. These are important factors in determining how decision-related behaviors are distributed throughout the organization. Their modification redistributes phases of decision processes, power distributions, communications processes, and social relationships. They are ways of manipulating the organizational and social forces.

Similarly, various organizational forms have emerged, as discussed above. Explicit evaluations of these forms are extremely difficult because each of them has manipulated not one but several of the structural characteristics. Hence, the quest for "optimal" organizational forms remains more of a puzzle than a reality.

SUMMARY AND CONCLUSIONS

The implications of organizational structure and form for future issues in decision making encompass a wide variety of processes. Technology innovation will play a major role both in terms of information processes and in the relationship between the individual and his job. Selection and training will increase the emphasis on matching the required decision skills of the position with those of the individual. Finally, numerous small group and organization-wide design strategies will be employed in an attempt to introduce flexibility and structure in the system.

Bibliography

Ackoff, R.L., Management misinformation systems. *Management Science*, 1967, 14, B-147–56.

Aguilar, F.J., *Scanning the Business Environment.* New York: Macmillan Publishing Co., 1967.

Alexander, R.A.; Barrett, G.V.; Bass, B.M.; and Ryterband, E.C., Empathy projection and negation in seven countries. In L.E. Abt and B.F. Reiss (Eds.) *Clinical Psychology in Industrial Organizations.* New York: Grune and Stratton, 1971, 29–49.

Alexis, M. and Wilson, C.Z., *Organizational Decision Making.* Englewood Cliffs, N.J.: Prentice-Hall, 1967.

Allee, W.C., *Cooperation Among Animals with Human Implications.* New York: Abelard-Schuman, 1951.

Allee, W.C., and Masure, R.H., A comparison of maze behavior in paired and isolated shell parakeets (*Melopsittacus undulatus* Shaw) in a two-alley problem box. *Journal of Comparative Psychology,* 1936, 22, 131–56.

Allen, T.J., and Cohen, S.I., Information flow in research and development laboratories. *Administrative Science Quarterly,* 1969, 14, 12–21.

Allen, V.L., Situational factors in conformity. In L. Berkowitz (Ed.) *Advances in Experimental Social Psychology*. New York: Academic Press, 1965, 2, 133–73.

Allport, F.H., *Social Psychology*. Boston: Houghton Mifflin, 1924.

Allport, Gordon W., Attitudes. In M. Fishbein (Ed.), *Readings in Attitude Theory and Measurement*. New York: John Wiley & Sons, 1967, 3.

Alutto, J.A., and Belasco, J.A., A typology for participation in organizational decision making. *Administrative Science Quarterly*, 1972, 17, 117–25.

Argyle, M., Social pressure in public and private situations. *Journal of Abnormal and Social Psychology*, 1957, 54, 172–75.

Aronson, E., and Mills, J., The effect of severity of initiation of liking for a group. *Journal of Abnormal and Social Psychology*, 1959, 59, 177–81.

Asch, S.E., Effects of group pressure upon the modification and distortion of judgments. In H. Guetzkow (Ed.), *Groups, Leadership and Men*. Pittsburgh: Carnegie Press, 1951, 177–90.

_____. Opinions and social pressure. *Scientific American*, 1955, 193, 31–35.

_____. *Social Psychology*. Englewood Cliffs, N.J.: Prentice-Hall, 1952.

_____. Studies of independence and submission to group pressure: I. a minority of one against a unanimous majority. *Psychological Monographs*, 70, No. 9 (whole No. 417), 1956.

Atkinson, J.W., Motivational determinants of risk taking behavior, *Psychological Review*. 1957, 64, 359–72.

Bachrach, P. and Baratz, M.S., Decisions and nondecisions: an analytical framework. *American Political Science Review*, 1963, 57, 632–42.

Back, K.W., Influence through social communication. *Journal of Abnormal and Social Psychology*, 1951, 46, 9–23.

Bales, Robert F., and Edgar F. Borgotta, Size of group as a factor in the interaction profile. In A. Paul Hare; Edgar F. Borgotta; and Robert F. Bales, *The Small Group: Studies in Social Interaction*. New York: Alfred A. Knopf, 1955, 403–05, 411–13.

Bales, R., and Slater, P., Role differentiation in small decision-making groups. In T. Parsons *et al.* (Eds.), *Family Socialization and Interaction Process*. Glencoe, Ill: Free Press, 1955.

Barnard, C.I., *The Functions of the Executive*. Cambridge, Mass.: Harvard University Press, 1938.

Barnlund, D.C., A comparative study of individual, majority, and group judgment. *Journal of Abnormal and Social Psychology*, 1959, 58, 55–60.

Bass, A.R.; Fiedler, F.E.; and Krueger, S., Personality correlates of assumed similarity (ASO) and related scores. Urbana, Ill.: University of Illinois, Group Effectiveness Research Laboratory, 1964.

Bavelas, A., Communication patterns in task-oriented groups. *Journal of the Acoustical Society of America*, 1950, 22, 725–30.

_____. A mathematical model for group structures. *Applied Anthropology*, 1948, 7, 16–30.

Beaty, W.E., and Shaw, M.E., Some effects of social interaction on probability learning. *Journal of Psychology*, 1965, 59, 299–306.

Begum, B.O., and Lehr, D.J., Effects of authoritarianism on vigilance performance. *Journal of Applied Psychology*, 1963, 47, 75–77.

Bellman, R.E., *Dynamic Programming*. Princeton, N.J.: Princeton University Press, 1957.

Bennis, W.G.; Berkowitz, N.; Affinito, M.; and Malone, M., Reference groups and loyalties in the out-patient department. *Administrative Science Quarterly*, 1958, 2, 481–500.

Berg, I.A., and Bass, B.M. (Eds.), *Conformity and Deviation*. New York: Harper & Row, 1961.

Berkowitz, L., Groups standards, cohesiveness, and productivity. *Human Relations*, 1954, 7, 509–19.

———. Shared leadership in small decision making groups. *Journal of Abnormal and Social Psychology*, 1953, 48, 231–38.

Bieri, J., Cognitive complexity-simplicity and predictive behavior. *Journal of Abnormal and Social Psychology*, 1955, 51, 263–68.

Blake, R.R., and Mouton, Jane S., The dynamics of influence and concern. *International Journal of Social Psychiatry*, 1957, 2, 263–305.

Blankenship, L.V. and Miles, R.E., Organizational structure and managerial decision behavior. *Administrative Science Quarterly*, 1968, 13, 106–20.

Blau, P.M., *Exchange and power in social life*. New York: John Wiley & Sons, 1964.

Block, J., and Block, Jeanne, An interpersonal experiment on reactions to authority. *Human Relations*, 1952, 5, 91–98.

Bouchard, T.J., Jr. and Hare, Melana, Size, performance and potential in brainstorming groups. *Journal of Applied Psychology*, 1970, 54, 51–55.

Boulding, K.E., The ethics of rational decision. *Management Science*, 1966, 12, B-161–69.

Bower, J.L., Group decision making: a report of an experimental study. *Behavioral Science*, 1965, 10, 277–89.

Bowman, E.H., Consistency and optimality in managerial decision making. *Management Science*, 1963, 9, 310–21.

Brehm, J.W., Post-decision changes in desirability of alternatives. *Journal of Abnormal and Social Psychology*, 1956, 52, 384–99.

Brehmer, B., Cognitive dependence on additive and configural cue-criterion relations. *The American Journal of Psychology*, 1969, 32, 490–503.

Brim, O.G., Jr., The acceptance of new behavior in child-rearing. *Human Relations*, 1954, 7, 473–91.

Brim, O.G., Jr., and Hoff, D.B., Individual and situational differences in desire for certainty. *Journal of Abnormal and Social Psychology*, 1957, 54, 225–29.

Brody, N., The effect of commitment to correct and incorrect decisions on confidence in a sequential decision task. *American Journal of Psychology*, 1965, 78, 251–56.

Bross, I.D., *Design for Decision*. New York: Macmillan Publishing Co., 1953.

Brown, D.S., Shaping the organization to fit people. *Management of Personnel Quarterly*, 1966, 5, 12–16.

Bruner, J.S., and Goodman, C.C., Value and need as organizing factors in perception. *The Journal of Abnormal and Social Psychology,* 1947, 42, 33–44.

Bruner, J.S.; Goodnow, J.J.; and Austin, G.A., *A Study of Thinking.* New York: John Wiley & Sons, 1956.

Brunswick, E., Representative design and probabilistic theory in a functional psychology. *Psychological Review,* 1955, 62, 193–217.

Burlingame, J.F., Information technology and decentralization. *Harvard Business Review,* 1961, 39, 121–26.

Burns, T. and Stalker, G.M., *The Management of Innovation.* London: Tavistock Publications, 1961.

Burnstein, E., An analysis of group decisions involving risk. *Human Relations,* 1969, 22, 381–95.

Burnstein, E.; Miller, H.; Vinokur, A.; Katz, S.; and Joan Crowley, Risky shift is eminently rational. *Journal of Personality and Social Psychology,* 1971, 20, 462–71.

Burton, A., The influence of social factors upon the persistence of satiation in school children. *Child Development,* 1941, 2, 121–29.

Byrne, D., Interpersonal attraction and attitude similarity. *Journal of Abnormal and Social Psychology,* 1961, 62, 713–15.

Byrne, D., and Buehler, J. A., A note on the influence of propinquity upon acquaintanceships. *Journal of Abnormal and Social Psychology,* 1955, 51, 147–48.

Byrne, D.; Clore, J.L., Jr.; and Worchel, P., Effect of economic similarity–dissimilarity on interpersonal attraction. *Journal of Personality and Social Psychology,* 1966, 4, 220–24.

Campbell, J.P.; Dunnette, M.D.; Lawler, E.E., III; and Weick, K.E., Jr., *Managerial Behavior, Performance and Effectiveness.* New York: McGraw-Hill Book Co., 1970.

Carter, L.F., Some research on leadership in small groups. In H. Guetzkow (Ed.), *Groups, Leadership, and Men: Research in Human Relations.* Pittsburgh: Carnegie Press, Carnegie Institute of Technology, 1951, 146–57.

Cartwright, D.A., Power: a neglected variable in social psychology. In D.A. Cartwright (Ed.), *Studies in Social Power.* Ann Arbor, Mich.: Institute for Social Research, 1959a, 1–14.

Cartwright, D.A., Field theoretical conception of power. In D.A. Cartwright (Ed.), *Studies in Social Power.* Ann Arbor, Mich.: Institute for Social Research, 1959b, 183–220.

Cartwright, D., and Zander, A. (Eds.), *Group Dynamics.* New York: Harper & Row, 1968.

Castellan, N.J., Multiple cue probability learning with irrelevant cues. *Organizational Behavior and Human Performance,* 1973, 9, 16–29.

Castore, Carl H., Peterson, Kevin; and Goodrich, Thomas A., Risky shift: social value or social choice? an alternative model. *Journal of Personality and Social Psychology,* 1971, 20, 487–94.

Chapanis, N.P., and Chapanis A., Cognitive dissonance five years later. *Psychological Bulletin,* 1964, 61, 1–22.

Charnes, A., and Cooper, W.W., *Management Models and Industrial Applica-*

tions of Linear Programming, Vols. I and II. New York: John Wiley & Sons, 1961.

Clark, K.B., Problems of power and social change: toward a relevant social psychology. *Journal of Social Issues,* 1965, 4–20.

Clark, R.D., III, Group-induced shift toward risk: a critical appraisal. *Psychological Bulletin,* 1971, 76, 251–70.

Clark, Russell D., III; Crockett, Walter H.; and Archer, Richard L., Risk-as-value hypothesis: the relationship between perception of self, others, and the risky shift. *Journal of Personality and Social Psychology,* 1971, 20, 425–29.

Clarkson, G.P.E., *Portfolio Selection: A Simulation of Trust Investment.* Englewood Cliffs, N.J.: Prentice-Hall, 1962.

Coch, L., and French, J.R., Overcoming resistance to change. *Human Relations,* 1948, 1, 512–32.

Cohen, A.R., Communication discrepancy and attitude change: a dissonance theory approach. *Journal of Personality,* 1959, 27, 386–96.

———. Need for cognition and order of communication as determinants of opinion change. In C.I. Hovland (Ed.), *Order of Presentation in Persuasion.* New Haven, Conn.: Yale University Press, 1957, 79–97.

Cohen, D. J.; Whitmyre, J. W.; and Funk, W. H., Effect of group cohesiveness and training upon group thinking. *Journal of Applied Psychology,* 1960, 44, 319–22.

Cohen, J. B. and Golden, E., Informational social influence and product evaluation. *Journal of Applied Psychology,* 1972, 56, 54–59.

Coleman, J.F.; Blake, R.R.; and Mouton, J.S., Task difficulty and conformity pressures. *Journal of Abnormal and Social Psychology,* 1958, 57, 120–22.

Collins, B.E., and Guetzkow, H., *A Social Psychology of Group Processes for Decision Making.* New York: John Wiley & Sons, 1964.

Collins, B.E., and Raven, B.H., Group structure: attraction, coalitions, communication and power. In G. Lindzey and E. Aronson (Eds.), *The Handbook of Social Psychology.* Reading, Mass.: Addison-Wesley, 1969, 4, 102–204.

Constanzo, P.R., Conformity development as a function of self blame. *Journal of Personality and Social Psychology,* 1970, 14, 366–74.

Costanzo, P.R., and Shaw, M.E., Conformity as a function of age level. *Child Development,* 1966, 37, 967–75.

Costello, T.W. and Zalkind, S.S., *Psychology in Administration: A Research Orientation.* Englewood Cliffs, N.J.: Prentice-Hall, 1963.

Coyle, Grace L., *Social Process in Organized Groups.* New York: The Richard R. Smith Co., 1930.

Cravens, D.W., An exploratory analysis of individual information processing. *Management Science,* 1970, 16, B-656-70.

Crawford, J.L. and Haaland, G.A., Predecisional information seeking and subsequent conformity in the social influence process. *Journal of Personality and Social Psychology,* 1972, 23, 112–19.

Crutchfield, R.S., Conformity and character. *American Psychologist,* 1955, 10, 191–98.

Cyert, R.M.; Dill, W.R.; and March, J.G., The role of expectations in business decision making. *Administrative Science Quarterly,* 1958, 3, 307–40.

Cyert, R.M.; Feigenbaum, E.H.; and March, J.G., Models in a behavioral theory of the firm. In J.M. Dutton and W.H. Starbuck (Eds.), *Computer Simulation of Human Behavior.* New York: John Wiley & Sons, 1971, Chapter 11.

Cyert, R.M., and March, J.G., *A Behavioral Theory of the Firm.* Englewood Cliffs, N.J.: Prentice-Hall, 1963.

Dahl, R.A., The concept of power. *Behavioral Science,* 1957, 2, 201–18.

Dahle, T.L., An objective and comparative study of five methods of transmitting information to business and industrial employees. In G.A. Yukl and K.N. Wexley, (Eds.), *Readings in Organizational and Industrial Psychology.* New York: Oxford University Press, 1971, 63–70.

Dahlstrom, E., Exchange, influence and power. *Acta Sociologica,* 1966, 9, 237–84.

Dalton, M., In W. F. Whyte, *Money and Motivation.* New York: Harper & Row, 1955, Chapter 6.

Davis, J.H.; Hornik, J.A.; and Hornseth, J.P., Group decision schemes and strategy preferences in a sequential response task. *Journal of Personality and Social Psychology,* 1970, 15, 397–408.

Davis, K., Management communication and the grapevine. In G.A. Yukl and K.N. Wexley, (Eds.), *Readings in Organizational and Industrial Psychology.* New York: Oxford University Press, 1971, 93–101.

Dawes, R.M., A case study of graduate admissions: application of three principles of human decision making. *American Psychologist,* 1971, 26, 180–88.

Dearborn, D.C., and Simon, H.A., Selective perception: a note on the departmental identifications of executives. *Sociometry,* 1958, 21, 140–44.

Delbecq, A.L., The management of decision making within the firm: three strategies for three types of decision-making. *Academy of Management Journal,* 1967, 10, 329–39.

Deutsch, M., A theory of cooperation and competition. *Human Relations,* 1949a, 2, 129–52.

_____. An experimental study of the effects of cooperation and competition. *Human Relations,* 1949b, 2, 199–32.

Deutsch, M., and Gerard, H.B., A study of normative and informational social influences upon individual judgment. *Journal of Abnormal and Social Psychology,* 1955, 51, 629–36.

DeWhirst, H.D., Influence of perceived information-sharing norms on communication channel utilization. *Academy of Management Journal,* 1971, 14, 305–15.

Dill, W.R., The impact of environment on organizational development. In S. Mailick and E.H. Van Ness (Eds.), *Concepts and Issues in Administrative Behavior.* Englewood Cliffs, N.J.: Prentice-Hall, 1962, 94–109.

Dion, K.L.; Baron, R.S.; and Miller, N., Why do groups make riskier decisions than individuals? In L. Berkowitz (Ed.), *Current Advances in Experimental Social Psychology,* Vol. 5. New York: Academic Press, 1970.

Di Vesta, F.J., Effects of confidence and motivation on susceptibility to informational social influence. *Journal of Abnormal and Social Psychology,* 1959, 59, 204–09.

Doob, A.N.; Carlsmith, J.M.; Freedman, J.L.; Landauer, T.K.; and Tom, S., Jr., Effect of initial selling price on subsequent sales. *Journal of Personality and Social Psychology*, 1969, 11, 345–50.

Driver, M.J., A structural analysis of aggression, stress and personality in an internation simulation. Working paper, Purdue University, Institute for Research in the Behavioral Economic and Management Sciences, Paper No. 97, 1965.

———. Conceptual structure and group processes in an internation simulation. Part one: the perception of simulated nations. *Educational Testing Service Research Bulletin:* 62-15. Princeton: N.J., 1962.

———. The relationship between abstractness of conceptual functioning and group performance in a complex decision making environment. Master's thesis, Princeton University, 1960.

———. Threat, communication rate and the complexity of social perception. Paper given at Western Psychological Association meeting, Vancouver, B.C., 1969.

Driver, M.J., and Streufert, S., Integrative complexity: an approach to individuals and groups as information-processing systems. *Administrative Science Quarterly*, 1969, 14, 272–85.

DuCharme, W.M., A response bias explanation of conservative human inference. *Journal of Experimental Psychology*, 1970, 85, 66–74.

Dudycha, L., and Naylor, J.C., Characteristics of human inference process in complex choice behavior situations. *Organizational Behavior and Human Performance*, 1966a, 1, 110–28.

———. The effect of variations in the cue R matrix upon the obtained policy equation of judges. *Educational and Psychological Measurement*, 1966b, 26, 583–603.

Dulany, Don, Awareness, rules and propositional control: a confrontation with S-R behavior theory. In D. Horton and T. Dixon (Eds.), *Verbal Behavior and S-R Theory*. Englewood Cliffs, N.J.: Prentice-Hall, 1967.

Dunnette, M.D.; Campbell, M.D.; and Jaastad, Kay, The effect of group participation on brainstorming effectiveness for two industrial samples. *Journal of Applied Psychology*, 1963, 47, 30–37.

Ebert, R.J., Time horizon: implications for aggregate scheduling effectiveness. *AIIE Transactions*, 1972a, 4, 298–307.

———. Environmental structure and programmed decision effectiveness. *Management Science*, 1972b, 19, 435–45.

———. Human control of a two-variable decision system. *Organizational Behavior and Human Performance*, 1972c, 7, 237–264.

Edwards, W., Conservatism in human information processing. In B. Kleinmuntz (Ed.), *Formal Representation of Human Judgment*. New York: John Wiley & Sons, 1968, Chapter 2.

———. Dynamic decision theory and probabilistic information processing. *Human Factors*, 1962, 4, 59–73.

———. The theory of decision making. *Psychological Bulletin*, 1954, 51, 380–418.

Edwards, W., and Phillips, L.D., Man as transducer for probabilities in bayesian command and control systems. In M. W. Shelly, II and G. L. Bryan (Eds.), *Human Judgments and Optimality*. New York: John Wiley & Sons, 1964.

Edwards, W.; Phillips, L.D.; Hays, W.L.; and Goodman, B.C., Probabilistic information processing systems: design and evaluation. *IEEE Transactions on Systems Science and Cybernetics*, 1968, SSC-4, 248–65.

Einhorn, H.J., Use of nonlinear, noncompensatory models as a function of task and amount of information. *Organizational Behavior and Human Performance*, 1971, 6, 1–27.

Elbing, A.O., *Behavioral Decisions in Organizations*. Glenview, Ill.: Scott, Foresman and Co., 1970.

Emerson, R.M., Exchange theory, part one: a psychological basis for social exchange. In J. Berger; M. Zelditch; and B. Anderson (Eds.), *Sociological Theories in Progress*, Vol. II. Boston: Houghton Mifflin Co., in press (a).

——. Exchange theory, part two: exchange relations, exchange networks and groups as exchange systems. In J. Berger; M. Zelditch; and B. Anderson (Eds.), *Sociological Theories in Progress*, Vol. II. Boston: Houghton Mifflin Co., in press (b).

——. Power-dependence relations. *American Sociological Review*, 1962, 27, 31–40.

Emery, F.E., and Trist, E.L., The causal texture of organizational environments. *Human Relations*, 1963, 18, 20–26.

Emory, C.W., and Niland, P., *Making Management Decisions*. Boston: Houghton Mifflin Co., 1968.

England, G.W., Personal value systems of American managers. *Academy of Management Journal*, 1967, 10, 53–68.

——. Personal value systems of managers—so what? Manuscript, *Industrial Relations Center*, University of Minnesota, January 1973.

England, G.W., and Lee, R., Organizational goals and expected behavior among Americans, Japanese and Korean managers—a comparative study. *Academy of Management Journal*, 1971, 14, 425–38.

England, G.W.; Olsen, K.; and Agarwal, N., *A Manual of Development and Research for the Personal Values Questionnaire*. Manuscript, University of Minnesota, October 1971.

Ericson, R.F., The impact of cybernetic information technology on management value systems. *Management Science*, 1969, 16, no. 2, B-40–60.

Evan, W.M., and Zelditch, M., Jr., A laboratory experiment on bureaucratic authority. *American Sociological Review*, 1961, 26, 883–93.

Exline, R.V., Group climate as a factor in the relevance and accuracy of social perception. *Journal of Abnormal and Social Psychology*, 1957, 55, 382–88.

Fagen, S.A., The effects of real and experimentally reported ability on confidence and conformity. *American Psychologist*, 1963, 18, 357–58.

Farnsworth, P.R., and Behner, Alice, A note on the attitude of social conformity. *Journal of Social Psychology*, 1931, 2, 126–28.

Feldman, J., and Kanter, H.E., Organizational decision making. In J.G. March (Ed.), *Handbook of Organizations*. Chicago: Rand McNally and Co., 1965, Chapter 14.

Ference, T.P., Organizational communications systems and the decision process. *Management Science,* 1970, 17, B-83-96.

Festinger, L., *A Theory of Cognitive Dissonance.* Stanford, Ca.: Stanford University Press, 1957.

Festinger, L., and Carlsmith, J.M., Cognitive consequences of forced compliance. *Journal of Abnormal and Social Psychology,* 1959, 58, 203–10.

Festinger, L.; Schachter, S.; and Back, K.W., *Social Pressure in Informal Groups.* New York: Harper & Bros., 1950.

Fiedler, F.E., *A Theory of Leadership Effectiveness.* New York: McGraw-Hill Book Co., 1967.

––––––. Validation and extension of the contingency model of leadership effectiveness: a review of empirical findings. *Psychological Bulletin,* 1971, 76, 128–48.

Filley, A.C., and Grimes, A.J., The bases of power in decision processes. In R.W. Millman and M.P. Hottenstein (Eds.), *Academy of Management Proceedings: Twenty-Seventh Annual Meeting,* 1967, 133–60.

Filley, A.C., and House, R.J., *Managerial Process and Organizational Behavior.* Glenview, Ill.: Scott, Foresman and Co., 1969.

Fishbein, M., An investigation of the relationship between beliefs about an object and the attitude toward that object. *Human Relations,* 1963, 16, 233–40.

––––––. Attitude and the prediction of behavior. In M. Fishbein (Ed.), *Readings in Attitude Theory and Measurement.* New York: John Wiley & Sons, 1967.

Fishbein, M.; Landy, E.; and Hatch, G., Some determinants of an individual's esteem for his least preferred co-worker: an attitudinal analysis. Urbana, Ill.: University of Illinois, Group Effectiveness Research Laboratory, 1965.

Fishbein, M., and Raven, B.H., The AB scales: an operational definition of belief and attitude. In M. Fishbein (Ed.), *Readings in Attitude Theory and Measurement.* New York: John Wiley & Sons, 1967, 183–90.

Fisk, G., *The Psychology of Management Decision.* Lund, Sweden: CWK Bleerup, 1967.

Foa, U.G.; Mitchell, T.R.; and Fiedler, F.E., Differentiation matching. *Behavior Science,* 1971, 16, 130–42.

Forrester, J.W., *Industrial Dynamics.* New York: John Wiley & Sons, 1961.

Frank, F., and Anderson, L.R., Effects of task and group size upon productivity and member satisfaction. *Sociometry,* 1971, 34, 135–49.

Frank, J.D., Experimental studies of personal pressure and resistance: I. Experimental production of resistance. *Journal of General Psychology,* 1944a, 30, 23–41.

––––––. Experimental studies of personal pressure and resistance: II. Methods of overcoming resistance. *Journal of General Psychology,* 1944b, 30, 43–56.

––––––. Experimental studies of personal pressure and resistance: III. Qualitative analysis of resistant behavior. *Journal of General Psychology,* 1944c, 30, 57–64.

Freedman, J.L.; Carlsmith, J.M.; and Sears, D.O., *Social Psychology.* Englewood-Cliffs, N.J.: Prentice-Hall, 1970.

French, J.R.P., Jr., The disruption and cohesion of groups. *Journal of Abnormal and Social Psychology,* 1941, 36, 361–77.

French, J.R.P., Jr., Field experiments: changing group productivity. In J.G. Miller (Ed.), *Experiments in Social Process: A Symposium on Social Psychology.* New York: McGraw-Hill Book Co., 1950.

French, J.R.P., Jr., and Raven, B., The bases of social power. In D. Cartwright (Ed.), *Studies in Social Power.* Ann Arbor, Mich.: Institute for Social Research, 1959.

French, J.R.P., Jr., and Snyder, R., Leadership and interpersonal power. In D. Cartwright (Ed.), *Studies in Social Power.* Ann Arbor, Mich.: Institute for Social Research, 1959, 118–49.

Friedrich, C.J., *Constitutional Government and Democracy.* Boston: Little, Brown & Co., 1941.

Gage, N.L., Explorations in the understanding of others. *Educational and Psychological Measurement,* 1953, 13, 14–26.

Gamson, W.A., Experimental studies in coalition formation. In L. Berkowitz (Ed.), *Advances in Experimental Social Psychology,* Vol. 1. New York: Academic Press, 1964.

Gantt, Henry L., *Work, Wages and Profit.* New York: Engineering Magazine Co., 1910.

Gavett, J.W., *Production and Operations Management.* New York: Harcourt, Brace and World, 1968.

Gerard, H.B., and Mathewson, G.C., The effects of severity of initiation on liking for a group: a replication. *Journal of Experimental Social Psychology,* 1966, 2, 278–87.

Gerard, H.B.; Wilhelmy, R.A.; and Connolley, E.S., Conformity and group size. *Journal of Personality and Social Psychology,* 1968, 8, 79–82.

Ghiselli, E.E., and Lodahl, T.M., Patterns of managerial traits and group effectiveness. *Journal of Abnormal and Social Psychology,* 1958, 57, 61–66.

Gibb, C.A., Leadership. In G. Lindzey (Ed.), *Handbook of Social Psychology,* Vol. 2. Cambridge, Mass.: Addison-Wesley, 1954.

Goldberg, L.R., Diagnosticians vs. diagnostic signs: the diagnosis of psychosis vs. neurosis from the MMPI. *Psychological Monographs,* 1965, 79 (9, Whole No. 602).

———, Man versus model of man: a rationale, plus some evidence, for a method of improving on clinical inferences. *Psychological Bulletin,* 1970, 73, 422–32.

———. Simple models or simple processes? some research on clinical judgments. *American Psychologist,* 1968, 23, 483–96.

Goldhammer, H., and Shils, E.A., Types of power and status. *American Journal of Sociology,* 1939, 45, 171–82.

Goldman, M., A comparison of individual and group performance for varying combinations of initial ability. *Journal of Personality and Social Psychology,* 1965, 1, 210–16.

Goodstadt, B., and Kipnis, D., Situational influences on the use of power. *Journal of Applied Psychology,* 1970, 54, 201–07.

Gordon, K., Group judgments in the field of lifted weights. *Journal of Experimental Psychology,* 1924, 7, 389–400.

Gouldner, A.W., *Patterns of Industrial Bureaucracy*. Glencoe, Ill.: Free Press, 1954.

Graen, G., Instrumentality theory of work motivation: some experimental results and suggested modifications. *Journal of Applied Psychology Monograph*, 1969, 53, 1–25.

Graen, G.; Alvares, D.A.; Orris, J.; and Martella, J., The contingency model of leadership effectiveness. Antecedent and evidential results. *Psychological Bulletin*, 1970, 74, 285–96.

Greenspoon, J., The reinforcing effect of two spoken sounds on the frequency of two responses. *American Journal of Psychology*, 1955, 44, 221–48.

Griffitt, W., Interpersonal attraction as a function of self concept and personality similarity–dissimilarity. *Journal of Personality and Social Psychology*, 1966, 4, 581–84.

Gross, E., Primary functions of the small group. *American Journal of Sociology*, 1954, 60, 24–30.

Guetzkow, H.; Alger, C.; Brody, R.; Noel, R.; and Snyder, R., *Simulation in International Relations*. Englewood Cliffs, N.J.: Prentice-Hall, 1963.

Gurnee, H., A comparison of collective and individual judgments of facts. *Journal of Experimental Psychology*, 1937, 21, 106–12.

Guth, W.D., and Tagiuri, R., Personal values and corporate strategies. *Harvard Business Review*, 1965, 43, 123–32.

Haaland, H., Information seeking behavior and sources of influence in conformity, *Behavioral Science*, 1968, 13, 238–39.

Hadley, G., *Linear Programming*. Reading, Mass.: Addison-Wesley, 1962.

———. *Nonlinear and Dynamic Programming*. Reading, Mass.: Addison-Wesley, 1964.

Hammond, K.R., Probabilistic functioning and the clinical method. *Psychological Review*, 1955, 62, 255–62.

Hammond, K.R.; Hursch, C.J.; and Todd, F.J., Analyzing the components of clinical inference. *Psychological Review*, 1964, 71, 438–56.

Hammond, K.R., and Summers, D.A., Cognitive dependence on linear and nonlinear cues. *Psychological Review*, 1965, 72, 215–24.

Hammond, K.R.; Summers, D. A.;and Deane, D. H., Negative effects of outcome-feedback in multiple cue probability learning. *Organizational Behavior and Human Performance*, 1973, 9, 30–34.

Hampton, D., *Modern Management: Issues and Ideas*. Belmont, Calif.: Dickenson Publishing Co., 1969.

Hare, A., Paul, *Handbook of Small Group Research*. New York: The Free Press of Glencoe, 1962.

Harper, F.B.W., The sociometric composition of the group as a determinant of yielding to a distorted norm. Ph.D. dissertation. University of California, Berkeley, 1961.

Harsanyi, J.C., Measurement of social power in n-person reciprocal power situations. *Behavioral Science*, 1962b, 7, 81–91.

———. Measurement of social power, opportunity costs, and the theory of two-person bargaining games. *Behavioral Science*, 1962b, 7, 67–80.

Harvey, O.J.; Hunt, D.E.; and Schroder, H.M., *Conceptual Systems and Personality Organization*. New York: John Wiley & Sons, 1961.

Hathaway, S.R., and McKinley, J.C., *Minnesota Multiphasic Personality Inventory*. New York: Psychological Corporation, 1943.

Hays, W.L., *Statistics for Psychologists*. New York: Holt, Rinehart and Winston, 1963.

Hearn, G., Leadership and the spatial factor in small groups. *Journal of Abnormal and Social Psychology*, 1957, 54, 269–72.

Heider, F., Attitudes and cognitive organization. *Journal of Psychology*, 1946, 21, 107–12.

_____. *The Psychology of Interpersonal Relations*. New York: John Wiley & Sons, 1958.

Helson, H., Adaptation-level as a frame of reference for prediction of psychological data. *American Journal of Psychology*, 1947, 60, 1–29.

_____. *Theoretical Foundations of Psychology*. New York: D. Van Nostrand Co., 1951.

Hemphill, J.K., Relations between the size of the group and the behavior of "superior" leaders. *Journal of Social Psychology*, 1950, 32, 11–22.

Heneman, H.G., III and Schwab, D.P., An evaluation of research on expectancy theory predictions of employee performance. *Psychological Bulletin*, 1972, 78, 1–9.

Hitler, A., *Mein Kampf*, translated by E.T.S. Dugdale. Cambridge, Mass.: Riverside Press, 1933.

Hochbaum, G.M., The relation between group members' self confidence and their reactions to group pressure to conformity. *American Sociological Review*, 1954, 19, 678–87.

Hoffman, L.R., Homogeneity of member personality and its effect on group problem-solving. *Journal of Abnormal and Social Psychology*, 1959, 58, 27–32.

Hoffman, L.R., and Maier, N.R.F., Quality and acceptance of problem solutions by members of homogeneous and heterogeneous groups. *Journal of Abnormal and Social Psychology*, 1961, 62, 401–07.

Hoffman, P.J., Cue consistency and configurality in human judgment. In B. Kleinmuntz (Ed.), *Formal Representation of Human Judgment*. New York: John Wiley & Sons, 1968, Chapter 3.

_____. The paramorphic representation of clinical judgment. *Psychological Bulletin*, 1960, 57, 116–31.

Hoffman, P.J.; Slovic, P.; and Rorer, L.G., An analysis-of-variance model for the assessment of configural cue utilization in clinical judgment. *Psychological Bulletin*, 1968, 69, 338–49.

Hoge, R.D., and Lanzetta, J.T., Effects of response uncertainty and degree of knowledge on subjective uncertainty. *Psychological Reports*, 1968, 22, 1081–90.

Holloman, C.R., and Hendrick, H.W., Adequacy of group decisions as a function of the decision-making process. *Academy of Management Journal*, 1972, 15, 175–84.

Holt, C.C.; Modigliani, F.; Muth, J.F.; and Simon, H.A., *Planning Production, Inventories and Work Force*. Englewood Cliffs, N.J.: Prentice-Hall, 1960.

Hovland, C.I.; Harvey, O.J.; and Sherif, M., Assimilation and contrast effects in reaction to communication and attitude change. *Journal of Abnormal and Social Psychology*, 1957, 55, 244–52.

Hovland, C.I.; Lumsdaine, A.A.; and Sheffield, F.D., *Experiments in Mass Communications*. Princeton, N.J.: Princeton University Press, 1949.

Hovland, C.I., and Weiss, W., The influence of source credibility on communication effectiveness. *Public Opinion Quarterly*, 1952, 15, 635–50.

Huber, G.P., and Delbecq, A., Guidelines for combining the judgment of individual members in decision conferences. *Academy of Management Journal*, 1972, 15, 161–74.

Hursch, C.J.; Hammond, K.R.; and Hursch, J.L. Some methodological considerations in multiple-cue probability studies. *Psychological Review*, 1964, 71, 42–60.

Hurwitz, J.I.; Zander, A.F.; and Hymovitch, B., Some effects of power on the relations among group members. In D. Cartwright and A. Zander (Eds.), *Group Dynamics: Research and Theory*. Evanston, Ill.: Row, Peterson, 1953, 483–92.

Husband, R.W., Cooperative versus solitary problem solution. *Journal of Social Psychology*, 1940, 11, 405–09.

Ilgen, D.R., and O'Brien, G., *The Effects of Task Organization and Member Compatibility on Leader-Member Relations in Small Groups*. Urbana, Ill.: University of Illinois, 1968.

Irwin, F.W., and Smith, W.A.S., Value, cost, and information as determiners of decision. *Journal of Experimental Psychology*, 1957, 54, 229–32.

Iscoe, I.; Williams, M.; and Harvey, J., Modification of children's judgments by a simulated group technique: a normative developmental study. *Child Development*, 1963, 34, 963–73.

Ivancevich, J.M., An analysis of control, bases of control and satisfaction in an organizational setting. *Academy of Management Journal*, 1970, 13, 427–36.

Izard, C.E., Personality similarity, and friendship. *Journal of Abnormal and Social Psychology*, 1960a, 61, 47–51.

———. Personality similarity, positive affect, and interpersonal attraction. *Journal of Abnormal and Social Psychology*, 1960b, 61, 484–85.

Janis, I.L., and Feshbach, S., Effects of fear-arousing communications. *Journal of Abnormal and Social Psychology*, 1953, 48, 78–92.

Janis, I.L., and Terwilliger, R., An experimental study of psychological resistance to fear-arousing communications. *Journal of Abnormal and Social Psychology*, 1962, 65, 403–10.

Jellison, J.M., and Mills, J., Effect of public commitment upon opinions. *Journal of Experimental Social Psychology*, 1969, 5, 340–46.

Jenness, A., The role of discussion in changing opinion regarding a matter of fact. *Journal of Abnormal and Social Psychology*, 1932, 27, 279–96.

Johnson, C.D., and Davis, J.H., An equiprobability model of risk taking. *Organizational Behavior and Human Performance*, 1972, 8, 1–20.

Johnson, R.A.; Newell, W.T.; and Vergin, R.C., *Operations Management: A Systems Concept*. Boston: Houghton Mifflin Co. 1972.

Jones, E.E., *Ingratiation*. New York: Appleton-Century-Crofts, 1964.

Jones, H.R., and Johnson, M., LPC as a modifier of leader-follower relationships. *Academy of Management Journal,* 1972, 15, 185–96.

Julian, J.W.; Regula, C.R.; and Hollander, E.P., Effects of prior agreement from others on task confidence and conformity. Technical Report 9, ONR Contract 4679, Buffalo, N.Y.: State University of New York, 1967.

Julian, J.W.; Ryckman, R.M.; and Hollander, E.P., Effects of prior group support on conformity: an extension. Technical Report 4, ONR Contract 4679, Buffalo, N.Y.: State University of New York, 1966.

Julian, J.W., and Steiner, I.D., Perceived acceptance as a determinant of conformity behavior. *Journal of Social Psychology,* 1961, 55, 191–98.

Kahn, R.L., and Katz, D., Leadership practices in relation to productivity and morale. In D. Cartwright and A. Zander (Eds.), *Group Dynamics: Research and Theory.* New York: Harper & Row, 1953, 612–28.

Karlsson, G., Some aspects of power in small groups. In J. H. Craswell; H. Solomon; and P. Suppes, (Eds.), *Mathematical Methods in Small Group Processes.* Stanford, Cal.: Stanford University Press, 1962.

Katona, G., Rational behavior and economic behavior. *Psychological Review,* 1953, 60, 307–18.

Katz, D., and Kahn, R.L., *The Social Psychology of Organizations.* New York: John Wiley & Sons, 1966.

Katz, Elihu and Lazarsfeld, P., *Personal Influence: The Part Played by People in the Flow of Mass Communications.* Glencoe, Ill.: Free Press, 1955.

Kefalas, A., and Schoderbek, P.P., Scanning the business environment—some empirical results. *Decision Sciences,* 1973, 4, 63–74.

Kelley, H.H., and Thibaut, J.W., Group problem solving. In G. Lindzey and E. Aronson (Eds.), *Handbook of Social Psychology.* Reading, Mass.: Addison-Wesley, 1969, Vol. 4, 1–101.

Kelman, H.C., Compliance, identification and internalization: three processes of attitude change. *Journal of Conflict Resolution,* 1958, 2, 51–60.

Kelman, H.C., and Hovland, C.I., "Reinstatement" of the communicator in delayed measurement of opinion change. *Journal of Abnormal and Social Psychology,* 1953, 48, 327–35.

Kiesler, C.A. and Kiesler, S.B., *Conformity.* Reading, Mass.: Addison-Wesley, 1969.

Kinney, Elva E., A study of peer group social acceptability at the 5th grade level in a public school. *Journal of Educational Research,* 1953, 47, 57–64.

Kipnis, D., The effects of leadership style and leadership power upon the inducement of an attitude change. *Journal of Abnormal and Social Psychology,* 1958, 57, 173–80.

Kipnis, D., and Vanderveer, R., Ingratiation and the use of power. *Journal of Personality and Social Psychology,* 1971, 17, 280–86.

Kleinmuntz, B., (Ed.), *Formal Representation of Human Judgment.* New York: John Wiley & Sons, 1968.

Kleinmuntz, Benjamin, The processing of clinical information by man and machine. In B. Kleinmuntz (Ed.), *Formal Representation of Human Judgment.* New York: John Wiley & Sons., 1968, Chapter 6.

Knight, H.C., A comparison of the reliability of group and individual judgments. Master's thesis, Columbia University, 1921 (Cited in Lorge *et al.*, 1958).

Kogan, N., and Wallach, M.A., *Risk Taking: A Study in Cognition and Personality*. New York: Holt, Rinehart and Winston, 1964.

Kolasa, B.J., *Introduction to Behavioral Science for Business*. New York: John Wiley & Sons, 1969.

Korman, A.K., Consideration, initiating structure and organizational criteria: a review. *Personnel Psychology*, 1966, 17, 349–63.

Kornberg, A., and Perry, S.D., Conceptual models of power and their applicability to empirical research in politics. *Political Science*, 1966, 18, 52–70.

Kort, F., A nonlinear model for the analysis of judicial systems. *The American Political Science Review*, 1968, 62, 546–55.

Kostlan, A., A method for the empirical study of psychodiagnosis. *Journal of Consulting Psychology*, 1954, 18, 83–88.

Krech, D.; Crutchfield, R.S. ; and Ballachey, E.L., *Individual in Society*. New York: McGraw-Hill Book Co., 1962.

Kuhn, A., *The Study of Society: A Unified Approach*. Homewood, Ill.: Richard D. Irwin, 1963.

Lammers, C.J., Power and participation in decision making in formal organizations. *American Journal of Sociology*, 1967, 73, 201–16.

Lanzetta, J.T., and Kanareff, V.T., Information cost, amount of payoff and level of aspiration as determinants of information seeking in decision making. *Behavioral Science*, 1962, 7, 459–73.

La Piere, R.T., Attitudes versus action. *Social Forces*, 1934, 13, 230–37.

Laughlin, P.R.; Branch, L.G.; and Johnson, H.H., Individual versus triadic performance on a unidimensional complementary task as a function of initial ability level. *Journal of Personality and Social Psychology*, 1969, 12, 144–50.

Lawler, E.E., *Pay and Organizational Effectiveness: A Psychological View*. New York: McGraw-Hill Book Co., 1971.

Lawrence, P.R., and Lorsch, J.W., *Organization and Environment*. Homewood, Ill.: Richard D. Irwin, 1969.

Leavitt, H.J., and Mueller, R.A.H., Some effects of feedback on communication. In E.A. Fleishman (Ed.), *Studies in Personnel and Industrial Psychology*. Homewood, Ill.: Dorsey Press, 1967, 475–83.

Lee, S.M., Decision analysis through goal programming. *Decision Sciences*, 1971, 2, 172–80.

Lee, S.M., and Clayton, E.R., A goal programming model for academic resource allocation. *Management Science*, 1972, 18, B-395–08.

Lefkowitz, M.; Blake, R. R.; and Mouton, Jane S., Status factors in pedestrian violation of traffic signals. *Journal of Abnormal and Social Psychology*, 1955, 51, 704–06.

Leventhal, H., and Niles, P., A field experiment on fear arousal with data on the validity of questionnaire measures. *Journal of Personality*, 1964, 31, 459–79.

Levy, L., Studies in conformity behavior: a methodological note. *Journal of Psychology*, 1960, 50, 39–41.

Lewin, K., *Field Theory in Social Science.* New York: Harper & Bros., 1951.

Likert, R., An emerging theory of organization, leadership and management. In L. Petrullo and B. Bass (Eds.), *Leadership and Interpersonal Behavior.* New York: Holt, Rinehart and Winston, 1961, 290–309.

Lindblom, C.E., The science of muddling through. *Public Administration Review,* 1959, 19, 79–88.

Lippitt, R.; Polansky, N.; Redl, F.; and Rosen, S. The dynamics of power. *Human Relations,* 1952, 5, 37–64.

Lorge, I.; Fox, D.; Davitz, J.; and Brenner, M., A survey of studies contrasting the quality of group performance and individual performance, 1920–1957. *Psychological Bulletin,* 1958, 55, 337–72.

Lott, A.J., and Lott, B.E., Group cohesiveness as interpersonal attraction: a review of relationships with antecedent and consequent variables. *Psychological Bulletin,* 1965, 14, 259–309.

––––––. Group cohesiveness, communication level and conformity. *Journal of Abnormal and Social Psychology,* 1961, 62, 408–12.

Luchins, A.S., Social influences on perception of complex drawings. *Journal of Social Psychology,* 1945, 21, 257–73.

Luchins, A.S., and Luchins, E.H., On conformity with true and false communications. *Journal of Social Psychology,* 1955, 42, 283–04.

McClelland, D.C.; Atkinson, J.W.; Clark, R.A.; and Lowell, E.L., *The Achievement Motive.* New York: Appleton-Century-Crofts, 1953.

McDavid, J.W., and Sistrunk, F., Personality correlates of two kinds of conforming behavior. *Journal of Personality,* 1964, 32, 420–35.

McGuigan, F.J., *Experimental Psychology: A Methodological Approach.* Englewood Cliffs, N.J.: Prentice-Hall, 1960.

McGuire, W.J., The current status of cognitive consistency theories. In S. Feldman (Ed.), *Cognitive Consistency.* New York: Academic Press, 1966.

MacKenzie, K.D., An analysis of risky shift experiments. *Organizational Behavior and Human Performance,* 1971, 6, 249–66.

McWhinney, W.H., Organizational form, decision modalities and the environment. *Human Relations,* 1968, 21, 269–81.

Maier, N.R.F., Maximizing personal creativity through better problem solving. *Personnel Administration,* 1964, 27, 14–18.

––––––. *Problem Solving Discussions and Conferences: Leadership Methods and Skills.* New York: McGraw-Hill Book Co., 1963.

Maier, N.R.F., and Maier, R.A., An experimental test of the effects of "developmental" versus "free" discussions on the quality of group decisions. *Journal of Applied Psychology,* 1957, 41, 320–33.

Malof, M., and Lott, A.J., Ethnocentrism and the acceptance of Negro support in a group pressure situation. *Journal of Abnormal and Social Psychology,* 1962, 65, 254–53.

Mandler, G.; Mussen, P.; Kogan, N.; and Wallach, M., *New Directions in Psychology, Volume III.* New York: Holt, Rinehart and Winston, 1967.

Mann, R.D., A review of the relationships between personality and performance in small groups. *Psychological Bulletin,* 1959, 56, 241–70.

March, J.G., An introduction to the theory and measurement of influence. *American Political Science Review*, 1955, 49, 431–51.

March, J.G., and Simon, H.A., *Organizations*. New York: John Wiley & Sons, 1958.

Marple, C.H., The comparative susceptibility of three age levels to the suggestion of group versus expert opinion. *Journal of Social Psychology*, 1933, 10, 3–40.

Marquis, D.G.; Guetzkow, H.; and Heyns, R.W., A social psychological study of the decision-making conference. In H. Guetzkow (Ed.), *Groups, Leadership and Men*. Pittsburgh: Carnegie Press, 1951, 55–67.

Marsh, P.O., *Persuasive Speaking*. New York: Harper & Row, 1967.

Martin, N.H., Differential decisions in the management of an industrial plant. *The Journal of Business*, 1956, 29, 249–60.

_____. The levels of management and their mental demands. In W.L. Warner and N.H. Martin (Eds.), *Industrial Man*. New York: Harper & Bros., 1959.

Mason, R.O. and Moskowitz, H., Conservatism in information processing: implications for management information systems. *Decision Sciences*, 1972, 3, 35–54.

Matheson, J.E., Decision analysis practice: examples and insights. Manuscript, *Stanford Research Institute*, Menlo Park, Ca., 1969.

Matheson, J.E., and Roths, W.J., Decision analysis of space projects: voyager mars. Manuscript, *Stanford Research Institute*, Menlo Park, Ca., 1967.

Meadow, A.; Parnes, S.J.; and Reese, H., Influence of brainstorming instructions and problem sequence on a creative problem solving test. *Journal of Applied Psychology*, 1959, 43, 413–16.

Mechanic, D., Sources of power of lower participants in complex organizations. In W. W. Cooper; H.J. Leavitt; and M.W. Shelley II (Eds.), *New Perspectives in Organization Research*. New York: John Wiley & Sons, 1964, Chapter 9.

Meehl, P.E., *Clinical Versus Statistical Prediction*. Minneapolis: University of Minnesota Press, 1954.

Meunier, C., and Rule, B.G., Anxiety, confidence and conformity. *Journal of Personality*, 1967, 35, 498–504.

Michael, G.C., A review of heuristic programming. *Decision Sciences*, 1972, 3, 74–100.

Middleton, C.J., How to set up a project organization. *Harvard Business Review*, 1967, 65, 73–82.

Milgram, S., Behavioral study of obedience. *Journal of Abnormal and Social Psychology*, 1963, 67, 371–78.

Miller, G.A.; Galanter, E.; and Pribram, K.H., *Plans and the Structure of Behavior*. New York: Holt, Rinehart and Winston, 1960.

Miller, J.A., Information input overload and psychopathology. *American Journal of Psychiatry*, 1960, 116, 695–704.

Miller, L., and Hamblin, R., Interdependence, differential rewarding and productivity. *American Sociological Review*, 1963, 28, 768–78.

Miller, N., and Campbell, D.T., Recency and primacy in persuasion as a function of the timing of speeches and measurements. *Journal of Abnormal and Social Psychology*, 1959, 59, 1–9.

Mills, J., Opinion change as a function of the communicator's desire to influence and liking for the audience. *Journal of Experimental and Social Psychology,* 1966, 2, 152–59.

Mills, J., and Aronson, E., Opinion change as a function of communicator's attractiveness and desire to influence. *Journal of Personality and Social Psychology,* 1965, 1, 173–77.

Mills, J., and Harvey, J., Opinion change as a function of when information about the communicator is received and whether he is attractive or expert. *Journal of Personality and Social Psychology,* 1972, 21, 52–55.

Mitchell, T.R., Cognitive complexity and leadership style. *Journal of Personality and Social Psychology,* 1970, 16, 166–74.

———. The construct validity of three dimensions of leadership research. *Journal of Social Psychology,* 1970, 80, 89–94.

———. Motivation and participation: an integration. *Academy of Management Journal* (in press).

Mitchell, T.R., and Biglan, A., Instrumentality theories: current uses in psychology. *Psychological Bulletin,* 1971, 76, 432–54.

Mitchell, T.R.; Biglan, A.; Oncken, G.R.; and Fiedler, F.E. The contingency model: criticisms and suggestions. *Journal of the Academy of Management,* 1970, 253–67.

Mitchell, T.R., and Knudsen, B.W., Instrumentality theory predictions of students' attitudes towards business and their choice of business as an occupation. *Journal of the Academy of Management,* 1973, 16, 41–51.

Mitchell, T.R., and Nebeker, D.M., Expectancy theory predictions of academic performance and satisfaction. *Journal of Applied Psychology,* 1973, 57, 61–67.

Mitchell, T.R., and Pollard, W.E., Instrumentality theory predictions of academic behavior. *Journal of Social Psychology,* 1973, 89, 35–45.

Moran, G., Dyadic attraction and orientational consensus. *Journal of Personality and Social Psychology,* 1966, 4, 94–99.

Morlock, H., The effect of outcome desirability on information required for decisions. *Behavioral Science,* 1967, 12, 296–300.

Morlock, H.C., Jr., and Hertz, K.J., Effect on the desirability of outcomes on decision making. *Psychological Reports,* 1964, 14, 11–17.

Morris, W.T., On the art of modeling. *Management Science,* 1967, 13, B-707–17.

Moskowitz, H., The value of information in aggregate production planning–a behavioral experiment. *AIIE Transactions,* 1972, 4, 290–97.

Mosteller, F., and Nogee, P., An experimental measurement of utility. *Journal of Political Economy,* 1951, 59, 371–404.

Mouton, J.S.; Blake, R.R.; and Olmstead, J.A., The relationship between frequency of yielding and the disclosure of personal identity. *Journal of Personality,* 1956, 24, 339–47.

Mukerji, N.P., An investigation of ability in work groups and in isolation. *British Journal of Psychology,* 1940, 30, 352–56.

Mulder, M., Power equalization through participation? *Administrative Science Quarterly,* 1971, 16, 31–39.

Mulder, M., and Wilke, H., Participation and power equalization. *Organizational Behavior and Human Performance*, 1970, 5, 430–48.

Nagel, J.H., Some questions about the concept of power. *Behavioral Science*, 1968, 13, 129–37.

Naylor, J.C., and Clark, R.D., Intuitive inference strategies in interval learning tasks as a function of validity magnitude and sign. *Organizational Behavior and Human Performance*, 1968, 3, 378–99.

Naylor, J.C., and Schenck, E.A., The influence of cue redundancy upon the human inference process for tasks of varying degrees of predictability. *Organizational Behavior and Human Performance*, 1968, 3, 47–61.

Naylor, T.H.; Balintfy, J.L.; Burdick, D.S.; and Chu, D., *Computer Simulation Techniques*. New York: John Wiley & Sons, 1966.

Nebeker, D.M., Situational favorability and perceived environmental uncertainty: an integrative approach. DNR Technical Report No. 73-48, Seattle, Wash.: University of Washington, September 1973.

Newcomb, T.M., The prediction of interpersonal attraction. *American Psychologist*, 1956, 11, 575–86.

Newell, A., Judgment and its representation: an introduction. In B. Kleinmuntz (Ed.), *Formal Representation of Human Judgment*. New York: John Wiley & Sons, 1968, Chapter 1.

Newton, J.R., Judgment and feedback in a quasi-clinical situation. *Journal of Personality and Social Psychology*, 1965, 1, 336–42.

Nickols, S.A., A study of the additivity of variables influencing conformity Ph.D. dissertation, University of Florida, 1964.

Nystedt, L., and Magnusson, D., Cue relevance and feedback in a clinical prediction task. *Organizational Behavior and Human Performance*, 1973, 9, 100–09.

O'Brien, G.E., Groups structure and the measurement of potential leader influence. *Australian Journal of Psychology*, 1969, 21, 277–89.

Orne, M.T., On the social psychology of the psychological experiment: with particular reference to demand characteristics and their implications. *American Psychologist*, 1962, 17, 776–83.

Orne, M.T., and Evans, F.J., Social control in the psychological experiment: antisocial behavior and hypothesis. *Journal of Personality and Social Psychology*, 1965, 1, 189–200.

Osborn, A.F., *Applied Imagination*. New York: Charles Scribner's Sons, 1957.

Osgood, C.E., Cross-cultural comparability in attitude measurement via multilingual semantic differentials. In M. Fishbein (Ed.), *Readings in Attitude Theory and Measurement*. New York: John Wiley & Sons, 1965, 108–16.

Osgood, C.E.; Suci, G.J.; and Tannenbaum, P.H., *The Measurement of Meaning*. Urbana, Ill.: University of Illinois Press, 1957.

Osgood, C.E., and Tannenbaum, P.H., The principle of congruity in the prediction of attitude change. *Psychological Review*, 1955, 62, 42–55.

Parnes, S.J., Research on developing creative behavior. In C. W. Taylor (Ed.), *Widening Horizons in Creativity*. New York: John Wiley & Sons, 1964, 145–69.

Parsons, T., *Structure and Process in Modern Societies.* Glencoe, Ill.: Free Press, 1960.

Patel, A.A., and Gordon, J.E., Some personal and situational determinants of yielding to influence. *Journal of Abnormal and Social Psychology,* 1960, 61, 411–18.

Peak, H., Attitude and motivation. *Nebraska Symposium on Motivation,* 1955, 3, 149–59.

Perlmutter, H.V., and DeMontmollin, G., Group learning of nonsense syllables. *Journal of Abnormal and Social Psychology,* 1952, 28, 148–54.

Peterson, C.R.; DuCharme, W.M.; and Edwards, W., Sampling distributions and probability revisions. *Journal of Experimental Psychology,* 1968, 76, 236–43.

Peterson, C.R.; Hammond, K.R.; and Summers, D.A., Multiple probability learning with shifting weights of cues. *American Journal of Psychology,* 1965a, 78, 660–63.

———. Optimal responding in multiple-cue probability learning. *Journal of Experimental Psychology.* 1965b, 70, 270–76.

Pettigrew, T.F., The measurement and correlates of category width as a cognitive variable. *Journal of Personality,* 1958, 26, 532–44.

Piaget, J., *The Moral Judgment of the Child.* New York: Basic Books, 1954.

Pollard, W.E., and Mitchell, T.R., Decision theory analysis of social power. *Psychological Bulletin,* 1973, 78, 433–46.

Porter, L.W., *Organizational Patterns of Managerial Job Attitudes.* New York: American Foundation for Management Research, 1964.

Porter, L.W., and Lawler, E.E., Properties of organization structure in relation to job attitudes and job behavior. *Psychological Bulletin,* 1965, 64, 23–51.

Posthuma, A., Normative data on the least preferred co-worker and group atmosphere questionnaires. Technical Report No. 70-78, Organizational Research, Seattle, Wash., 1970.

Pounds, W.F., The process of problem finding. *Industrial Management Review,* Fall 1969, 1–19.

Pruitt, Dean G., Choice shifts in group discussion: an introductory review. *Journal of Personality and Social Psychology,* 1971, 20, 339–60.

———. Informational requirements in making decisions. *American Journal of Psychology,* 1961, 74, 443–39.

Raiffa, H., and Schlaifer, R., *Applied Statistical Decision Theory.* Cambridge, Mass.: Harvard University Press, 1961.

Rapoport, Amnon, A study of human control in a stochastic multistage decision task. *Behavioral Science,* 1966, 11, 18–32.

———. Dynamic programming models for multistage decision-making tasks. *Journal of Mathematical Psychology,* 1967, 4, 48–71.

Raven, B.H., Social influence on opinions and the communication of related content. *Journal of Abnormal and Social Psychology,* 1959, 58, 119–28.

Raven, B.H., and French, J.R.P., Jr., Group support, legitimate power, and social influence. *Journal of Personality,* 1958a, 26, 400–09.

———. Legitimate power, coercive power, and observability in social influence. *Sociometry,* 1958b, 21, 83–97.

Raven, B.H., and Rietsema, J., The effects of varied clarity of group goal and group path upon the individual and his relation to his group. *Human Relations,* 1957, 10, 29–45.

Raven, B.H., and Shaw, J.I., Interdependence and group problem solving in the triad. *Journal of Personality and Social Psychology,* 1970, 14, 157–65.

Ray, H.W., The application of dynamic programming to the study of multi-stage decision processes in the individual. Ph.D. dissertation, Ohio State University, Department of Psychology, 1963.

Read, W.H., Upward communication in industrial hierarchies. In G.A. Yukl and K.N. Wexley, (Eds.), *Readings in Organizational and Industrial Psychology.* New York: Oxford University Press, 1971, 71–101.

Reitan, H.T., and Shaw, M.E., Group membership, sex-composition of the group and conformity behavior. *Journal of Social Psychology,* 1964, 64, 45–51.

Rhine, R.J., and Polowniak, W.A.J., Attitude change, commitment and ego involvement. *Journal of Personality and Social Psychology,* 1971, 19, 277–80.

Rhine, R.J., and Severance, L.J., Ego-involvement, discrepancy, source credibility and attitude change. *Journal of Personality and Social Psychology,* 1970, 16, 175–90.

Rice, L.E., and Mitchell, T.R., Structural determinants of individual behavior in organizations. *Administrative Science Quarterly,* 1973, 18, 56–70.

Rigby, F.D., Heuristic analysis of decision situations. In M.W. Shelley and G.L. Bryan (Eds.), *Human Judgments and Optimality.* New York: John Wiley and Sons, 1964, Chapter 2.

Riker, W.H., Some ambiguities in the notion of power. *American Political Science Review,* 1964, 58, 341–49.

Ring, K., and Kelley, H.H., A comparison of augmentation and reduction as modes of influence. *Journal of Abnormal and Social Psychology,* 1963, 66, 95–102.

Roberts, J.C., and Castore, C.H., The effects of conformity, information and confidence upon subjects willingness to take risk following a group discussion. *Organizational Behavior and Human Performance,* 1972, 8, 384–94.

Roby, T.B.; Nicol, E.H.; and Farrell, F.M., Group problem solving under two types of executive structure. *Journal of Abnormal and Social Psychology,* 1963, 67, 550–56.

Roethlisberger, F.J., and Dickson, W.J., *Management and the Worker.* Cambridge, Mass.: Harvard University Press, 1939.

Rogers, R.W., and Thistlethwaite, P.L., Effects of fear arousal and reassurance on attitude change. *Journal of Personality and Social Psychology,* 1970, 15, 227–33.

Rokeach, M., and Kliejunas, P., Behavior as a function of attitude-toward object and attitude-toward situation. *Journal of Personality and Social Psychology,* 1972, 22, 194–210.

Rosenbaum, M., and Blake, R.R., Volunteering as a function of field structure. *Journal of Abnormal and Social Psychology,* 1955, 50, 193–96.

Rosenberg, L.A., Conformity as a function of confidence in self and confidence in partner. *Human Relations,* 1963, 16, 131–39.

———. Group size, prior experience and conformity. *Journal of Abnormal and Social Psychology*, 1961, 63, 436–37.

Rosenberg, M.J., Cognitive structure and attitudinal effect. *Journal of Abnormal and Social Psychology*, 1956, 53, 367–72.

Russell, B., *Power*. New York: Barnes and Noble, 1962.

St. Jean, R., Reformulation of the value hypothesis in group risk taking. *Proceedings of the 78th Annual Convention of the American Psychological Association*, 1970, 5, 339–40 (Summary).

Samelson, F., Conforming behavior under two conditions of conflict in the cognitive field. *Journal of Abnormal and Social Psychology*, 1957, 55, 181–87.

Sarbin, T.R.; Taft, R.; and Bailey, D.E., *Clinical Inference and Cognitive Theory*. New York: Holt, Rinehart and Winston, 1960.

Sayeki, Y., Allocation of importance: an axiom system. *Journal of Mathematical Psychology*, 1972, 9, 55–65.

Sayeki, Y., and Vesper, K.H., Allocation of importance in a hierarchical goal structure. *Management Science*, 1973, 19, 667–75.

Schachter, S., Deviation, rejection and communication. *Journal of Abnormal and Social Psychology*, 1951, 46, 190–207.

Schachter, S.; Ellertson, N.; McBride, D.; and Gregory, D., An experimental study of cohesiveness and productivity. *Human Relations*, 1951, 4, 229–38.

Scheibe, K.E., *Beliefs and Values*. New York: Holt, Rinehart and Winston, 1970.

Schenck, E.A., and Naylor, J.C., A cautionary note concerning the use of regression analysis for capturing the strategies of people. *Educational and Psychological Measurement*, 1968, 28, 3–7.

Schopler, J., Social power. In L. Berkowitz (Ed.), *Advances in Experimental Social Psychology*. New York: Academic Press, 1965, 2, 177–219.

Schroder, H.M.; Driver, M.J.; and Streufert, S., *Human Information Processing*. New York: Holt, Rinehart and Winston, 1967.

Scott, W.G., and Mitchell, T.R., *Organization Theory: A Structural and Behavioral Analysis*. Homewood, Ill.: Irwin-Dorsey, 1972.

Secord, Paul F., and Backman, Carl W., *Social Psychology*. New York: McGraw-Hill Book Co., 1964, 22–24.

Segall, M.H.; Campbell, D.T.; and Herskovits, J.J., *The Influence of Culture on Visual Perception*. Indianapolis, Ind.: Bobbs-Merrill Co., 1966.

Shapley, L.S., and Shubik, M.A., A method for evaluating the distribution of power in a committee system. *American Political Science Review*, 1954, 48, 787–92.

Shartle, C.L., *Executive Performance and Leadership*. Columbus: Ohio State University Research Foundation, 1952.

Shaw, Marjorie E., A comparison of individuals and small groups in the rational solution of complex problems. *American Journal of Psychology*, 1932, 44, 491–504.

Shaw, M.E., Communication networks. In L. Berkowitz (Ed.), *Advances in Experimental Social Psychology*, New York: Academic Press, Vol. 1, 1964, 111–47.

_____. Group Dynamics: *The Psychology of Small Group Behavior.* New York: McGraw-Hill Book Co., 1971.

Shaw, M.E.; Rothschild, G.H.; and Strickland, J.F., Decision processes in communication nets. *Journal of Abnormal and Social Psychology,* 1957, 54, 323–30.

Shaw, M.E., and Shaw, L.M., Some effects of sociometric grouping upon learning in a second grade classroom. *Journal of Social Psychology,* 1962, 57, 453–58.

Shelly, M.W., Jr., and Bryan, G.L., (Eds.), *Human Judgments and Optimality.* New York: John Wiley & Sons, 1964.

Sherif, M., A study of some social factors in perception. *Archivia Psychologia,* 1935, 27, 187.

Sherif, M., and Sherif, C.W., *An Outline of Social Psychology* (rev. ed.). New York: Harper & Row, 1969.

Sherman, S.J., Effects of choice and incentive on attitude change in a discrepant behavior situation. *Journal of Personality and Social Psychology,* 1970, 15, 245–52.

Shiflett, S.C., and Nealey, S.M., The effects of changing leader power: a test of "situational engineering." *Organizational Behavior and Human Performance,* 1972, 7, 371–82.

Shrode, W.A., and Brown, W.B., A study of optimality in recurrent decision-making of lower-level management. *Academy of Management Journal,* 1970, 13, 389–401.

Shull, F.A.; Delbecq, A.L.; and Cummings, L.L., *Organizational Decision Making.* New York: McGraw-Hill Book Co., 1970.

Sieber, J.E., and Lanzetta, J.T., Conflict and conceptual structure as determinants of decision making behavior. *Journal of Personality,* 1964, 32, 622–641.

Siegel, S., and Zajonc, R.B., Group risk-taking in professional decisions. *Sociometry,* 1967, 30, 339–50.

Silverthorne, Colin P., Information input and the group shift phenomenon in risk taking, *Journal of Personality and Social Psychology,* 1971, 20, 456–61.

Simon, H.A., A behavioral model of rational choice. *Quarterly Journal of Economics,* 1955, 69, 99–118.

_____. *Administrative Behavior.* New York: Macmillan Publishing Co., 1965.

_____. *Models of Man.* New York: John Wiley & Sons, 1957.

_____. *The New Science of Management Decision.* New York: Harper & Row, 1960.

_____. Theories of decision making in economics and behavioral science. *American Economic Review,* 1959, 49, 253–83.

Simon, H.A., and Barenfeld, M., Information-processing analysis of perceptual processes in problem solving. *Psychological Review,* 1969, 76, 473–83.

Simon, H.A., and Newell, A., Human problem solving: the state of the theory in 1970. *American Psychologist,* 1971, 26, 145–59.

Simons, H.W.; Berkowitz, N.N.; and Moyer, R.J., Similarity, credibility, and attitude change: a review and a theory. *Psychological Bulletin,* 1970, 73, 1–16.

Slater, Philip E., Contrasting correlates of group size. *Sociometry,* 1959, 21, 129–39.

Slovic, P., Analyzing the expert judge: a descriptive study of a stockbroker's decision processes. *Journal of Applied Psychology,* 1969, 53, 255–63.

――――. Cue consistency and cue-utilization in judgment. *American Journal of Psychology,* 1966, 79, 427–34.

Slovic, P.; Fleissner, D.; and Bauman, W.S., Analyzing the use of information in investment decision making: a methodological proposal. *Journal of Business,* 1972, 45, 283–301.

Slovic, P. and Lichtenstein, S., Comparison of Bayesian and regression approaches to the study of information processing in judgment. *Organizational Behavior and Human Performance,* 1971, 6, 649–744.

Smith, C.R.; Williams, L.; and Willis, R.H., Race, sex and belief as determinants of friendship acceptance. *Journal of Personality and Social Psychology,* 1967, 5, 127–37.

Soelberg, P., Unprogrammed decision making. *Papers and Proceedings, 26th Annual Meeting,* New York: The Academy of Management, December 27–29, 1966, 3–16.

Sommer, R., Studies in personal space. *Sociometry,* 1959, 22, 247–60.

Steiner, I.D., and Rajaratnam, N., A model for the comparison of individual and group performance scores. *Behavioral Science,* 1961, 6, 142–47.

Steinzor, B., The spatial factor in face-to-face discussion groups. *Journal of Abnormal and Social Psychology,* 1950, 45, 552–555.

Stephan, F.F., and Mishler, E.G., The distribution of participation in small groups: an exponential approximation. *American Sociological Review,* 1952, 17, 598–608.

Stogdill, R., Personal factors associated with leadership: a survey of the literature. *Journal of Psychology,* 1948, 25, 37–51.

Stogdill, R.M., and Coons, A.E., Leader behavior: its description and measurement. *Research Monograph No. 88,* Columbus: Ohio State University, 1957.

Stoner, J.A.F., A comparison of individual and group decisions involving risk. Master's thesis, Massachusetts Institute of Technology, School of Industrial Management, 1961.

――――. Risky and cautious shifts in group decisions: the influence of widely held values. *Journal of Experimental Social Psychology,* 1968, 4, 442–59.

Streufert, S., and Castore, C.H., Information search and the effects of failure: a test of complexity theory. *Journal of Experimental Social Psychology,* 1971, 7, 125–43.

Streufert, S., and Driver, M., Conceptual structure, information load and perceptual complexity. *Psychonomic Science,* 1965, 3, 249–50.

Streufert, S.; Suedfeld, P.; and Driver, M.J., Conceptual structure, information search, and information utilization. *Journal of Personality and Social Psychology,* 1965, 2, 736–40.

Streufert, S., and Taylor, E.A., Objective risk levels and subjective risk perception. *O.N.R. Technical Report No. 40,* Layfayette, Ind.: Purdue University, August 1971.

Stroebe, W.; Thompson, V.D.; Insko, C.A.; and Reisman, S.R., Balance and differentiation in the evaluation of linked attitude objectives. *Journal of Personality and Social Psychology,* 1970, 16, 38–47.

Stroop, J.R., Is the judgment of the group better than that of the average member of the group? *Journal of Experimental Psychology,* 1932, 15, 550–62.

Suedfeld, P., and Streufert, S., Information search as a function of conceptual and environmental complexity. *Psychonomic Science,* 1966, 4, 351–52.

Summers, D.A., The learning of responses to multiple weighted cues. *Journal of Experimental Psychology,* 1962, 64, 29–34.

――――. Adaptation to change in multiple probability tasks. *American Journal of Psychology,* 1969, 82, 235–40.

Summers, D.A., and Hammond, K.R., Inference behavior in multiple-cue tasks involving both linear and nonlinear relations. *Journal of Experimental Psychology,* 1966, 71, 751–57.

Taffel, C., Anxiety and the conditioning of verbal behavior. *Journal of Abnormal and Social Psychology,* 1955, 51, 496–501.

Tannenbaum, A.S., (Ed.), *Control in Organizations.* New York: McGraw-Hill Book Co., 1968.

Tannenbaum, P.H., The congruity principle revisited: studies in the reduction, induction and generalization of persuasion. In L. Berkowitz (Ed.), *Advances in Experimental Social Psychology,* Vol. III. New York: Academic Press, 1967, 272–320.

Tannenbaum, R., Managerial decision making. *The Journal of Business,* 1950, 23, 22–39.

Taylor, D.W.; Berry, P.C.; and Block, C.H., Does group participation when using brainstorming facilitate or inhibit creative thinking? *Administrative Science Quarterly,* 1958, 3, 23–47.

Taylor, D.W., and Faust, W.L., Twenty questions: efficiency of problem solving as a function of the size of the group. *Journal of Experimental Psychology,* 1952, 44, 360–63.

Teger, A.I., and Pruitt, D.G., Components of group risk-taking. *Journal of Experimental Social Psychology,* 1967, 3, 189–205.

Tesser, A., and Rosen, S., Similarity of objective fate as a determinant of the reluctance to transmit unpleasant information: the MUM effect. *Journal of Personality and Social Psychology,* 1972, 23, 46–53.

Thibaut, J.W., and Kelley, H.H., *The Social Psychology of Groups.* New York: John Wiley & Sons, 1959.

Thibaut, J.W., and Strickland, L.H., Psychological set and social conformity. *Journal of Personality,* 1956, 25, 115–29.

Thomas, R.E., Development of new techniques for analysis of human controller dynamics. *Technical Documentary Report No. MRL-TDR-62-65,* Wright-Patterson Air Force Base, Ohio, June 1962.

Thompson, J.D., Decision making, the firm, and the market. In W.W. Cooper *et al.* (Eds.), *New Perspectives in Organization Research.* New York: John Wiley & Sons, 1964.

——. *Organizations in Actions.* New York: McGraw-Hill Book Co., 1967.

Thompson, J.D., and Tuden, A., *Comparative Studies in Administration.* Pittsburgh: University of Pittsburgh Press, 1959.

Todd, F.J., and Hammond, K.R., Differential feedback in two multiple-cue probability learning tasks. *Behavioral Science,* 1965, 10, 429–35.

Travis, L.E., The effect of a small audience upon eye-hand coordination. *Journal of Abnormal and Social Psychology,* 1925, 20, 142–46.

Triandis, H.C., *Attitude and Attitude Change.* New York: John Wiley & Sons, 1971.

Triandis, H.C.; Hall, E.R.; and Ewen, R.B., Member heterogeneity and dyadic creativity. *Human Relations,* 1965, 18, 33–55.

Triplett, N., The dynamogenic factors in pacemaking and competition. *American Journal of Psychology,* 1897, 9, 507–33.

Tuddenham, R.D.; MacBridge, P.; and Zahn, V., The influence of the sex composition of the group upon yielding to a distorted norm. *Journal of Psychology,* 1958, 46, 243–51.

Uhl, C.N., Learning of interval concepts: I. Effects of differences in stimulus weights. *Journal of Experimental Psychology,* 1963, 64, 264–73.

Van Doorn, J.A.A., Sociology and the problem of power. *Sociologica Neerlandica,* 1962–63, 1, 3–51.

Vannoy, J.S., Generality of cognitive complexity-simplicity as a personality construct. *Journal of Personality and Social Psychology,* 1965, 2, 385–96.

Van Zelst, R.H., Sociometrically selected work teams increase production. *Personnel Psychology,* 1952, 5, 175–86.

Vesper, K.H., and Sayeki, Y., A quantitative approach for policy analysis. *California Management Review,* 1973, 15, 119–26.

Vinokur, A., Review and theoretical analysis of the effects of group processes upon individual and group decisions involving risk. *Psychological Bulletin,* 1971, 76, 231–50.

Von Neumann, J., and Morgenstern, O., *Theory of Games and Economic Behavior* (2nd ed). Princeton, N.J.: Princeton University Press, 1947.

Vroom, V.H., *Work and Motivation.* New York: John Wiley & Sons, 1964.

Vroom, V.H., and Pehl, B., Relationship between age and risk taking among managers. *Journal of Applied Psychology,* 1971, 55, 399–405.

Vroom, V.H., and Yetton, P.W., Leadership behavior on standardized cases. Technical report No. 3, New Haven, Conn.: Yale University, 1973.

Wagner, H.M., *Principles of Management Science,* Englewood Cliffs, N.J.: Prentice-Hall, 1970.

Wahba, M.A., The effect of some dimensions of social power on cooperation in mixed-motive games. *Organizational Behavior and Human Performance,* 1971, 6, 235–47.

Wald, A., *Sequential Analysis.* New York: John Wiley & Sons, 1947.

Walker, C.M., and Bourne, L.E., Jr., Concept identification as a function of amounts of relevant and irrelevant information. *American Journal of Psychology,* 1961, 74, 410–17.

Wallach, M.A., and Kogan, N., Sex differences and judgment processes. *Journal of Personality,* 1959, 27, 555–64.

Wallach, M.A.; Kogan, N.; and Bem, D.J., Group influence on individual risk taking. *Journal of Abnormal and Social Psychology*, 1962, 65, 75–86.

Wapner, S., and Alper, Thelma, G. The effect of an audience on behavior in a choice situation. *Journal of Abnormal and Social Psychology*, 1952, 47, 222–29.

Warner, W.L., and Abegglen, J.C., *Big Business Leaders in America*. New York: Harper & Row, 1955.

Watson, D., Effects of certain social power structures on communication in task-oriented groups. *Sociometry*, 1965, 28, 322–36.

Watson, D., and Bromberg, B., Power, communication, and position satisfaction in task-oriented groups. *Journal of Personality and Social Psychology*, 1965, 2, 859–64.

Watson, G.B., Do groups think more effectively than individuals? *Journal of Abnormal and Social Psychology*, 1928, 23, 328–36.

Watson, J.B., Psychology as the behaviorist views it. *Psychological Review*, 1913, 20, 158–77.

Weber, Max, *The Protestant Ethic and the Spirit of Capitalism*. London: Allen and Unwin, 1930.

Wiggins, N., and Hoffman, P.J., The three models of clinical judgment. *Journal of Abnormal Psychology*, 1968, 73, 70–77.

Wilson, C.Z., and Alexis, M., Basic framework for decisions. *Journal of the Academy of Management*, 1962, 5, 151–64.

Winkler, R.L., The quantification of judgment: some methodological suggestions. *Journal of the American Statistical Association*, 1967, 62, 1105–20.

Winters, P.R., Forecasting sales by exponentially weighted moving averages. *Management Science*, 1960, 6, 324–42.

Wood, M.T., Effects of decision processes and task situations on influence perceptions. *Organizational Behavior and Human Performance*, 1972, 7, 417–27.

Woodward, J., *Industrial Organization: Theory and Practice*. London: Oxford University Press, 1965.

Wrong, D.H., Some problems in defining social power. *American Journal of Sociology*, 1968, 73, 673–81.

Wyer, R.S., Jr., Information redundancy, inconsistency, and novelty and their role in impression formation. *Journal of Experimental Social Psychology*, 1970, 6, 111–27.

Yntema, D.B., Keeping track of several things at once. *Human Factors*, 1963, 5, 7–17.

Yntema, D.B., and Mueser, G.E., Keeping track of variables that have few or many states. *Journal of Experimental Psychology*, 1962, 63, 391–95.

Yuker, H.E., Group atmosphere and memory. *Journal of Abnormal and Social Psychology*, 1955, 51, 17–23.

Yukl, G.A., and Wexley, K.N., eds. *Readings in Organizational and Industrial Psychology*. New York: Oxford University Press, 1971.

Zajonc, R.B., The requirements and design of a standard group task. *Journal of Experimental Social Psychology*, 1965, 1, 71–88.

Zajonc, R.B., and Sales, S.M., Social facilitation of dominant and subordinate responses. *Journal of Experimental Social Psychology,* 1966, 2, 160–68.

Zander, A., and Curtis, T., Effects of social power on aspiration setting and striving. *Journal of Abnormal and Social Psychology,* 1962, 64, 63–74.

Zani, W.M., Blueprint for MIS. *Harvard Business Review,* 1970, 48, 95–100.

Zimbardo, P.G., and Ebbesen, E.B., Experimental modification of the relationship between effort, attitude and behavior. *Journal of Experimental Social Psychology,* 1970, 16, 207–13.

Zimbardo, P.G., and Ebbesen, E.B., *Influencing Attitudes and Changing Behavior.* Reading, Mass.: Addison-Wesley Publishing Co. 1969.

Zimbardo, P.G.; Ebbesen, E.B.; and Fraser, S.C., Emotional persuasion: arousal state as a distractor. Unpublished manuscript, Stanford University, 1968.

Zipf, Sheila G., Resistance and conformity under reward and punishment. *Journal of Abnormal and Social Psychology,* 1960, 61, 102–09.

Author Index

Subject Index